A Nuclear Family Vacation

Also by Sharon Weinberger

*Imaginary Weapons: A Journey Through
the Pentagon's Scientific Underworld*

A Nuclear Family Vacation

Travels in the World of
Atomic Weaponry

Nathan Hodge
and
Sharon Weinberger

BLOOMSBURY

Published by Bloomsbury USA, New York
Distributed to the trade by Macmillan

All papers used by Bloomsbury USA are natural, recyclable products made from wood
grown in well-managed forests. The manufacturing processes conform to the
environmental regulations of the country of origin.

LIBRARY OF CONGRESS CATALOGING-IN-PUBLICATION DATA

Hodge, Nathan.
A nuclear family vacation: travels in the world of atomic weaponry / Nathan Hodge and
Sharon Weinberger.—1st U.S. ed.
p. cm.
ISBN-13: 978–1–59691–378–3
ISBN-10: 1–59691–378–9
1. Nuclear weapons—Popular works. 2. Nuclear engineering—Popular works. 3. Nuclear
nonproliferation—Popular works. I. Weinberger, Sharon. II. Title.

U264.H635 2008
623.4′5119—dc22
2008002013

First U.S. Edition 2008

1 3 5 7 9 10 8 6 4 2

Typeset by Hewer Text UK Ltd, Edinburgh
Printed in the United States of America by Quebecor World Fairfield

For our parents,
Brien and Marjorie Hodge,
Miles Weinberger and
Bernice Koslow-Weinberger (1932–2002)

Contents

"Buddy," the motel manager said, "You know what'll happen if you call up and ask to see some missile silos? Why, those OSI boys will be down here bangin' on your door in about three minutes. And you know what? They won't be polite, either."

—Barney Greinke, *Nuke Tourist*

PROLOGUE

How to Be an Armageddon Tourist

In most wars, the battles end and the survivors go home, leaving historians and strategy buffs to argue over the weapons and tactics. Eventually, tourists visit the battlegrounds. Some travelers go to Normandy to see the landing sites; others visit Civil War battlefields across the United States. Standing on hallowed ground, they try to summon a distant vision of carnage from the landscape. Politicians, in their turn, evoke memories of the war—good and bad—to justify one or another policy. But the Cold War was not like other wars, and its deadliest weapon, the thermonuclear bomb, was never used in battle. It was used to keep a sort of peace.

Once upon a time, the logic of nuclear weapons seemed clear, even if not everyone agreed with the underlying premise. Two superpowers— the United States and the Soviet Union—maintained huge nuclear arsenals, ready at a moment's notice to strike the other side. The concept of mutual assured destruction, and the potential end of mankind, preserved a stalemate that avoided direct military confrontation between East and West for nearly fifty years. In 1991, that war ostensibly ended when the Soviet Union spun apart and the United States declared victory. The nuclear arsenals, however, remained in place.

What happens when a war ends, but the warriors don't go home? One summer, we decided to tour those Cold War nuclear battlefields, the places where atomic combat never took place. That trip led us further into the world of nuclear weaponry, a complex with global reach. Eventually our trip took us to destinations in five countries and ten U.S. states.

Nuclear tourism is experiencing something of a renaissance. Decommissioned Cold War bunkers are opening to the public, not just in the United States but in other countries as well. Former missile silos—some privately owned—now welcome tourists eager to turn the launch key. Even sites of nuclear disaster, like Chernobyl, attract explorers. Sites linked to the Manhattan Project, the top secret World War II program to develop the atomic bomb, are particularly popular. For example, Hanford, in Washington State, the original plutonium production plant and dubbed "the most contaminated place in North America," is now open to the public; tours of the facility are overbooked. And New Mexico, birthplace of the atomic bomb, is naturally a main attraction.

An article in the travel section of the *Financial Times* extols the virtues of what it calls the "Nuclear Trail," which begins with Trinity, site of the first test of a nuclear device. "This 1,000 mile trip up Interstate I-25 from the Mexican border to Wyoming is a glorious drive through the empty spaces of the American West," writes Leslie Woodhead, a documentary filmmaker who traveled some of the atomic landscape. "It's also a journey tracking the epic story of America's obsession with the bomb."

Tour guides to the world of atomic weaponry are also proliferating. The Bureau of Atomic Tourism Web site presents an eclectic mix of popular and esoteric nuclear destinations, while *The Traveler's Guide to Nuclear Weapons: A Journey Through America's Cold War Battlefields* chronicles every nuclear-related site, no matter how obscure. Museums dedicated to the history of nuclear weapons have sprung up, from Los Alamos, New Mexico, to Kurchatov, Kazakhstan. Scholars, too, are beginning to take note of this surge in nuclear tourism fueled by a mix of Cold War nostalgia and morbid curiosity. "Many visitors, even those who are anti-nuclear, are drawn to the nuclear in New Mexico by a sense of awe and mystery," notes Hugh Gusterson, an anthropologist who has studied the nuclear complex.

The idea of a nuclear family vacation first occurred to us in early 2005, around the time of year when many families begin thinking about trips to Disneyland or the Jersey Shore. We faced the same dilemma as any married couple: how to see some new sights, visit family, and have fun, all in the space of a few short weeks. During our discussions, we hit on the somewhat whimsical idea of a "nuclear family vacation," a trip to key nuclear weapons sites. Conveniently enough, these sites were located in proximity to assorted family members: a cousin in Los Alamos, birthplace of the atomic bomb, an aunt in Las Vegas, near the site where nuclear weapons were once set off on a regular basis, and a brother in northern California, not far from the lab that physicist Edward Teller built.

While places of historical interest—Trinity, for instance—are scattered around the map, visiting only those sites would have limited us to the past. And although we did visit some of those popular destinations, we wanted to see something that the average traveler can't: the working complex. As we researched our itinerary, we discovered that there were nuclear sites of one sort or another close to just about everyone's homes (although we drew the line when a brother in Colorado offered to sneak us into a decommissioned Atlas missile silo now used for a garbage dump). While it would be amusing to think that our families had somehow gravitated toward nuclear weapons, this was not quite the case. Rather, the sites, facilities, and laboratories that support nuclear weapons work, even today, have great geographic reach. The nuclear world was closer than we'd thought.

We timed our first nuclear road trip to coincide with the sixtieth anniversary of Trinity. The next summer, after following a parallel itinerary through Russia and Kazakhstan, we realized that our vacation was more than a Cold War nostalgia trip. After all, a quick survey of the headlines—news of a nuclear proliferation ring based in Pakistan, reports of a nuclear-armed North Korea, and questions about the nuclear aspirations of Iran—seemed to suggest that nuclear weapons had never really gone away. We wanted to understand the powerful role nuclear weaponry still plays in today's world.

Our search began near our home in Washington, D.C.

In June 2005, shortly before our first trip, we walked into the Washington office of National Nuclear Security Administration (NNSA) chief Linton Brooks. He was leaning over his shoes, looking slightly flummoxed. He paused and looked up at us, still holding his shoelaces. "Yes, there's the headline," he sighed. "The man responsible for nuclear weapons can't even tie his own shoes."

Brooks's fatalism was not unfounded. Recent news reports had not been kind to his agency, an arm of the Department of Energy that oversees the nuclear weapons complex. In particular, reporters were fixated on security woes at Los Alamos National Laboratory, where the disappearance of classified computer disks had prompted a months-long shutdown of the facility. Those "missing" disks, in fact, never existed; they were phantoms created by a faulty inventory list. But the snafu was a major blow to the NNSA's credibility, and it amplified perceptions of mismanagement at Los Alamos. Unfortunately for Brooks, Los Alamos had been unable to shed its image as the problem child of the nuclear labs family.

"I've been a little surprised at the insatiable desire—a combination of the twenty-four-hour news cycle and the Congress—to know every-thing now," he said of the security lapses. "In fact, when problems occur, the one thing you can almost always be certain of is that your initial understanding is wrong." An example of that, Brooks continued, was the case of the Los Alamos disks. "Almost everything we thought was true in the first ninety-six hours turns out not to have been true."

Today, the NNSA is an obscure agency within the Department of Energy. It was created in 2000 amid the fallout from the Wen Ho Lee scandal, in which a Los Alamos employee was falsely suspected of providing nuclear secrets to China. NNSA's official status is "quasi-autonomous." That means the NNSA, though a part of the Department of Energy, has its own management structure. In other words, the work of nuclear weapons was essentially pulled out of the Department of Energy and consolidated in a single organization whose primary function is to oversee the nuclear weapons stockpile and the infra-structure responsible for maintaining it. It was not, however, the panacea that some had hoped for.

The U.S. nuclear weapons complex consists of the vast network of laboratories and production and test facilities that once built—and now maintains—the U.S. nuclear weapons stockpile. Of the twenty-seven sites the United States opened between the start of the Manhattan Project in 1942 and the end of the Cold War, just eight remain: Los Alamos National Laboratory, Lawrence Livermore National Labora-tory, Sandia National Laboratories, the Nevada Test Site, Kansas City

Plant, Pantex Plant, Y-12 National Security Complex, and Savannah River Site. These facilities are all multipurpose—and in this book, we explore some of their work in detail—but generally speaking, it's helpful to understand that Los Alamos, Livermore, and Sandia are involved in the design of nuclear weapons; the Nevada Test Site, as its name suggests, is used for testing nuclear weapons; and the remaining facilities are production plants, where the actual weapons components are fabricated and, in the case of Pantex, assembled into weapons.

In 1966, the United States had a staggering 32,193 weapons in its stockpile. By 2006, the exact number of deployed warheads was classified, but it was estimated to be around 6,000 and dropping. Despite the consolidation of nuclear facilities and the decline in the number of weapons, the cost of maintaining the nuclear stockpile has not decreased. In 2006, the United States spent $6.61 billion on the nuclear weapons complex. In 1984, that amount (in 2006 dollars) was $6.34 billion. In other words, the United States is spending today about the same amount of money on nuclear weapons that it was at the height of the Cold War.

And at the center of this vast enterprise is the NNSA, which manages the far-flung complex from Washington. The new agency's quasi-autonomous status goes to the heart of the problem. The NNSA was assigned multiple lines of authority and overlapping responsibilities that made decision making hard and accountability elusive. In the seven years since the agency was created, problems seemed to multiply, with proliferating reports of mismanagement and security violations. "In theory, it was a good idea to separate nuclear weapons from the day-to-day White House political considerations that encumber any cabinet-level agency," said Philip Coyle, a former associate director of Lawrence Livermore National Laboratory. "But in practice it has only played into the perception that the NNSA and its contractors are not accountable to higher-level authorities, in this case the secretary of energy."

With all the bad press over lost computer disks, it was easy to lose sight of the bigger picture: The NNSA was embarking on an ambitious project, called Complex 2030, to modernize U.S. nuclear weapons facilities. The plan, which had attracted very little public attention, focused on consolidating and securing facilities while, in line with international political agreements, dismantling nuclear weapons. That meant, however, rebuilding some facilities and, controversially, resuming production of plutonium pits, used to trigger thermonuclear weapons. At the heart of Complex 2030, and perhaps its most controversial component, was a plan to develop and produce a new (or in the words of the NNSA, "replacement") nuclear weapon, the first such weapon to be designed since the end of the Cold War. Complex 2030 would shrink the nuclear landscape, but it would also in effect rebuild it.

Complex 2030 was a result of a series of moves on the part of the Bush administration, beginning with its decision in late 2001 to withdraw from the Anti-Ballistic Missile Treaty in order to deploy a missile defense system. President George W. Bush had declared that he was "committed to achieving a credible deterrent with the lowest-possible number of nuclear weapons consistent with our national security needs." How many weapons was that? By 2002, that number, after negotiations with Russia, ended up being between seventeen hundred and twenty-two hundred. While that was a substantial reduction from Cold War highs of over thirty thousand, it was still enough to obliterate both countries several times over.

Reductions in the nuclear arsenal were greeted enthusiastically, but a couple of the administration's proposed nuclear initiatives quickly became—excuse the pun—politically radioactive. One was a study for a Robust Nuclear Earth Penetrator, a weapon frequently referred to as a nuclear bunker buster, a nuclear-tipped bomb that would be able to destroy enemy command centers or weapons of mass destruction situated deep underground. The other was something dubbed Advanced Concepts, explained as an investigation into new nuclear weapon designs. The former proposal was greeted with stiff congressional opposition, while the latter proposal, which also proved controversial, soon evolved into the Reliable Replacement Warhead (RRW). The RRW was essentially a new nuclear weapon, although its advocates argued that it was not a new model, just an upgrade. Whatever form the RRW would take, it would mark a major shift for the nuclear complex: the return to design and production of new nuclear weapons.

Democrats balked at Bush's nuclear proposals. Republicans, however, were not necessarily supportive of the administration's nuclear ambitions either. Representative David Hobson, then the Republican chairman of the House Energy and Water Development Appropriations Subcommittee, had the power to decide whether the administration would get funding for its nuclear initiatives, and he was one of the first to question what was going on. Concerns about the administration's approach to nuclear weapons extended abroad as well. There were increasing worries that terrorists could obtain nuclear material, or worse yet, a complete nuclear weapon. But there was declining support for programs to help secure loose nuclear material in places like Russia and the former Soviet republics.

And the United States was sending a very mixed message on the world stage when it came to nukes. In 1998, India and Pakistan emerged as declared nuclear powers. Yet, while it first condemned those actions, and supported sanctions, the U.S. government later embraced both countries as a reward for their support after 9/11. For a brief moment in the early 1990s, the threat of nuclear war had seemed the stuff of kitschy Reagan-era movies like *WarGames* or *The Day After*. Nuclear deterrence had belonged to the era of duck and cover. But now, all that had changed.

By the summer of 2005, when we began our first nuclear vacation, the United States was over two years into Operation Iraqi Freedom, a war that began as a hunt for weapons of mass destruction. "We cannot wait for the final proof—the smoking gun—that could come in the form of a mushroom cloud," Bush warned in 2002. As we later found out, there were no weapons of mass destruction in Iraq at that time, let alone nuclear weapons. However, not long after, the Bush administration would begin ratcheting up the pressure on Iran over its nuclear program. The atom bomb was back in vogue.

It was with all these issues in mind that we embarked on our journey.

How does one plan a nuclear vacation? We knew that the major focus of our travels would be the U.S. nuclear arsenal, not out of patriotic bias, but because the United States has, along with Russia, one of the two largest nuclear arsenals in the world. There are six other countries that officially acknowledge having nuclear weapons: the United Kingdom, France, China, India, Pakistan, and North Korea (which, after a fizzled test, promised in 2007 to rid itself of its small stockpile). Israel, though undeclared, is presumed to possess nuclear weapons.

In planning our itinerary, we balanced what we thought would be the value of visiting a given place with our ability to get access and see something that would be relevant. Though a visit to North Korea would have been fascinating in its own right, we doubt it would have revealed much about the country's nuclear ambitions. Similarly, in Israel, visiting a nuclear weapons facility that the country doesn't admit exists would have been a nonstarter. India and Pakistan—which guard their arsenals closely—have little to offer the nuclear tourist. Iran ended up on our list, though we were unsure until the very last minute that we would be allowed in the country.

Secrecy is a long-standing, and in many cases necessary, corollary of nuclear weapons, and it presents a certain logistical challenge to planning a nuclear vacation. Asking to tour a nuclear facility might strike foreign officials as absurd, though in the United States the nuclear laboratories have long recognized, and even encouraged, tourism. There are perfectly legitimate reasons for keeping nuclear facilities secure and nuclear weapons knowledge tightly controlled, though there are times when such restrictions border on the paranoid. In some cases, we learned something valuable even when confronted with restrictions. In Russia, the regime of President Vladimir Putin has imposed new layers of secrecy, making it all but impossible for journalists (let alone tourists) to visit the country's closed nuclear cities. Still, we learned— through our attempts—how closed this world has become, and how little we may really know about the threat of a nuclear black market.

Sometimes, the places we expected to be open were anything but. The United Kingdom and France, both signatories to the Nuclear Non-Proliferation Treaty (NPT) and declared nuclear states, are surprisingly secretive about their nuclear facilities. They are also—like the United States—in the process of modernizing their strategic nuclear arsenals. Other than periodic press conferences, there has been, unfortunately, little in the way of access to the individuals and places involved in these projects.

At home, we faced similar issues. We wanted to see a part of the production complex, but Pantex, we learned, requires a "Q" clearance (the Department of Energy's version of "top secret") to even get in the door. We settled instead on Y-12, a production facility in Oak Ridge, Tennessee. While our focus was on current sites, we occasionally made historic detours where we thought it would aid us substantially in understanding the current complex, such as to the former congressional bunker at the Greenbrier resort in West Virginia. There was even one case—the secretive Site R underground bunker in Pennsylvania—where we thought it worthwhile to sneak a peek of the area, even though we couldn't get in. We did, however, visit all three nuclear weapons laboratories in the United States.

We hope this book serves as a guide, so that those who visit the historical sites understand the modern context and those who are interested in nuclear strategy can learn a bit more about the unique culture and history of the nuclear complex. Neither view is complete without the other. Nuclear strategy does not exist in a vacuum; it is formed in large part by the people who labor within the complex's diverse institutions.

This book is not designed to be an encyclopedia of the world of atomic weapons. Rather, we want to give the reader a sense of what it is like to travel in this world. For that same reason, we have kept quotes and interviews with nuclear scholars to a minimum, referring to their views and positions as they were relevant to our travels. This is not to say we ignored their views. In between our "vacations," we attended countless roundtables and press conferences with experts and officials from government, think tanks, and nonprofit groups.

We began to perceive a general lack of public debate and awareness on nuclear weapons issues. While the nuclear standoff between NATO and the Warsaw Pact may belong to the past, the various elements of the nuclear complex are now looking for new roles and struggling to create a new reason for being. Nuclear history is still being written. And the greatest challenge—and perhaps danger—we face is not a specific threat, be it from nuclear terrorism or all-out nuclear war. It is the lack of any coherent nuclear strategy for dealing with these threats.

A couple of notes with regard to our travels and choice of words. When people speak about the nuclear weapons complex as a formal institution, they are usually referring to those sites involved in the design, production, and testing of nuclear weapons. However, for our purposes, we expanded this to include more broadly those places involved in using and defending against nuclear weapons. Thus we included a number of military installations in our travels.

We have attempted to order the chapters somewhat in line with our original itinerary, but we made exceptions where we thought the story

should be dictated by the chronology of nuclear weapons developments, and not the whims of our schedule. Although we use the term
"we" throughout the book, we were not joined at the hip the whole
time. There were several cases—typically a specific interview—when,
for reasons of either expediency or necessity, only one of us was
present. We use the first person plural for two reasons: we did not
want to confuse the reader, and more importantly, this book ultimately
is about our travels together, on what started as a two-week road trip
out west and grew into a worldwide tour. It is about a shared travel
experience.

This is a travelogue comprising just over two years of vacations, not
two years of solid travel, meaning that every vacation day we got, we
went, well, someplace nuclear. While our friends went to Florida, Crete,
or the south of France, we waited in lines for visas, begged the U.S.
Army to let us into a secretive base in the middle of the Pacific, or poked
around in underground silos where the keys to nuclear Armageddon
were locked in little boxes. Just like some real vacations, there were
trips that didn't go quite right; there were momentary regrets, and even
the occasional argument. In other words, it wasn't always fun, and
sometimes—when we actually arrived where we were going—we indeed wished we were somewhere else, even back at home. But like on all
memorable vacations, the good outweighed the bad, and we came back
a bit richer than when we left. And after all, how many vacation
itineraries allow you to see Iranian yellowcake?

Finally, while we do not mean to make light of nuclear weaponry,
we found it a topic that lends itself to dark humor. That dark humor is
something that even translates across borders, as we discovered at
Iran's Esfahān Uranium Conversion Facility, where an Iranian official
sidled up and asked us: "Are you having a nice nuclear family
vacation?"

He was smiling broadly; clearly he had come upon some of our
reporting via Google and understood exactly what we were doing there.

While our book explores the role of nuclear weapons, it would be
misleading to say that serious policy issues inspired us to take the first
trip. The most common question we were asked on our travels was why
we chose this unusual form of sightseeing. That was hard to answer at
first. Why, after all, does anyone go anywhere on a vacation that
doesn't involve a beach or a ski slope? Perhaps because people want to

see something of the world, not just read about it in a book. There is something ineffable about the experience of travel.

"What exactly do you expect to get out of this trip?" asked a chipper young Kazakh journalist after our return from a former Soviet nuclear test site. We wished, at the time, we had the answer—but that emerged only when we began to think about writing a book. What could we say? That we wanted to go on vacation, but Walley World was closed? That Iraq was getting a little dicey? Or that nuclear tourism was the next big thing? We mumbled something about nuclear weapons being very important, looked down at our shoes, and wondered if they might set off a radiation detector. Maybe we should have just told her the truth. Family vacations, like love, are all about compromises—Sally might want Hawaii, Johnny might want the Alamo. In the end, you try to choose something that is meaningful and memorable for everyone. As two defense reporters wedded to our work (and each other), we couldn't think of any place we'd rather be than a former Soviet test site, on ground zero. It had meaning. It was memorable. Maybe next year we'll visit the DMZ.

CHAPTER 1

Priscilla, Queen of the Desert
A Visit to the Nevada Test Site

On June 24, 1957, the U.S. military touched off a thirty-seven-kiloton nuclear device over Frenchman Flat, a dry lake bed about seventy-five miles northwest of Las Vegas. The atmospheric test, code-named Priscilla, was part of Operation Plumbbob, a series of atomic detonations. The provenance of that code name remains obscure. The earliest tests were ordered on the old military alphabet (Able, Baker, Charlie); in later years, Los Alamos National Laboratory scientists named their tests after Western ghost towns, while their counterparts at Lawrence Livermore National Laboratory—for reasons unknown—favored names of cheese. Several in the 1950s were named after women. Test site lore persists that some were named for local prostitutes. Rumor had it Priscilla was a whore from Pahrump. But it didn't matter to those who knew her; everyone agreed Priscilla was beautiful.

The most powerful of the bombs detonated on Frenchman Flat, Priscilla was designed to test the effects of a nuclear explosion on construction. The military placed a handful of structures downrange from ground zero, including several buildings, bomb shelters, and even a bank vault built by the Mosler Safe Co. Priscilla's blast loosened the trim on the ten-inch-thick safe door and peeled away the rebar from the vault. The explosive force collapsed six-inch-thick concrete domes, flattened aluminum fallout shelters, and displaced the wall of a windowless brick structure that faced ground zero.

But Priscilla was also a thing of beauty. An incandescent cloud, a perfectly formed column of red dust ringed with a halo of fire, rose above the Nevada desert. It was seductive, terrible, and beautiful—a nuclear money shot.

Over the course of four decades, the United States conducted 1,054 nuclear tests, mostly at the Nevada Test Site. During the era of aboveground testing, the glow from atomic detonations could be seen as far away as Los Angeles. The last atmospheric test—Little Feller I—was conducted in 1962; underground tests continued for another three decades, ending with the 1992 Divider test. An official moratorium followed in 1994, and the Nevada Test Site—where 928 nuclear devices had been detonated—finally went quiet.

But the site does not belong completely to the past. While busloads of tourists now visit, the Nevada Test Site is still a working part of the U.S. nuclear weapons complex. It is also ready, if necessary, to resume nuclear tests. How prepared it should be was the question in the summer of 2005, as we prepared to make the first stop on our nuclear vacation.

The issue was not whether the government would resume testing, but how quickly it would be able to do it. As Linton Brooks, the head of the NNSA, explained it to us, in 2001 "test readiness" (the time required to prepare for an underground nuclear test) was at about thirty-six months, which the administration thought wasn't nearly good enough. It wanted to be test ready within eighteen months. "We picked eighteen months, which is not random, but it's not highly precise science," Brooks admitted. "[Because] we looked back and we said, 'When there have been problems with our stockpile in the past that caused you to want to test, either to make sure you understood the problem or to make sure that the fix worked, how long has it typically taken you to design and field that test?' And eighteen months seemed to be a reasonable level."

Congress was not willing to pay for anything more than twenty-four-months readiness. The difference between the administration's proposal and what Congress was ready to fund was just five million dollars. Congress didn't understand why the administration felt it had to be ready in the shortest conceivable amount of time. Others suspected the whole enterprise was a pretext for hastening a return to nuclear testing. Brooks did not offer any particular rationale. "The president's budget supports it, and I support the president's budget," he told us in 2005, employing the standard phrase used to defer to an official position.

But how, exactly, did the administration come up with the figure of eighteen months? After all, an NNSA advisory panel in 2002 had concluded that the United States could resume testing in as little as three to six months. And the same panel had concluded that the current thirty-six-month figure was a distortion of what was in fact only a very rough estimate.

The panel had gone on to note that the only "bottlenecks" for testing would be at the most basic level of finding qualified work crews and equipment. The report contradicted Brooks's assertion that eighteen months was the minimum amount of time in which scientists could resume testing, but they also undermined the administration's argument that it needed the extra money in order to shorten that time period. In either case, the issue was moot: The NNSA disbanded that advisory panel in 2003.

Nonetheless, the administration seemed determined to forge ahead with enhancements at the Nevada Test Site. A member of the disbanded NNSA advisory panel, who had recently visited the Nevada Test Site, noted at least one sign that activity was ramping up in the desert: the number of buses used to transport workers from Las Vegas. "A few years ago they were down to twenty busloads; now they are up to sixty busloads," he told us. "At the heyday of testing, they were somewhere around eighty to one hundred busloads."

Not all of that was directly related to nuclear testing, of course. Some of it may have been related to nearby Yucca Mountain, which was slated to become the nation's nuclear waste repository. The Defense Department also used the site for nonnuclear tests. But the busloads of workers pouring into the site seemed to be sending one clear signal, the former panel member said: "They're back into a height of Cold War–level of activity."

The Nevada Test Site is just over an hour's drive north from Las Vegas, the mecca of American tourism. We booked a room in the Luxor, the massive pyramid rising on Las Vegas Boulevard, on the south end of the city's famed Strip. Our room overlooked a windowless atrium, where the Egyptian-themed decor was bathed in a hallucinatory casino glow, set against the background of chiming slot machines. We absorbed the numbing vibe of the gambling industry, watching retirees line up for the Pharaoh's Pheast Buffet while tourists in cargo shorts played quarter slots and threw back free drinks. The card tables and roulette wheels are always open, and without clocks or sunlight, it could have been day or night, weekend or weekday. Las Vegas entices you to live in the moment.

But Las Vegas is not just about gambling. Perhaps not surprisingly, nuclear weaponry has joined Celine Dion and Siegfried and Roy's Secret Garden as another attraction. The Atomic Testing Museum, which opened in 2005, is located just a few miles from the glitz and lights of Las Vegas Boulevard, though with its pale concrete exterior and nondescript blue awning, it stands out only because of the distinctive atom sign on the facade. Tickets are sold at the "Wackenhut Guard Station," a tribute to Nevada Test Site security contractor Wackenhut, which also put up a significant chunk of money to open the museum. The vestibule features a sign that reads: "The entry gallery is made possible by the generous support of Lockheed Martin."

The main exhibit area of the museum is covered in fake granite, meant to replicate the deep shafts where underground tests were conducted. We spent a few minutes browsing a collection of Cold War kitsch: everything from cereal boxes and comic books featuring the atomic motif to toys and Christmas decorations. We passed by a life-size mock-up of a 1950s-era fallout shelter stuffed with a family of mannequins in period costume and watched a short film that helpfully explains how a nuclear bomb works. Next we stepped into the "Ground Zero Theater"—where a chilling reenactment of the Trinity test comes complete with a rush of air from the vents to simulate the shock wave from that first nuclear blast. "There was never a detonation where you weren't scared," one of the movie's narrators pronounces.

For those seeking more than a museum tour, the Department of Energy offers regular bus excursions out to the Nevada Test Site, making the place a popular destination for retiree tour groups. In planning our trip to Nevada, we briefly debated the merits of tagging along with a busload of regular tourists, but we decided the rules (no photography or recording devices permitted) were too restrictive. Instead, we requested permission to go on a press tour, which afforded us the opportunity to take pictures and explore some areas not accessible to tourists.

When we arrived at the NNSA's office in North Las Vegas early the next morning, we were greeted with the worrisome news that a wildfire had enveloped part of the Nevada Test Site, which meant that our entire tour might be canceled for the day. Our hosts from the public affairs office decided to investigate the situation, leaving us in the company of Ghazar Papazian, a Los Alamos National Laboratory scientist. Papazian, a loquacious man who went by the nickname Raffi, was the director of test site activities for Los Alamos. His job, essentially, was to oversee the New Mexico–based lab's testing activities at the Nevada site. We were lucky for the introduction: Papazian had a knack for explaining some very complex technical matters.

Papazian came to the site in 1981 as a Westinghouse employee working on the Peacekeeper missile program. Three years later, he was hired by Los Alamos in New Mexico, but was assigned to the Nevada Test Site, where he worked on underground nuclear tests. In 1992, when testing ceased, Papazian transferred down to New Mexico, but he would not stay there long. During the Clinton administration, the Department of Energy began the Stockpile Stewardship Program, which was meant to ensure the reliability of the nuclear arsenal without conducting nuclear tests. Papazian took the opportunity to return to Nevada to oversee tests on plutonium pits, the core of a modern thermonuclear weapon. These tests—called "subcritical" because they don't involve a self-sustaining chain reaction—are now the focus of work at the Nevada Test Site.

Subcritical tests are now as close as the Nevada Test Site comes to the full-scale nuclear tests of years past. Back in the days of full-scale testing, an underground shot was the ultimate way of proving out a new warhead design. Now Papazian and his colleagues have to design ways of testing nukes without a full-scale nuclear detonation. They do this by testing the individual parts of the bomb. The plutonium pit is often described as the trigger of a thermonuclear weapon. It works by implosion: The plutonium core achieves supercriticality when it is compressed in on itself by high explosives.* And to ensure that these triggers work, the testers focus on understanding the physical properties of the plutonium pits—how they age and how they react when compressed by a detonation wave.

Take, for instance, the phenomenon called "spalling." Papazian

---

* The original bomb detonated at the Trinity site in 1945 was a grapefruit-size plutonium core squeezed by an array of high-explosive "lenses"—shaped something like patches on a soccer ball. The precise shape of the "physics package" inside a modern nuclear warhead is still a closely held secret.

patiently explained how spallation occurs as a shock wave passes through rigid material, breaking apart the inner surfaces. If you were to punch a brick wall hard enough, the inner surfaces would start to crumble. "If a car hits a cement barrier, it tends to fall apart," Papazian said. "Well, when plutonium is shocked, it has the tendency to fall apart internally. So, we're trying to understand . . . what the inner layers [of plutonium] are looking like."

Another issue with plutonium is "ejecta," the fragments that fly off material that has been subjected to a shock. "When you pour a Coke into a glass, you'll see small particles of bubbles of Coke," Papazian said. "Ejecta is something like that, but it happens inside a pit, because it's being shocked. We're trying to understand how much ejecta comes off that pit of plutonium—to try to understand . . . the condition of the plutonium after it has been shocked, so the modeler can put that data into his computer models to be able to do the assessments."

Why all the fuss over the behavior of plutonium pits? In the past, no one really needed all that data, especially in an era when nuclear weapons were continuously being built and replaced. But plutonium is a notoriously fickle element: Exposed to air, it oxidizes; in powder form, it can ignite at relatively low temperatures. When it's used in pits, their outer surface corrodes, while radioactive decay inside the spheres can cause further detrimental effects. And, particularly at the beginning of stockpile stewardship, no one was sure how aging plutonium pits would behave.

Papazian served as the test director on the first two subcritical tests: Rebound and Stagecoach. These types of tests are all done in underground facilities that Papazian likened to a passageway with a series of doors. He took out a pen and quickly began sketching a diagram on a piece of paper, drawing a series of the nested "bottles" that contain the hazardous experiments on the pits.

The subcritical tests at the Nevada Test Site are classified as "high-hazard activities"—an understatement, because they involve putting plutonium and high explosives in close proximity. In addition to those tests, another chore at the site focuses on studying how the components of a nuclear weapon age. The challenges of that task are manifold. Scientists conduct tests in the U1a Facility, a tunnel complex one thousand feet beneath the desert floor. The work there also involves understanding all the materials—metals, plastics, and electronics—that go into a nuclear device.

While today's work focuses on subcritical tests, that doesn't mean the older parts of the test site—the "subsidence craters" left behind by nuclear tests—are merely a historical curiosity. Each subsidence crater has special meaning for nuclear weapons designers. Papazian said the craters reflect a weapons designer's skill: The lack of a subsidence crater can indicate the failure of a nuclear device. (Papazian was simplifying for our sake; subsidence depends on a bomb's yield and the particular geology of a test site. Craters can take weeks, sometimes years, to form—or they might never form at all. That said, the lack of a subsidence crater is at least one visual indication of a failed test.)

Now, a decade and a half after the end of nuclear testing, senior weapons designers take the next generation of scientists out to the Nevada Test Site. "One of the most interesting things they do is they put them on a bus and let them loose with somebody who knows the test site," Papazian said. "They go to places where failures occurred. The old designer explains the failures, and why that design failed for him or her."

It's a humbling experience when designers go to a test site where the ground didn't subside because of a failure, Papazian explained. "You'll see subsidence craters, huge subsidence craters, as huge as can be. That's an indicator of how well it performed. Some of them are as flat as can be. Cables are coming out, but they haven't subsided; it didn't work." For the nuclear weapons designers, he said, these flat areas bear a lesson: They are the topography of failure. "Gee, I made a mistake. I assumed something; I used a different material that I thought would work. My codes were wrong."

After the first nuclear test was conducted at the Trinity site, near Alamogordo, New Mexico, in 1945, the U.S. government initially conducted its postwar tests far out in the Pacific. But the logistics of conducting tests thousands of miles from the continental United States proved burdensome, and the Soviet Union's first test of a nuclear weapon in 1949 only heightened U.S. concerns about its own nuclear program. The government set its sights on a more convenient location. Thus began Operation Nutmeg, a secret effort to select a test site in the continental United States. Despite the fact that an 1863 treaty had promised the lands that now constitute the Nevada Test Site to the Shoshone Indians, the land was deemed uninhabited and suitable for tests. An official history of the test site begins in 1826, with the "first White man to enter northern Nevada."

Nancy Tufano, a spokeswoman employed by Bechtel Nevada, the company that runs the Nevada Test Site for the NNSA, chauffeured us out to the site in a white, government-issue SUV. As we drove north along Route 95, Tufano explained that at the peak of atomic testing, about ten thousand employees made the daily trek up this same highway, once known as the "widow maker"; the government eventually had to expand the treacherous two-lane road into a divided freeway. Now, most of the fifteen hundred or so workers at the site live in Las Vegas or in Pahrump, a suburb that is around forty miles from the site.

The southern boundary of the Nevada Test Site is sixty-five miles north of Las Vegas. Given the size of Las Vegas, one of the fastest-growing metropolitan areas in the United States, it seems odd today that the government would choose this place for top-secret testing. But much has changed in the past half century. Las Vegas has grown from a poky town of around twenty-five thousand to a city of three million. The site itself is bounded on three sides by the restricted airspace of the Nevada Test and Training Range, an Air Force combat training area and gunnery range; to the north it is protected by mountains. As we neared the site, Tufano gestured out the window. "We'll be passing the holding cells," she said, pointing to the chain-link pens where anti-nuclear demonstrators who trespassed on the site would be placed until they could be processed. Near the pens, a sign clearly marked the boundaries: NEVADA TEST SITE, NO TRESPASSING. Tufano noted that conflicts with protesters had been much more frequent during the days of nuclear testing. "Now they come about once a year, near Easter time," she continued. "They're very peaceful."

We passed through the main gates and into the Nevada Test Site, and Tufano pointed out sites of interest, like the Desert Rock Airstrip, one of several airstrips at the site. "They put soldiers in trenches in close proximity to atmospheric testing," she explained. They would be about five miles away from the actual test—the purpose was to study the effects of a nuclear weapon on soldiers. "What were the effects?" we asked.

"Probably not good. I don't really know," she replied.

We arrived in Mercury, the once-bustling town that served as the daytime home to workers at the height of testing. There was once even a bowling alley and a movie theater here, though both have long since closed. Mercury is now essentially a ghost town. And the end of testing not only depopulated the site, it stripped it of its sense of urgency. While security is still tight, times have changed since the Cold War. *New York Times* journalist William J. Broad described a visit to the site in 1986, when he observed armed guards roaming the territory with standing orders of "shoot to kill" in case someone tried to make off with a nuclear weapon. Today, officers from Wackenhut patrol the perimeter.

In the employee cafeteria, we collected our box lunches. The room was a 1950s holdover; until just a few years ago, a steak dinner cost barely a dollar. It was eerily quiet. The linoleum floors were freshly mopped, the cafeteria tables were set in neat rows, and someone had decorated the interior columns with American flags. There were no customers. Safety posters were plastered across the walls—some offering cheery motivational slogans, others warning against casual handling of machinery ("Think of safety as a hand up, not a hand off!"). The piped-in music added to the *Twilight Zone* feel. The only humorous touch was a vending machine with frozen burritos and chimichangas; its sign advertised "nukeables" over a photo of a mushroom cloud. Someone had taped a small handwritten note to the machine that identified the exact name of the test: Ivy Mike, 1952.

After a few minutes, Tufano reappeared. She had located our security escort. We were introduced to Darrel McPherson, a man with closely cropped white hair and a neatly trimmed mustache, tidily attired in a red polo shirt. He had worked at the Nevada Test Site for some forty-one years. Back when he started, the site was run by Reynolds Electric; Bechtel Nevada took over in 1995. McPherson was a miner who had been working in northern California when he heard they were looking for miners in Nevada. "This was the next place, so I came down here," he explained matter-of-factly.

He remained underground for much of his career, helping dig miles of tunnels for nuclear weapons tests until 1976, when he left for a few years to become a federal mine inspector. When we asked him what it was like to work here now, as opposed to during the Cold War, his response was economical: "It was much busier in those days."

*   *   *

The Nevada Test Site was a sandbox for nuclear weapons developers. It was the place where scientists could test the effects of nuclear weapons on human beings, the structures they inhabited, and the machinery they waged war with. Over four decades of active testing, they tested new nuclear weapons to see if they would work. They pulled older weapons out of the inventory to make sure they still worked. They tried new ways of launching nuclear warheads. And they learned about the basic physics of nuclear weapons.

Over several decades, the place was littered with nuclear debris. Like pottery shards, each artifact belongs to an era, reflecting the shifting priorities of the nuclear complex. Weapons laboratories wanted to resolve basic questions of weapons design. Civil defense planners hoped to build better shelters. And the military, of course, needed to practice for atomic warfare. There was always a bit of show business as well. Military and civilian observers watched the tests, as did members of the press. News Nob, an outcropping of rock on the east side of Mercury Highway in Area 6, offered the best view. Empty benches where reporters once sat remain there today.

We began our tour at Frenchman Flat in Area 5. Between January 1951 and July 1962, Frenchman Flat was ground zero for atmospheric nuclear tests. A total of fourteen nuclear devices were detonated here, starting with the one-kiloton Able, which was dropped from the bay of a B-50 bomber. The names of atomic tests always held a certain mystique, even when they were prosaic (Able was the first letter of the military alphabet at the time). Cultural sensitivity was not always a strong point. For a test conducted by the Defense Nuclear Agency, for example, someone designed a logo of an Indian straddling a bomb with his fingers stuck in his ears: The test was named Huron Landing. Another, Misty Rain, depicted a bikini-clad woman holding an umbrella.

The remnants of testing are scattered around Frenchman Flat. A single-track railway bridge was built for an atmospheric test (code name: Encore) by Army engineers. The structure was blasted apart by 450 pounds per square inch of dynamic overpressure—the twisted remains of the steel beams are still in place. Reinforced concrete buildings still lie in forlorn ruins, destroyed by the Priscilla test. McPherson pointed to the Hotel, a dilapidated structure with a number of rooms. The facade was used to test different kinds of building materials; the wood portion was blown away. In fact, just about every kind of structure that could be subjected to an atomic blast was tested at Frenchman Flat.

There were tests on living creatures as well. Because pigskin is remarkably similar to human flesh, the U.S. government experimented on live pigs. Tests in 1957 exposed some twelve hundred pigs to atomic detonation. Some of the pigs survived, but all that was left of their presence as we walked the test site was the wire mesh of their former holding pens—appropriately called the Pork Sheraton.

As we wandered among the ruins at Frenchman Flat, we asked McPherson about the dangers, if any, of radiation on the site. "There's less radiation here than in your house," he replied confidently. After four decades, the desiccated soil was essentially "at background"—showing only radiation levels from natural sources. But the place still had the look and feel of a *Mad Max* movie set, a blasted landscape bereft of inhabitants. We felt like lone survivors of a postapocalyptic America.

Later, we drove to the Apple II site—where two colonial-style houses, one wood and one brick, built to mimic American suburbia, remained standing. The two-story structures were part of the euphemistically dubbed Survival Town, created so scientists could gauge the effects of nuclear weapons on civil infrastructure. The Apple II houses, constructed as part of the Operation Teapot test series, were perhaps the most recognizable landmarks at the test site. The windowless shells were the surviving remnants of a mock town hit with a twenty-nine-kiloton nuclear blast. For the test, which took place on St. Patrick's Day, 1953, researchers from the Federal Civil Defense Administration placed mannequins inside various rooms of the houses to see how well they would survive. "They didn't do very well," Tufano said, adding that the ones in the basements did fare a little better.

Perhaps because the Apple II houses were meant to resemble Middle America, it was tempting to think about the effects of a nuclear blast on our own modest home. Our house was brick (that was good), but there was no basement (that was bad). Glass doors led to the balcony (very, very bad). Survival Town contained more than just residential buildings—the testers built everything from radio broadcast stations to electrical power systems, throwing in a few donated automobiles for good measure. Most of the debris has long since been cleared from the site, though, leaving the houses of Survival Town standing in a wide-open desert where they never belonged, an ominous relic of the era of nuclear testing.

In the afternoon, we drove up to the Monastery, which had once been used as a vantage point from which to observe tests in the Yucca Flat basin. Later, it was a communications relay point and—more prosaically—a warehouse. Now it was a place to break for lunch, a picnic spot with a panoramic view of the test site below. The Nevada Test Site was often a picnicker's delight. In the era of atmospheric testing, Las Vegans liked to drive to the outskirts of the range to watch the colorful fireballs blossom in the sky.

The 1963 Limited Test Ban Treaty—which prohibited testing in the atmosphere, in space, and underwater—put an end to the fireworks show. The final aboveground test—Little Feller I—must have been a bit of a disappointment for those in attendance. The yield was relatively tiny, less than twenty kilotons. Testing then went completely underground, and attempts to limit the power of weapons testing came later.

In the era of underground tests, Mercury became a city of miners, who carved out hundreds of miles of underground caverns. Men like McPherson were recruited from around the country to come to Nevada to build this netherworld where a new era of nuclear weapons testing would commence. Work on a test—which might take up to a year to prepare for—began with miners drilling the deep underground holes where the nuclear devices would be emplaced. A canister packed with diagnostic tools—ultrasensitive instruments used to measure the nuclear shot—was suspended at the top of a prefabricated "bogey tower" that crowned the site. In the last step, the nuclear device and the instrumentation canister were lowered into the ground. Diagnostic cables snaking out from the canister led to a trailer, where the data from the blast would be recorded.

With the end of atmospheric testing in 1963, the topography of the test site was transformed. Instead of blasted railroad trestles or ghostly Survival Towns, the relics of underground testing were the massive subsidence craters that pockmarked the desert floor. A nuclear detonation vaporized tons of rock beneath the ground, collapsing the soil above in a saucer-shaped depression. Seen from the air, the Nevada Test Site—with its miles of barren soil marked by perfectly spherical craters—looks like the surface of the moon. Underground nuclear weapons testing may not have been quite the spectator sport that drew Las Vegans in the 1950s, but it had its own sense of drama and mystique. William J. Broad described in the *New York Times* how an underground test proceeded:

> On "D Day," the test site is cleared of all personnel except a small group of scientists and security guards who drive out to a trailer known as the "red shack" to electronically arm the weapon. Two of the scientists carry a special briefcase and a bag of tiny cubes that have numbers painted on their sides. They alternately pick cubes out of the bag and punch the numbers into an "arm enable" device in the briefcase, generating a random code that is sent to the weapon on a special electrical cable.
>
> The scientists then drive across the desert to the "control point" in a mountain pass overlooking the test site. Here, in a high-technology complex surrounded by armed guards and barbed wire, they again open their briefcase and send the same random code to the weapon. It is now armed.
>
> [. . .]
>
> If everything is ready, the test controller gives the go-ahead and a secret coded signal is sent to the red shack. There is no single "button." Instead, the signal starts a computer that automatically cycles through a 5-to-15-minute program that ends with the detonation of the weapon. At any point, the controller can halt the test by pressing the red stop button.

If all went as planned, the weapon would detonate, and in a flash, tons of bedrock would disappear. There would be no mushroom cloud, just a seismic tremor. The actual explosion—which millions of dollars in equipment were dedicated to measuring—was over in just a fraction of a second. "If you had a camera that took a million frames per second, you'd only get a few frames," McPherson explained.

At Area 3—the Yucca Flat basin—we stopped to visit Bilby, one of the largest subsidence craters. Bilby was the result of a 1963 underground test with a yield of some 249 kilotons, which created an aftershock that could be felt all the way to Las Vegas. The crater that formed in its wake was 1,800 feet in diameter and 80 feet deep. Bilby was impressive, but it was nothing next to Sedan, a monstrous crater excavated in 1962 by a shallowly buried 104-kiloton device. The explosion moved around twelve million tons of earth, carving out a crater 1,280 feet in diameter and 230 feet deep, according to the *Nevada Test Site Guide*. The seismic energy released equaled that of an earthquake measuring 4.75 on the Richter scale. Perhaps no other place at the Nevada Test Site gives a more immediate sense of the awesome destructive power of a thermonuclear weapon.

The irony of Sedan, however, was that the test that created it was meant to demonstrate that the hydrogen bomb could be put to constructive use. The test was part of Operation Plowshare, which sought "peaceful" uses for thermonuclear weapons. The Sedan test was designed to see whether nuclear weapons could be used to dig canals. Technically, it was a success, evidenced by the massive crater spanning before us. There was one minor hitch: The ground was radioactive.*

Over the years, pressure to restrict testing increased. The Threshold Test Ban Treaty of 1974 limited weapons tests to 150 kilotons. The next major move to limit testing didn't come until after the Cold War.

On September 23, 1992, the U.S. conducted an underground nuclear test code-named Divider. No one at the time knew that it would be the last U.S. nuclear test of the twentieth century. Less than a month later, President George H. W. Bush signed a bill restricting any further nuclear tests. President Bill Clinton in 1993 extended the moratorium through 1995. The next year, Clinton signed the Comprehensive Nuclear-Test-Ban Treaty, the last of three treaties limiting nuclear tests. While the Senate never ratified the treaty—and eventually rejected it in 1999—the United States has continued an indefinite moratorium on testing.

The last remnants of underground nuclear testing stand like lone sentries at the Nevada Test Site. They are named Icecap and Gabbs, tests scheduled for 1993 that never took place. Their tall bogey towers still loom over the desert, monuments to tests that never were. On our

---

* The aftershock of Sedan was felt again in 2005, when Sudanese officials discovered a reference in an official U.S. government document to the "Sudan" nuclear test. That surprising revelation was the result of a typo in the *Congressional Record*, but officials in Khartoum nonetheless launched an official inquiry.

way back, we stopped off at Gabbs, a test that would have been conducted by Lawrence Livermore National Laboratory. Today, the site looks much like it did some fifteen years ago: A tower stands in place over the shaft where the nuclear weapon would have been emplaced. Diagnostic cables run across the field to trailers that are no longer there. After fifteen years of sitting under the sun, the tower and testing equipment are still in reasonable shape, though bits of metal littered the area around them.

We wandered around the bogey tower, stopping to look at the "mouse hole" where the nuclear device would have been lowered for the test. It was covered by a metal plate that looked rather like a manhole. A few jackrabbits raced through the dust on the other side of the tower, while a lizard slithered over the nearby concrete. The test site today is filled with wildlife. Back in the days of testing, the animals followed the test crews, McPherson explained. When the site workers would go out to get ready for a test, crows would circle above, hoping for some bits of food. Later came the coyotes.

When President Bush suspended testing in 1992, no one was sure how long the moratorium would last. The irony, as Papazian had pointed out to us earlier that day, was that weapons scientists today must rely on data from the era of testing to determine whether or not nuclear weapons will work. And yet that data collected during the era of testing was not envisioned for stockpile stewardship.

As we contemplated that dilemma, we noticed more vehicles traveling down the desert highway that bisects the test site. Earlier that morning, the road had been strangely empty, but over the course of the afternoon, we had seen an increasing number of vehicles traveling deeper into the test site. Some were carrying large equipment. McPherson explained that most of the routine work at the test site goes on Monday through Thursday (we visited on a Thursday), with most workers taking Fridays off. Since the site is virtually empty on Fridays, this scheduling makes it easier to cordon off workers from potentially hazardous areas, and also to ensure secrecy, if need be. "They're doing a test tomorrow," McPherson said.

So could he tell us what, exactly, tomorrow's test would involve?

"No," he said, replying in a manner that was polite but didn't invite further questions.

We decided to press our luck a bit. Could it be a subcritical test of plutonium pits, we asked? "No," McPherson replied. "When we do subcritical tests, they are announced the day before." He then offered a hint. Some of the testing done at the Nevada Test Site for other "customers," like the Defense Department, isn't always announced, he explained. As we talked, a flatbed truck trundled down the road, towing the wingless fuselage of a C-130 cargo plane. "What's that for?" we asked. McPherson shook his head firmly. "I didn't see anything," he said, like a devoted atheist asked to confirm an apparition of the Virgin Mary.

We understood, at that point, that we weren't meant to have seen it either.

The C-130 was likely part of ongoing military and homeland security testing. The military uses the Nevada Test Site for chemical and biological weapons preparedness, as well as to test some of its own high explosives. That sort of testing didn't seem to inspire a veteran of atomic testing like McPherson, who said such tests were "not anything that spectacular."

We stood silently for a moment as the vehicles drove by, taking in the incongruous scene of a seemingly abandoned test site suddenly gearing up for action. Rather than being closed or abandoned, the test site had the distinct feeling of a play at intermission—like a stage that at any point could be filled with actors springing back to action.

The disembodied aircraft fuselage faded off into the distance, and we got back into the SUV. As we drove toward the Strip, we saw in clear view the strange parallels between Las Vegas—a city dominated by imitation skyscrapers and faux monuments—and the test site, where abandoned houses, train trestles, and even aircraft mimic real-world places. Even the Boneyard at 5119 Cameron Street—the final resting place for vintage neon signs from the Strip—summons the landscape of a postapocalyptic America.

That the test site itself had become a part of the Vegas tourism experience was not completely strange; in a sense, the site was always about showmanship. Whether it was picnickers watching the mushroom clouds or reporters parked at News Nob, the test site was meant to provide a vivid show of might, not just to the American people, but also to their enemies.

There may never again be a war quite like the Cold War, and there is no other battlefield quite like the Nevada Test Site, where a country nuked its own territory nearly a thousand times to demonstrate to its adversaries the devastating strength of its arsenal. The town of Mercury—and the Nevada Test Site—may never again be the bustling place of the Cold War, but it seems quite probable that the vast tract of land, meant to help deter an opposing superpower, will find new purpose. As we watched the C-130 fuselage disappear down the road, we realized the war on terror was providing a new rationale for the Nevada Test Site.

CHAPTER 2

When Knowledge Is an Endangered Thing

Travels Through New Mexico's Nuclear Landscape

It was nearing 100 degrees, we were almost twenty miles from the nearest town, and we desperately needed something a mere twenty feet away. The sentry looked at us sympathetically but shook his head no: We wouldn't be allowed to use the portable toilet on the other side of the gate until our security escort arrived. Rules were rules, and this was an Army base.

Visiting the birthplace of the atomic bomb sounds like a great idea until you reach the north entrance of the White Sands Missile Range. It's an hour-and-a-half drive from Albuquerque to the Stallion Gate, where we had been instructed to wait for an escort to lead us through security. The U.S. military owns this remote stretch of New Mexico desert, and anyone who wants to visit Trinity—site of the world's first detonation of a nuclear device—must be accompanied by an Army chaperone.

It was early June, just one month before the sixtieth anniversary of the 1945 Trinity atomic test. The next month, thousands of atomic tourists were expected to make the pilgrimage. The Trinity site is a tribute to the scientists who devised the world's most powerful weapon, an achievement that brought World War II to a swift close and kept the United States and the Soviet Union from a direct military confrontation. We had come to New Mexico with our own nuclear agenda: to figure out if the bomb makers were still needed.

The Trinity test was conducted in the early-morning hours of July 16, 1945, a culmination of the Manhattan Project, the marathon wartime effort to design and build the atomic bomb. A team of scientists working at the project's secret laboratory in Los Alamos, New Mexico, led the final assembly, and the road to Trinity retraces their journey south. The plutonium core for the bomb was transported from Los Alamos in the back of an Army sedan. A convoy delivered the high-explosives assembly in the middle of the night. The test site, 210 miles from Los Alamos, was selected because of its remote location—and because a mountain ridge shielded it from the nearest population centers. Six decades later, Trinity is still remote.

If nuclear weapons played a part in winning the Cold War, they also shaped the geography of New Mexico. A vast weapons complex grew out of the Manhattan Project, and today, the Department of Energy, which runs the nuclear weapons industry, is the single biggest employer in the state. We had come to New Mexico to explore that link between history and the present day. Yet Trinity is not a place that automatically lends itself to profound thoughts about the nuclear age. About forty-five minutes after we parked at the Stallion Gate, two cheerful Army public affairs officials—Debbie Bingham and Jim Eckles—arrived to take us down to the Jornada del Muerto (often translated, if incorrectly, as the "journey of death"), the remote valley where the test took place. Accompanying us were a Japanese camera crew and a Fox News team from El Paso, Texas. Members of the San Francisco Opera, which was readying *Doctor Atomic*, a production on the life of Manhattan Project leader J. Robert Oppenheimer, had been scheduled to come but couldn't make it.

Once our IDs were checked, we drove in a small convoy the approximately twenty miles from the Stallion Gate to Trinity, passing the yucca trees that guard the route toward the Sierra Oscura. As we approached the final stretch of road leading to the site, we could make out the faint outline of ground zero, a barren circle of earth. The scorching heat from the blast had carved out a shallow crater a thousand feet across; it had vaporized the shot tower that cradled the bomb; and it had melted the sand into pieces of shiny glass, called Trinitite. A famous photograph of the time shows Oppenheimer and Major General Leslie Groves, the hard-driving military officer in charge of the Manhattan Project, standing by a few pieces of twisted rebar jutting from the desert floor. That was all that remained of the tower. Today, the area around ground zero is demarcated by a fence.

The White Sands Missile Range holds "open houses" for the public twice a year. On the day we visited, officials were gearing up for the sixtieth anniversary open house, and expecting a record turnout. New portable toilets were lined up outside the gates leading to ground zero. Parked nearby was Jumbo, a reminder that all weapons development— even when successful—has the potential to become a boondoggle. The 214-ton steel container was meant to contain the priceless plutonium used in the Trinity device in case the explosives failed to set off the fission reaction. In the end, Manhattan Project designers decided not to use the $12 million vessel, suspending it instead from a test tower several hundred yards from ground zero. The container survived the atomic blast (as well as a later attempt to demolish it). Jumbo now sits at the Trinity gate, ready to greet visitors.

For years, no one knew what to do about Trinitite, the radioactive remnants of desert sand that the bomb melted into glass. Until recently, the eerie bluish green rocks sat unprotected around the site, disappearing into the pockets of tourists. Now a bunkerlike structure sits opposite ground zero to protect pieces for future generations, although small, random bits can still be easily spotted scattered around the grounds.

Today, the site is safe for tourists, we were told, although it's still slightly radioactive. Yes, the radiation is slightly "above background," said Bingham, but "you'd have to eat your weight in Trinitite" for the radiation to harm you. Visitors wouldn't be let in if it weren't safe. "After all, we're the government," she added without a hint of irony.

The device tested at Trinity was an "implosion device." A series of high-explosive lenses fired simultaneously to compress a six-kilogram sphere of plutonium to form a supercritical mass. Though there were two bomb designs at the time, one based on plutonium and the other on uranium, the reason for testing the plutonium implosion device was simple: There was only enough uranium for one bomb, and its designers were reasonably sure that it would work. Trinity proved the implosion design, paving the way for the decision to drop two nuclear weapons on Japan. The Little Boy device—essentially a cannon that fired a slug of uranium-235 at another uranium "target" to kick off a fission reaction—was dropped untested on August 5, 1945, over Hiroshima. Fat Man, a weapon similar to that tested at Trinity, was dropped on Nagasaki on August 9, 1945.

Trinity, in that respect, was the first nuclear battlefield. We followed the perimeter fence at ground zero, where the Army had commemorated its achievement. A series of photos showed the first milliseconds of the atomic era, captured by a high-speed camera. Other photos featured Manhattan Project workers; another, a newspaper headline from the day the first nuclear weapon was dropped. The ground zero site itself was somewhat ahistorical, however. The obelisk marking it was made from local lava for no particular reason, and a plaque acknowledged White Sands base commander Major General Frederick Thorlin, whose only contribution, Eckles admitted, was "chipping in the money" for the memorial that was erected in 1965. Other elements seem equally out of place. Signs tell visitors to beware of oryx, an African big-game species that the state of New Mexico introduced for trophy hunting.

Standing at ground zero did little to fire the imagination; there wasn't much left here that reflected the awesome power of a nuclear bomb. The Japanese television crew, which was finding few things of interest to tape, began trying to interview the other journalists at the site. We did what most people do after handling fragments of Trinitite: We brushed off our hands and drove with our escorts the two miles over to the McDonald Ranch House, where scientists had assembled the plutonium core of the Trinity device. The building is now restored and decorated with historic bric-a-brac. We wandered through the musty rooms, looking at the exhibits. A copy of Albert Einstein's now-famous 1939 letter to President Franklin Roosevelt—outlining the possibility of building an atomic weapon—was on prominent display.

Trinity, in essence, had been transformed into something of a remote tourist trap, another addition to the National Register of Historic Places. Yet none of the mundane items on display at the McDonald Ranch House spoke to the tremendous power of nuclear weaponry.

On our way out of the White Sands Missile Range, we had passed by facilities operated by the Defense Threat Reduction Agency (DTRA), an arm of the Pentagon that, among other things, tests the effects of nuclear weapons on military equipment. At the range's Large Blast Thermal Simulator, scientists work to re-create some of the conditions of a nuclear blast, such as the massive shock wave. DTRA has also touched off a number of giant bombs—using fertilizer and fuel oil, the same basic formula used to level the Alfred P. Murrah Federal Building in Oklahoma City—to mimic the effects of a nuclear blast. Our escorts had witnessed some of those tests, including one that simulated the equivalent of an eight-kiloton shock wave. It was close enough to the experience of a fission explosion. Bingham described how the humidity in the air created a rainbow that moved outward with the blast. "You could see the shock wave coming at us," Eckles added.

After leaving Trinity, we stopped briefly in the tiny New Mexico town of San Antonio to eat a late lunch in the darkened interior of the Owl Bar and Cafe, a restaurant and bar known for its green chili cheese-burgers. An old haunt of Manhattan Project scientists, it didn't look like it had changed much since the 1940s. A man in a cowboy hat sat on a bar stool, enjoying a can of Schlitz. Rather than joining him, we opted for iced tea and studied the directions to Los Alamos.

The drive from Trinity to Los Alamos took us about four and a half hours. The landscape slowly transformed as we left the flat scrub and desert vegetation of southern New Mexico for the dramatic Pajarito Plateau, the volcanic mesa on which the city is built. Even in the era of modern highways and well-paved roads, the trip is a reminder of how distant the city is from a major metropolitan area. And that physical isolation—which had made the location ideal for national security— was now causing problems for the historic Los Alamos National Laboratory.

Arriving in Los Alamos, with its neat rows of retro suburban houses, we had the distinct feeling we had been transported back to the *Leave it to Beaver* era. We stayed overnight with a cousin, who lived in the community of White Rock, a small town adjacent to Los Alamos. Founded in the 1940s by the Atomic Energy Commission to house construction workers for Los Alamos, White Rock was reborn in the 1970s to house Los Alamos' growing community. Today, it has the white-picket-fence feel of the old Los Alamos. Despite the idyllic setting, however, the place was going through something of an upheaval.

In the weeks preceding our trip to Los Alamos, the lab had been on the receiving end of some devastating press. The Project on Government Oversight (POGO), a watchdog group that frequently criticized the nuclear labs, hosted a dramatic press conference to publicize a brutal assault on Los Alamos whistle-blower Tommy Hook. The assault,

POGO hinted, was linked to Hook's upcoming congressional testimony on fraud at the lab. At the press conference, Hook's wife tearfully stood in for her husband, who was still recovering in the hospital. Her appearance sparked a flurry of press stories and speculation that Hook could have been the victim of a lab reprisal.

In fact, the truth was more banal. According to later accounts, Hook's night of whistle-blowing activities included a lap dance and drinks at Cheeks, a Santa Fe strip club, followed by a drunken altercation in the parking lot. The incident was part of a broader pattern of bad headlines that had plagued the lab for the better part of a decade. In 1999, Wen Ho Lee, a Taiwanese American scientist at Los Alamos, was accused of providing nuclear weapons secrets to China. The scandal made national headlines and brought Los Alamos under greater scrutiny, even as the criminal case against Lee fell apart. In the end, Lee pleaded guilty to the much-lesser charge—still a felony—of mishandling classified data. At that point, he had served 278 days in solitary confinement. (We contacted Wen Ho Lee's daughter, who politely informed us that her father was, perhaps understandably, not speaking to the press.)

After the Wen Ho Lee case, things got worse at Los Alamos. Missing computer disks, laboratory accidents, and alleged fraud and theft were all reported out of the lab. Security infractions—a major concern, given the highly sensitive nature of nuclear weapons design—multiplied, and critics began to wonder if the scientists of Los Alamos were capable of being trusted with national security. Los Alamos, the birthplace of the atomic bomb, the epitome of science in the service of national security, seemed incapable of competently managing its own affairs.

Part of the problem was the peculiar culture of Los Alamos, described to us by one scientist as a combination of living "out in the boondocks" and in a "one-company town." The eccentric atmosphere of Los Alamos dated back to the Manhattan Project. Oppenheimer—who once wrote a friend, "My two great loves are physics and desert country"—selected the site based on the beauty and isolation of the mesa. But the austerity of the desert, for others, was nothing more than a curse. "Nobody can think straight in a place like that," exclaimed the eminent Hungarian American physicist Leo Szilard. "Everybody who goes there will go crazy."

There was a lot to be said for Szilard's observation. In the wake of the Wen Ho Lee scandal, the press seized on an image of Los Alamos as a sort of nuclear cloud-cuckoo-land, populated with scientists too preoccupied with theoretical problems to bother with the mundane issues of laboratory safety and handling classified data. Government watchdog groups took careful note of each scandal at the lab, from mishandling of radioactive materials to multiple security lapses. Every bit of news—no matter how small or insignificant—was picked up and amplified in the national press. The missing computer disks, credit card fraud, and laboratory accidents all danced across the national front pages. In one case, a Los Alamos employee allegedly tried to buy a thirty-thousand-dollar Mustang using a government-issued credit card. And that view of a dysfunctional laboratory, unfortunately, was reinforced by remarks made by the lab director, George "Pete" Nanos, a former Navy admiral who referred publicly to a "culture of arrogance" at the lab—and who berated scientists for being "cowboys" and "butt-heads."

By 2004, after the reports of missing classified computer disks surfaced, Los Alamos seemed to be in free fall. Nanos ordered a complete shutdown of operations. "This willful flouting of the rules must stop, and I don't care how many people I have to fire to make it stop," he wrote in a company-wide memo. "If you think the rules are silly, if you think compliance is a joke, please resign now and save me the trouble."

The unpopular decision left thousands of already-disgruntled employees even angrier—and unable to perform their work. By the time it emerged that the missing computer disks were phantoms—a mistake made on an inventory list—the damage had been done. Some parts of Los Alamos would remain shut down for months, leaving employees essentially twiddling their thumbs.

Full operations at the lab finally resumed after seven months. But the turmoil at Los Alamos had come at a critical point. The contract for the laboratory, which had been run since its inception by the University of California on behalf of the federal government, was up for competition. The university, paired with federal contractor Bechtel, was pitted against the University of Texas, which was bidding with defense contractor Lockheed Martin. Along with simple financial considerations (staying within the university's pension system, for instance), many scientists worried that a change of management would create a more corporate culture at the lab. And a large defense company, many feared, would be less concerned about science.

There was another concern, one voiced particularly by opponents of nuclear weapons. Stockpile stewardship, the effort to maintain nuclear weapons without full-scale testing, was a decade old by 2005, and questions were being raised about its long-term prospects. Under Complex 2030, however, Los Alamos potentially could take on new roles: as the home to a new plutonium production facility and as the designer of warheads to replace the current stockpile. "Stockpile stewardship is not a growth program," observed Greg Mello, the director of a local antinuclear group and a frequent lab critic. "It doesn't have the potential for lighting up the weapons complex with new production."

Los Alamos was born in secrecy. During the Manhattan Project, when the facility was designated as "Site Y," mail to Los Alamos residents was sent to a post office box in Santa Fe. The authorities concealed the existence of not only the laboratory but the entire community, and the town was closed off from the world until 1957. Today, security at Los Alamos National Laboratory is still tight. The morning after our arrival, we showed up at the lab early for a full day of interviews only to be informed by our public affairs escort that our digital recorders had been flagged as a concern by the security office. Rather than going "behind the gate"—i.e., inside the classified facilities—we would do all our interviews in unclassified areas. That meant being locked for the better part of the day inside a small, windowless conference room with a sign that read: THE TRUSTED, COMPETITIVE SCIENTIFIC SOLUTION FOR TODAY'S AND TOMORROW'S NATIONAL SECURITY CHALLENGES.

Despite that platitudinous mission statement, the lab's main job is still nuclear weapons, where more than half of its approximately two-billion-dollar budget goes each year. Most of that money goes to ensuring that nuclear weapons still work. As it happened, our visit to Los Alamos coincided with a significant event at the lab. John Immele, the lab's associate director for national security, informed us that the interim lab director, Robert Kuckuck, was holding a four-hour review of the B-61 gravity bomb—one of the primary nuclear weapons in the U.S. stockpile. It had been fourteen years since the United States had last detonated a nuclear weapon in a test, and two decades since a new nuclear weapon had entered the stockpile. So now, each year, the labs had to certify—in a secret document—that the nuclear weapons in the stockpile were still reliable. "There are significant issues that have come up," Immele told us. "But the answer has not been testing, the answer has been work-arounds."

In other words, Los Alamos' main job is to make sure that each and every individual component of the physics package of a nuclear warhead works, a task that has expanded, in one case, to remanufacturing plutonium triggers. But beyond nuclear weapons, the lab does significant work in everything from medical research to homeland security, and its budget, like that of the other nuclear labs, has crept up significantly despite the fact that nuclear weaponry is no longer a growth business.

The current situation, as Immele described it, is as much about politics as science. When, in 1995, the lab director realized that the debate over a test ban was inevitable, a number of key Department of Energy officials worked out a compromise. They proposed the Stockpile Stewardship Program as a way of monitoring and maintaining the nuclear arsenal without testing. The Democrats wanted the Comprehensive Nuclear-Test-Ban Treaty (CTBT); the Republicans wanted a weapons program that sustained nuclear deterrence. Both parties saw an end to nuclear testing as an acceptable political trade. The labs gave up developing nuclear weapons, and in turn, they received a tremendous infusion of funds—money that supporters argued would support the basic science and experimental work needed to maintain nuclear weapons without testing and to attract new talent to the labs.

But for critics, stockpile stewardship was little more than a bribe paid to the labs in return for endorsing the test ban. Richard Garwin, a prominent physicist and longtime weapons adviser, described the bargain between laboratory directors and the Clinton administration as a political expediency. "What could they get?" Garwin said. "Sandia got the microelectronics research center, which had minimal relevance to the CTBT. Los Alamos got the Dual-Axis Radiographic Hydrodynamic Test Facility. Livermore got the National Ignition Facility—the white elephant eating us out of house and home. [The laboratory directors] all maintained these were essential to stockpile stewardship, which they are not."

In other words, Garwin concluded that the labs were bought off with fancy science experiments. But Immele disagreed that the goodies bestowed on the lab were a bribe. " 'Bought off' is derogatory," he insisted, when we asked him about the implications of such a plan, which funneled billions of dollars into a laboratory system that critics argue should have been scaled back rather than expanded with the end of the Cold War. According to Immele, the matter was already decided when then-president Bill Clinton arrived at the lab in 1993. As Los Alamos lore has it, Clinton got into the car with Siegfried Hecker, the director of the lab at the time, and said something to the effect of, "We don't need nuclear testing, do we?" A decision had been made, but the nuclear labs had seen it coming. They had prepared a blueprint for a program that would maintain the stockpile—and ensure their survival.

Ten years later, however, the question remained whether stockpile stewardship would continue to work. After all, if you are going to launch a nuke, you had better be sure it goes off with the right kind of bang. "We realized as we went through the nineties without nuclear testing, the Department of Defense . . . didn't have a way to say, 'I understand,' " Immele said. "We came up with this engineering margin scheme. It's sort of well known in the strength of bridge girders. You design it only to flex it to a certain amount, under a certain amount of weight."

Take, for instance, the "primary," the nuclear fission device that creates the necessary radiation, heat and pressure to set off a "secondary" component that yields a much larger fusion reaction. The bombs dropped on Hiroshima and Nagasaki were "fission" devices. Thermonuclear weapons are dramatically more powerful. They derive most of their power from fusion, the process that fuels the sun. In a modern thermonuclear weapon, like the Los Alamos–designed W88, a plutonium fission device—the primary—is used to touch off the secondary fusion reaction. If the primary doesn't generate enough explosive power, then the secondary won't go off. The problem is that not everyone agrees on how much margin is enough to ensure the weapon will work.

During the Cold War, when new weapons were constantly being produced, riskier designs allowed the military to fit warheads in ever-smaller packages. But as the stockpile aged without being tested or replaced by new weapons, there was, over time, more uncertainty about whether bombs would go off as designed. "The Navy saw this coming and said: 'Will you guys look at having a warhead that has more margins?'" Immele recalled. "At the time it was called Robo-bomb."*

Thus emerged the concept for a new bomb, at least in theory. Robo-bomb was kicked around as an idea until 2003, when, as Immele explained it, a "seminal event" took place. During a stockpile steward-ship conference that brought together officials from the military and the Department of Energy—essentially the buyers and sellers of nuclear weapons—the proposal for a Reliable Replacement Warhead was put forward. "Pete [Nanos], with a lot of support from within the lab—he deserves the credit as the leader on this—said: 'Why don't we look again at what we call RRW?'"

In a sense, it was good timing, Immele explained. The Department of Energy was thinking about affordability, the Pentagon was interested in the idea of a new weapon, and there was concern, in general, about the ability of the labs to make new weapons. "It all came together at that meeting," he said.

Did that mean Nanos, who had just been forced out of Los Alamos in the days prior to our visit, was the proverbial father of the RRW?

Immele replied: "Pete's talk was the high point of the meeting."

Nuclear weapons scientists sometimes hang pictures of their favorite tests above their desks; they can describe, in loving detail, the very personal reasons for their choices. Sometimes it has to do with the limits of a particular design or the start of a new generation of weapons. One prominent government weapons scientist, upon his retirement, was presented with a life-size mock-up of a nuclear weapon—a throwback to one of the final scenes of *Dr. Strangelove*, when Slim Pickens rides the bomb to its target like a rodeo cowboy on a bull. Another admitted that he named his son after Ivy Mike, the 1952 hydrogen bomb test.

Yet the glamour of the nuclear weapons club faded with the end of the Cold War, leaving weapons designers at Los Alamos in a state of suspended animation, unable to do the primary job they had been trained to do: design new weapons. The lab has not designed a new

---

* Immele told us that the name Robo-bomb, short for "robust bomb," was later changed to avoid confusion with the Robust Nuclear Earth Penetrator, the controversial nuclear bunker buster.

nuclear weapon since the 1980s, which raises an obvious question. In an era when the United States is no longer designing nuclear weapons, what purpose does a nuclear design laboratory serve? Are nuclear weapons scientists an anachronism?

With his starched white shirt and somber black sport coat, James Mercer-Smith, better known to his colleagues at Los Alamos as "Jas," looked a bit like a cross between a Protestant minister and a small-town undertaker. In fact, he is, by a certain measure, one of the most powerful men on Earth. He is a thermonuclear weapons designer, something of a rarity in a country that no longer makes nuclear weapons. The last new nuclear weapon entered the U.S. arsenal in 1987, and in 1995, the United States launched stockpile stewardship to maintain its current weapons indefinitely.

The program has had one troubling side effect, at least for those who believe the United States must retain its ability to build nuclear weapons. As Linton Brooks, the head of the NNSA, told us in his office in Washington, nuclear weapons designers are now an endangered species. "The people who have brought a weapons system from concept to fielding, who are still working at the labs, could all be carried in one bus," he said. And with a few exceptions, Brooks added, most of those designers could "retire tomorrow."

At some point soon, very soon, the last scientist to have actually designed a nuclear weapon will retire, and with that, some fear, a trove of knowledge may be lost, possibly forever. But does that matter? Mercer-Smith, who came to Los Alamos in the early eighties, is a member of that dwindling band, and he affects a certain gravitas. As he began our interview, he thoughtfully folded his hands together as if about to say grace. The gesture seemed almost stylized, as if it had been rehearsed in a mirror for maximum effect. "Thermonuclear weapons are wonderful weapons," he told us with an ever-so-slight smile. "It's the only one in history that has never, ever been used."

Mercer-Smith was arguing that the potential devastation of these weapons—classic nuclear deterrence—was what had maintained the peace. It was enduring Cold War logic, particularly at the time when he was studying. Mercer-Smith was an undergraduate student in physics at the New College of Florida. "I will brag about my college," he said. "It gets about the same number of Fulbrights and National Merit Scholarships as the rest of the Florida university system combined." He went on to study astronomy and astrophysics at Yale—a typical background for a nuclear weapons designer. Understanding the complex processes involved in the birth, life, and death of stars is similar to mastering the concept of thermonuclear weapons.

Mercer-Smith came to the lab in 1983, rising to be the group leader of the thermonuclear design group and then deputy associate director for nuclear weapons. He had worked on half a dozen nuclear tests at the Nevada Test Site. His first shot, Duoro, was named after a New Mexican ghost town. Then the lab began naming tests after major cities in Texas. His last shot was Lubbock, in 1991, the year before the United States stopped testing nuclear weapons. "It should tell you how people from New Mexico feel about Texas," he joked. When we met with Mercer-Smith, he was back in the thermonuclear design group, except that Los Alamos no longer designed new thermonuclear weapons.

While making a name for himself as a top-notch designer, Mercer-Smith had also cultivated a media image, giving interviews to journalists—such as us—who parachuted into Los Alamos. He was always ready with pithy quotes about nuclear annihilation. In Jo Ann Shroyer's 1997 book on Los Alamos, *Secret Mesa*, he described his role as the "evil witch in Grimm's fairy tales" who "scare[s] little children into behaving." His flair for words made him popular with the press, though he admitted to us now that at least one time it had gotten him in hot water. Fond of literary allusions and historical references, Mercer-Smith told us that nuclear weapons were part of a Faustian bargain: The price of peace was the threat of Armageddon. Part of that bargain, of course, was also personal. To be a weapons designer, particularly a good one, you had to take pride in doing something that was, in the classic sense of the word, quite terrible: creating weapons of mass destruction.

He especially liked the topic of extinction. "I've always been interested in the plague of the fourteenth century," he announced, gazing off to the other end of the conference room, as if searching for a nonexistent window that would look out over the desert mesa. "You're in New Mexico now, so you know the bubonic plague is endemic in the state. You didn't know that, did you?"

As Mercer-Smith explained, plague is still relatively common in New Mexico. It's not a problem for local residents, whose doctors understand the symptoms. The problem is for out-of-state residents who visit, leave, and then see doctors unfamiliar with the disease. But plague, he pointed out, once had a far more devastating reach. "In 1346, when the plague got to Constantinople, and then spread through the Mediterranean very quickly, a third of Europe died," he said. "But civilization didn't die because the infrastructure was there. Nuclear weapons are qualitatively different in that they will not only kill very large numbers of people in a very grotesque fashion, but they also destroy civilization. They will destroy that infrastructure. You can't build back."

That sense of doom—a future that can only be deterred by possessing nuclear weapons—did not leave Mercer-Smith with much room for optimism. "We stall for time," he said, explaining the laboratory's duty. So when we asked him what he thought about the entire notion of stockpile stewardship, his response was predictably dark. "What we're trying to do is . . . maintain a nuclear deterrent and to do it without nuclear testing," he said. "From a purely technical standpoint, that doesn't make any sense."

He continued, "As a political decision, the United States, and the other major powers, have said, 'We're going to try to have our cake and eat it too. We're not going to test, we don't want anyone else to test, but we're going to maintain a nuclear stockpile for the foreseeable future.' "

Mercer-Smith took a far darker view of the stockpile than Immele. Yet some of his views were nostalgic. Back in the days of nuclear testing, he and other designers would go to the Nevada Test Site to witness the craters left by the underground detonation of bombs they'd designed. Some designers, as we were told, visit the craters to understand failure, tourists go to gawk at nuclear aftermath, but Mercer-Smith went to revisit something far more personal. "You have this odd relationship with your holes," he said, again gathering his hands in front of his face. He paused to ensure that he had our full attention and then continued, "I love my holes, I visit them whenever I go to the test site." Conscious that he had said something quite provocative, he paused for several seconds before adding, "On the other hand, in a rational way, that's a very terrifying dilemma."

Only Mercer-Smith didn't look particularly terrified. What seemed to worry him, rather, was the professional obsolescence of nuclear weapons designers. He came to the lab because he was concerned that the best Soviet physicists were disappearing into Russia's closed nuclear cities to work on weapons, while U.S. students were pursuing academic careers. Now, Mercer-Smith said, he again worried that the American public had lost touch with the threat of nuclear annihilation.

Recruiting top-notch scientists to Los Alamos was becoming an uphill battle, particularly in an era when new graduates didn't see the need for nuclear weapons. Those who did come were often lured by the promise of funding for basic science. As Tracy Ellen Lavezzi-Light, a young scientist at the lab, told us, she was initially uncomfortable with the idea of working on weapons. "I want to help people, I don't want to blow them up," she said. Scientists like Lavezzi-Light were allowed to split their time between basic science and work supporting nuclear weapons. "You don't just do science," she said. "The deal you make is: I'm going to do some science, if I'm lucky, and I'm also going to do technical work in support of missions."

But with the contract for Los Alamos set to change hands, and the lab possibly moving into plutonium production, many scientists were concerned that the facility would also lose its money for basic science. Without science, and without nuclear testing, recruitment would become even harder. After all, what scientist wants to perform the equivalent of custodial work on nuclear weapons? We asked Mercer-Smith whether, if he were just graduating now, he would still come to Los Alamos.

"I don't think so, because if I had been outside the labs, I don't think I would recognize how important what we do is," he replied. "Growing up in the sixties and seventies, I think I had a much better understanding of why the work that is done here is important. The students who grew up in the eighties or nineties are graduating today; I don't think they have any notion of why deterrence really does matter to them and their children. If you ask me would I come today, no, because I wouldn't have even thought of it as an important thing to do."

Despite the efforts of the lab's media relations department to give us a balanced picture during our visit, it was clear the mood at the lab hovered somewhere between depression and despair. Along with the impending contest over management of the lab, Pete Nanos, the unpopular lab director, had resigned under pressure the month before we arrived. A Department of Energy scientist who had come to Los Alamos on official business the week of Nanos's departure described his visit as "like arriving in a banana republic on the day the dictator has been dispatched and all the would-be dictators are out with swords and pistols."

And not unlike in a banana republic after the coup, a good number of people were simply packing their bags. As it turned out, three of the scientists we interviewed at Los Alamos were retiring that very week, including Doug Roberts, a Los Alamos computer scientist whose blog, LANL: The Real Story, was credited with helping unseat Nanos. Roberts's blog had become such a sensation that the Bradbury Science Museum, an annex to the laboratory that is open to the general public, was thinking of adding it to its permanent collection.*

We had dinner with Roberts in a brewery in Santa Fe, where, over draft microbrews, the man known as the "Los Alamos Blogger" explained the origins of his now-infamous work. It started, he told us, in a moment of desperation at a fast-food restaurant off Interstate 25. When we met with him, he had just completed his last day as a computer scientist at Los Alamos.

The lab employees are divided between technical staff, the scientists who are involved in research activities, and support staff, everyone— from the janitors to the lab spokespeople—who supports the scientists. Roberts was a member of the technical staff, which placed him firmly in a more privileged stratum of the lab hierarchy. He'd been born into the lab and its culture. His father, a chemist, came to work at Los Alamos in 1949, when the entire city of Los Alamos was still very much an isolated outpost, hidden from the world behind fences and heavy security. His father worked at the lab until 1963, when Roberts was thirteen. In 1984, Roberts came to work at Los Alamos, where he had been ever since.

Perhaps Roberts's long-standing connection to the lab was part of what motivated him to launch a blog that would do more damage to the lab's leadership than even the Wen Ho Lee scandal. "To tell you the truth, the reasons that I created that blog were purely selfish," he told us. "I found myself going home every day since July 16, the shutdown, and, without realizing it, [getting] just a little bit more angry at the management of the laboratory."

---

* LANL: The Real Story is archived at www.parrot-farm.net/~roberts/lanl-the-real-story.

Adding to the insult, Roberts and his colleagues suddenly discovered that the main outlet for airing their professional grievances—the letters-to-the-editor section of the *Los Alamos National Laboratory Daily News Bulletin*—had essentially been shut down. Laboratory management had imposed a six-week review process, and it wouldn't publish anything more controversial than letters about the parking situation at Los Alamos. Roberts's colleagues started talking about the situation and decided there needed to be some alternative forum in which to discuss lab management.

What actually sparked the blog, however, was an empty stomach. On December 28, 2004, Roberts was on his way to Albuquerque to visit his father. "I see this Arby's," he explained. "I never stop at Arby's, but they had a big plastic banner out front that said, FREE WIRELESS INTERNET. I thought, 'Well, OK, I can stop and get something to eat, catch up on my mail.'"

He ordered food, sat down, and opened his laptop, and within two hours, LANL: The Real Story was born.

At first, he just posted a few articles that had been rejected from the *News Bulletin* but then published by the *Los Alamos Monitor*, the town paper. And he just let the blog sit there. "I wasn't sure I wanted to subject myself to the scrutiny that a public act like that would cause," he explained. "You have to remember, back in late July, early August, mid-August, there was an atmosphere of fear and retribution at Los Alamos lab. People were getting fired for speaking out against management. But in the end I said, 'I can't keep it in any longer.'"

He finally told a handful of friends, and from there, the blog took off. Suddenly thousands of contributions poured in, taking Roberts—and the laboratory's leadership—by surprise. The blog began receiving national media attention, as anonymous postings laid bare the extent of the lab's difficulties. It was unprecedented to have employees of a secretive nuclear laboratory airing their dirty laundry for the whole world to see. Why Roberts didn't face retribution is unclear. Perhaps his visibility saved him. The response to the blog was so overwhelming—and the support from Los Alamos staff so strong—that it would have been difficult to punish him.

But aside from revealing the inner workings of the lab, Roberts's blog unearthed a more fundamental issue. Many of the people working at Los Alamos—though emotionally attached to the place—were still grasping for a new role and mission in life. And they felt the outside world did not quite understand the value of their work. The historical stature of Los Alamos, it turns out, was a mixed blessing. When it was revealed in 2003 that the head of security for Livermore had been having an affair with a Chinese spy, the news was no more than a blip on the radar screen of newspapers.

The malaise at Los Alamos underscored a more subtle issue for the lab in the post–Cold War era. What was its purpose? Being a repair shop for nuclear weapons didn't inspire much enthusiasm among its staff. In the absence of a clear mission, there was nothing left but to argue over management. For employees like Roberts, it was harder and harder to justify staying on. Though now retired from the lab, Roberts said he had no plans to leave the area. After a motorcycle trip with a friend, he was going to work for a small company receiving federal contracts. And despite all the problems at Los Alamos, he seemed sad to leave the lab behind.

"That was when the weirdness really struck me, but I'm getting used to the idea of leaving people that I've worked with for a long time that I like and respect. We've been through a lot together, and that part is not easy," he said. "But the lab has invited me to come back as an associate. So maybe I'm not leaving forever."

CHAPTER 3

Wicked Things

Exploring the Future of Nuclear Weapons at Sandia and Livermore

One of the most fascinating artifacts on display in the National Atomic Museum in Albuquerque is easy to miss. It's a backpack nuke that sits unobtrusively on the exhibit floor, parked next to the sleek metallic casing of a Mark 7 bomb. It could be mistaken for an old garbage can.

The Special Atomic Demolition Munition (SADM) was perhaps the strangest—and also one of the smallest—nuclear weapons in the U.S. inventory. What made it strange was not the design of the weapon, but its means of delivery. It would be strapped to a commando. Army and Navy special warfare units were trained to deploy the SADM, a sub-kiloton nuclear explosive designed to knock out strategic targets like dams, bridges, or harbors. The plan was for a two-man team to parachute into hostile territory with a SADM, evade detection or capture, and then plant the weapon at its target. And then, well, it's not quite clear what would happen next. The team members would then escape, theoretically. Or would they?

Though some popular references to the weapon suggest an escape plan was involved, a newspaper article from 1994—about five years after the SADM was withdrawn from the inventory—depicted a less Hollywood ending. "If that meant staying inside the hydroelectric plant, standing 20 feet away from the warhead, that's where you stayed," a former trained SADM mission member told a *Houston Chronicle* reporter. "It was suicide, and we all knew it."

We paused at the SADM—just the original casing, sans MK-54 warhead, of course. The SADM was not the only small tactical nuclear weapon in the U.S. inventory. There were others, like the M-388 Davy Crockett, a nuclear warhead designed to be launched from a recoilless rifle. But the SADM, which was in service between 1964 and 1989, was the closest thing the United States had to the "suitcase nuke" of spy thrillers. Operating the weapon was tricky, though. In order to work the bomb's hardwired detonator, the operator had to be within one hundred meters of the device—bringing new meaning to the phrase "danger close." One critic described the bomb as "comical."

It's hard to believe now, but the SADM exemplifies one vision scientists and strategists had for the practice of nuclear warfare. Tactical weapons would be used against tank columns or troop concentrations, or in the case of the SADM, against dams or bridges. However, the SADM was rendered obsolete by the advent in the U.S. military of precision-guided munitions and more-powerful chemical explosives that allowed conventional weapons to do what once only nuclear weapons could accomplish. Want to blow up a bridge? Just drop a satellite-guided bomb on each of the supports. Destroy an airfield? Just decide how evenly spaced you'd like the craters on the runway to be. After the fall of the Soviet Union, tactical nuclear weapons were the first to be pulled out of the inventory.

Even before the first nuclear device was successfully tested, scientists were thinking about how big a bang they needed to produce. Some subscribed to the bigger-is-better school. Edward Teller, for instance, pushed during the Manhattan Project to develop a class of powerful, fusion-fueled thermonuclear weapons. Leo Szilard, father of fission, theorized a cobalt bomb—a sort of enhanced dirty bomb—that could wipe out the planet. Others argued that a better weapon might be one that was smaller, more efficient, or perhaps even less destructive, like the enhanced-radiation neutron bomb. Some of these ideas were fanciful, but others, ultimately, were adopted as military planners hedged their bets. The United States developed a diverse arsenal of nuclear weapons that ranged from sub-kiloton tactical devices like the SADM to city-busting nukes like the W-88, the most advanced U.S. warhead.

The National Atomic Museum is perhaps the best place to explore the rich variety of nuclear weapons. The museum—which advertises itself as an "intriguing place to learn the story of the Atomic Age"—is housed in a nondescript building in downtown Albuquerque marked by an old Redstone missile fuselage. Before 9/11, the museum was on the grounds of Kirtland Air Force Base, where Sandia National Laboratories is also located. But the threat of domestic terrorism made all U.S. military bases more restrictive to the public, so the museum was relocated to this modest-size building, forcing it to mothball some of its larger exhibits. Like the Bradbury Science Museum in Los Alamos, it was designed with children in mind. Exhibits include "Little Al's Lab," an interactive science exhibit. The museum can even be rented for birthday parties.

We arrived an hour before closing on a blazing summer afternoon just before the Fourth of July, the perfect time to take refuge in an air-conditioned museum. We wandered into the main hall, stopping briefly to browse in the Up 'N' Atom gift shop, which stocks a good assortment of nuclear paraphernalia, books, and do-it-yourself science projects. The main hall of the museum features the history of nuclear weapons, beginning with the bulky nuclear bombs dropped on Hiroshima and Nagasaki. The exhibits begin with a static display of bomb casings for Fat Man (the Nagasaki-type bomb) and Little Boy (the Hiroshima-type bomb). From there, a visitor can view the progression of the nuclear arms race, from small munitions like the SADM to mega-weapons like the Mark 5 bomb.

A particularly fascinating exhibit is devoted to the Palomares incident of 1966—a famous nuclear mishap—when a B-52 bomber carrying nuclear weapons and a KC-135 aerial refueling tanker collided over Spain. Four B28 nuclear weapons tumbled out over the Spanish countryside. The high explosives in two of the bombs detonated, scattering plutonium across hundreds of acres; had one of the warheads gone off, it would have vaporized a good swath of eastern Andalusia.

But the message of the museum remains generally upbeat. The lower hall features a series of signs explaining radiation and its effects on humans. Inside the alcove, behind glass display cases, are examples of everyday radioactive materials, like a Donald Duck wristwatch with radium hands to make them glow in the dark.

The stated goal of such exhibits is to demystify radiation. One placard, for instance, lists a series of average radiation doses that a person might receive in the course of everyday life, from standing next to the Statue of Liberty to getting a chest X-ray. In fact, atmospheric testing, another display notes, contributes less than one millirem per year to radiation exposure. The National Atomic Museum correctly emphasizes how radiation fears, in some cases, have been overblown. Other highlights of nuclear hysteria—like the meltdown at the Three Mile Island plant in Pennsylvania—are illustrated by kitschy artifacts, such as the lamp shaped like a cooling tower from the infamous reactor.

Yet during the years of atmospheric testing, people were not exposed to an average dose of fallout radiation, but rather to varying levels that depended on their location and the prevailing weather patterns during a nuclear test. As author Richard L. Miller notes in *Under the Cloud*, radioactive debris from the 1953 Simon test was carried from the Nevada Test Site all the way to Troy, New York, where one physicist estimated that exposure to residents was "equivalent to a whole series of pelvic X-rays."*

We stopped at the end of our tour to watch a brief film showing the devastation in Hiroshima and Nagasaki. The video—with its dramatic depiction of burn victims—was powerful, but it was also not a centerpiece exhibit. On the whole, the National Atomic Museum seemed to be a tribute to the softer side of nuclear weaponry. Exhibits focused on science, not on the devastation of nuclear weapons (perhaps that was why they were planning to rename it the National Museum of Nuclear Science and History). The museum had to balance two almost contradictory goals: showing that nuclear weapons weren't all that scary, while also demonstrating that nuclear weapons were terrifying enough to make anyone think twice about using them. As we browsed the gift store sifting through Little Boy shot glasses and Albert Einstein action figures, we couldn't help but wonder what message—if any—the young children targeted by the museum got out of the exhibits.

*   *   *

---

* Most famously, the cast and crew of *The Conqueror*, a John Wayne movie, were downwind from a series of atmospheric tests while shooting on location in St. George, Utah, in 1956. Though there was no way to make a direct connection to the tests, it was later reported that by the 1980s, nearly half of the original crew had developed cancer (skeptics, however, also noted the several-pack-a-day cigarette habits of actors like Wayne).

After seeing so many nuclear weapons on display, we started wondering about their purpose. If nuclear weapons aren't all that effective in the era of precision weaponry, then how *do* they contribute to deterrence, particularly in an age when traditional deterrence is effectively dead? Would all the work of the nuclear weapons labs end up in the National Atomic Museum as relics of the nuclear age? While staying in Albuquerque, we went to visit Sandia National Laboratories to learn more about the future of nuclear weaponry.

Los Alamos and Livermore are frequently called design labs, and the scientists there ponder the complex problems of designing the physics package (fission and fusion components) for a nuclear weapon. Sandia National Laboratories, by contrast, was established originally as the Z Division of the Manhattan Project. Located initially just outside Albuquerque, it was charged with developing the nonnuclear components of a nuclear device and packaging it as a deliverable weapon. While it, too, was first managed by the University of California, by 1949 it was run by Western Electric, confirming its role as more of a corporate—as opposed to academic—lab. When we visited, it was operated by defense megalith Lockheed Martin, which was described, both positively and negatively, as running a tight ship.

The difference between the culture of Sandia and that of the design labs is immediate. Unlike the academic atmosphere that Los Alamos and Livermore try to cultivate, Sandia's focus—reflected in its Air Force base location and in signs and posters scattered throughout every building—is on safety, security, and defense. The difference is also apparent in conversation. Designers like James Mercer-Smith at Los Alamos might make lofty allusions to Herodotus or hint at the Faustian bargains involved in creating weapons of mass destruction. Sandia, on the other hand, is typically described as an "engineering facility." Joan Woodard, who headed the lab's nuclear weapons program, insisted to us that Sandia, too, was a design lab. The difference, she said, was that Sandia focused on usable technology. "We really have a strong ethic of science brought to an application," she told us in an interview held in a small conference room. "That's a core aspect of our culture."

Woodard was a friendly, no-nonsense woman with a look and demeanor that would fit in well on the board of a private corporation. In talking about Sandia's nuclear weapons work, she spoke frequently in the language one might use in a car factory, throwing around terms like "manufacturability" and "life-cycle and cost management." In fact, that's precisely how she saw the concept of "responsive infrastructure," the Department of Energy's plan for revitalizing the nuclear weapons complex. "It's the phrase you often hear in commercial industry: faster, better, cheaper," she noted. It's the same for nuclear weapons: "How can you maintain the deterrent in the most cost-effective way?"

Sandia, in many ways, was well positioned for survival in the post–Cold War world. Since it was teamed with both Livermore and Los Alamos in the competition to design the Reliable Replacement Warhead, it was assured a contract award. Like the other labs, Sandia got its share of stockpile stewardship dollars to certify the reliability of its components in the arsenal. And then there was Sandia's pride and joy, the Microsystems and Engineering Sciences Applications (MESA) Complex, which lab officials described as "crucial . . . to support a certifiable stockpile for the future."

Yet stockpile stewardship—and even a potential role in the RRW—was not necessarily reflective of how the lab viewed its future. We had asked to meet with Gerold Yonas, a longtime Sandia employee involved in far-out thinking, because we wanted to find out how scientists at a nuclear weapons laboratory envisioned the future. Or, perhaps more precisely, how they imagined their role in a future where nuclear weapons would perhaps no longer play as critical a part as they did during the Cold War.

With his neatly trimmed beard and regimental tie, Yonas looked every bit the Reagan-era policy wonk. A longtime Sandia employee, he served during President Ronald Reagan's administration as the chief scientist for the Strategic Defense Initiative—better known as Star Wars, the "peace shield" meant to protect America from Soviet nuclear attack. He had experience, by his own admission, with some pretty wild weapons ideas. One by one, the weapons that were supposed to be a part of Reagan's peace shield proved to be technically daunting, if not outright technological fantasies. At a conference, Yonas once humbly joked, "My career has not been marred by a single success," an acknowledgment that many of the Star Wars–era weapons—ranging from a nuclear-pumped X-ray laser to a Buck Rogers–style particle beam weapon—had come to an ignominious end. Yonas was a man who, for better or worse, seemed forever tied to the future. Perhaps that made his present career—dreaming up outlandish scenarios and future technologies—all the more appropriate.

Yonas was also known for his quick wit and wry sense of humor. One scientist related to us how Yonas, infuriated by a solar tower project at the lab, joked about taking a blowtorch to a frozen turkey and throwing it at the base of the tower. His hope, the story went, was that environmentalists would think solar rays had roasted an endangered whooping crane and would push to cancel the boondoggle (Yonas denied the story, or at least acting on the impulse). Since 1998, Yonas had run a division at Sandia called the Advanced Concepts Group, a sort of in-house think tank whose mission was to look at the future.

The Advanced Concepts Group thought about what Yonas called "wicked things." By "wicked," what he really meant was complex—a problem that changes when you apply a solution. "The nature of complex, wicked problems is they tend to involve people," Yonas said, sliding a neat sheaf of briefing papers toward us. "We tend to be complicated and wicked."

A chipper secretary placed a cup of coffee on the table in the unclassified conference room where we sat. Yonas thanked her politely, staring intently at the pile of printed-out PowerPoint slides. "So much easier than a slap in the face," he said, glancing at the caffeinated sludge. He didn't crack a smile.

His group, which included historians, anthropologists, and political analysts, in addition to scientists, held "fests" to think about "wicked problems." Essentially, Yonas created problems for Sandia to solve. As he put it, "We're in the mess-making business. We try to invent how to destroy the fabric of American society." What sort of messes? Race warfare, for starters. For a while, Yonas's group thought about how race warfare might be triggered in the United States. The scenarios his group invented involved biological attacks that would pit one race against another, possibly leading to the destruction of American society. Asked to name the specific races involved in the warfare, Yonas replied with a curt "No."

Of course, the problem with those wicked scenarios, at least in the old days, was that they didn't seem all that wicked. An early 1998 simulation concluded that an attack on the homeland was impossible, or that if it did happen, it wouldn't elicit a disastrous response. It ended with a sort of happy face. We were all OK. What, then, did Yonas think on September 11, 2001? As he recalled it, he turned on the television that morning and said, "Oh, darn."

The problem of terrorism was wickeder than he'd thought, so it was back to the drawing board. Yonas's solution was a new acronym. "I told my group that day that here forward we're going to focus our attention on dealing with UTAW," he said. UTAW (pronounced "Utah") is Ultra-Terrorism, Asymmetric Warfare. How should one solve UTAW? "That's the nature of a wicked problem," Yonas replied. "You don't ever come up with solutions."

That apparently didn't mean you shouldn't try. One of his ideas was to create computer programs, or "hypothesizers," that could predict the future by tracking complex data. But if people were so complex and wicked, how on earth could any computer program ever provide the sort of clarity needed to predict the future? "It worked in the movie *Minority Report*," he offered, referring to the Steven Spielberg film.

Yonas quickly added that he knew that was only fiction. "Many of our ideas, if you look hard, you'll find them in movies. People accuse me of going to movies rather than thinking hard." He shrugged his shoulders.

"Another thing we're really pushing very hard is golf balls," Yonas said, again without cracking a smile. Was that an acronym, we asked? "No," he replied. "It's a real golf ball: one that can feel, think, and decide, autonomously guiding itself into the hole." It would also make for a great golf game, he added. We wondered if Yonas meant unmanned aerial vehicles, robotic systems? No, he replied, laughing. "I want a golf ball."

"The notion," he said, "was a golf ball you could hit off the tee, and no matter how good a golfer you are, it'll always go right in the cup. I hit the pin; it bounces out, but it always goes in the cup. A lot of people would invest. The concept was a device that could see, could sense, it could decide, it could act, and it could communicate. That's S-D-A-C. Our idea was to develop enough of these at a low-enough cost that you could distribute a network of these SDAC [golf balls] that have precision awareness of a situation. And we still think that's a heck of a good idea."

Yonas said he wanted to take advantage of Sandia's MESA facility and its "micro-mechanical miniature gadgetry." The lab, he said, could miniaturize GPS and sensors and make the components cheaper. "Can you imagine? People [will] want to play golf with it. It has to be sufficiently rugged so that you could tee up and get it out there," he said. "I think it's doable, but it's a concept. Like everything we do, it's a concept."

Of course, the idea of scientists inventing technological solutions to complex, "wicked" problems is not really new, as Yonas himself was quick to point out. In the 1960s, a group of elite scientists known as the Jasons attempted to come up with their own technological panacea. Frustrated by the war in Vietnam, they conceived a sensor barrier that eventually became part of the quixotic McNamara Line. Sandia helped build the sensors, which Yonas cited as the precursor to his golf balls. The sensor barrier was intended to slow infiltration down the Ho Chi Minh Trail; sensors developed for the project were credited with helping break the siege of Khe Sanh in 1968. Yonas's "golf balls" concept was supposed to do a similar thing in urban terrain—letting troops know what was going on around the corner.

Of course, Yonas acknowledged the McNamara Line faced a wicked problem: discrimination. "One of my good friends in the Pentagon said, 'You know how many orangutans we bombed because of your damned sensors? This is useless, we bombed orangutans.' I used to say to him, 'But those orangutans were Viet Cong wearing orangutan suits.' He said, 'That's the problem: Deception will always beat a sensor.'"

Yonas paused and gave an audible sigh. "We still don't have the golf balls."*

With his far-out problems and elusive solutions, Gerold Yonas recognized that the labs needed to find new purpose in the age of terrorism and unconventional warfare. We were curious to see how Lawrence Livermore National Laboratory was wrestling with that same question.

We flew from Albuquerque to Oakland, California, choosing to stay with family just outside San Francisco. We set off the next day for Livermore, located about forty-eight miles southeast of San Francisco,

---

* Two years after our interview, Yonas not only didn't have his golf balls, he didn't have his group. The Advanced Concepts Group was disbanded in 2007.

driving against the crushing rush hour traffic. Commuting from Livermore to San Francisco once would have been unthinkable, but in the era of sky-high real estate and the area's tech-fueled economic boom, such a punishing commute is now considered common. If Livermore was once a rural community, the economic and geographic expansion of the Bay Area has transformed it to merely an outlying city.

Writers like William J. Broad, who visited Livermore in the 1980s, when the lab was embroiled in the politics of Star Wars, described a very different place than the one we found. "The seven-mile drive to the heart of Livermore highlighted the area's rural nature," he wrote. "I passed a red farmhouse, a giant semitrailer loaded with hundreds of bales of hay, and wide fields dotted with cows."

We, by contrast, passed a series of coffee shops and strip developments. During the 1980s, Livermore, though less isolated than Los Alamos, was still regarded as something of a backwater. Particularly in the mid-1980s, the lab attracted outsiders seeking a glimpse of its closed, secretive culture. Broad, for example, spent time with the top-secret O Group, a sort of Skunk Works composed of young geniuses who attracted high-level attention during the Star Wars years. Hugh Gusterson, the anthropologist, even enmeshed himself in the culture of Livermore weapons designers by spending two years in the town, observing them the way that anthropologists might study the tribes of Papua New Guinea. Livermore, no doubt, still maintains a unique culture, but it is less distinguishable than that of Los Alamos, particularly as the acreage around the lab has steadily transformed from ranch land and farms to bedroom community, a shift reflected in both the pricey real estate and the invasion of gourmet grocery stores and coffeehouses.

Livermore lab occupies approximately one square mile, it has an annual budget of some $1.6 billion, and it employs eighty-three hundred people. The directions to the main entrance took us past some strip developments and finally to a small visitors' center, where we stood in line with what looked like contractors and assorted lab guests, waiting for temporary badges. We spent the morning on a tour of the lab grounds, looking at the array of mostly low-slung concrete buildings intermixed with trailers. Despite the high security, Livermore resembles a college campus. Employees dress casually—many in sandals—and the primary mode of transport within the lab's confines is communally owned bikes, parked randomly at various buildings. For lunch, our public affairs escort took us to a Livermore winery, where we were served gourmet cheeses and a selection of the region's wines. Livermore may be a nuclear weapons lab—an atmosphere associated with the conservative mores of national security—but in culture, at least, it is California through and through.

Livermore's origins date back to acrimonious Cold War debates over the nuclear arsenal. Even during the Manhattan Project, Hungarian-born physicist Edward Teller clashed with Oppenheimer over the hydrogen bomb. Teller, a brilliant theorist, was already convinced that work should begin on a thermonuclear weapon, a device that would use a primary fission bomb to trigger a secondary fusion explosion. His clash with Oppenheimer sidelined him during the latter part of the Manhattan Project. The divisions continued even after the war. Unsatisfied with support for the hydrogen bomb at Los Alamos, Teller began to advocate for a second nuclear weapons lab. In 1952, he got his wish and Lawrence Livermore National Laboratory was established in a former naval air station in northern California. While not officially the director of the lab at its inception, Teller had vast powers over research and decision making, and weapons research largely followed his direction, which proved perhaps somewhat problematic. The first two tests of Livermore-designed weapons in the Nevada desert were embarrassing fizzles.

Teller's penchant for what is sometimes dubbed "nuclear optimism" extended to a number of ideas, ranging from hydrogen bombs to lasers. In the 1980s, for example, a group of bright young scientists in the O Group developed a concept for an X-ray laser powered by a thermonuclear explosion. Dubbed Excalibur, this so-called third-generation nuclear weapon was one of several notional beam weapons that the Pentagon funded research for as part of a proposed shield to defend against Soviet intercontinental ballistic missiles. Eventually, however, the project was terminated following a decade of controversial test results and accusations of scientific fraud.

When we visited Livermore, the largest single project at the lab was the National Ignition Facility (NIF), a massive 192-beam experimental laser facility still under construction. Tours of the facility were so common that the lab stocked extra pairs of steel-toed boots, hard hats, and smocks. Posters explaining the purpose of NIF were carefully set up in the entrance, near a model of the "target," a tiny pellet that contains a mix of tritium and deuterium. When the facility is complete, 192 lasers will be focused on that small target, compressing it and—hopefully—creating a fusion reaction. The ultimate goal is to create the ideal conditions for "ignition," when the right temperature and pressure spark a chain reaction. According to Livermore management, NIF is essential to stockpile stewardship, because once the facility is fully operational, it will be able to reproduce the fusion processes that take place inside a star or a thermonuclear weapon. If the project works— and NIF achieves ignition—it could also pave the way to fusion as a usable energy source.

Critics of the program have long questioned whether the massive facility is really essential for stockpile stewardship. And as the costs have grown and the schedule has lagged, patience has worn thin with the project. In 2001, the General Accounting Office (since renamed the Government Accountability Office) informed Congress that the project was already six years behind schedule and $1.4 billion over budget. The report blamed poor oversight and management for the facility's troubles. In the summer of 2005, when we visited, the mood was not good. One congressional committee had zeroed out money for the facility, raising the possibility that the whole project could come to a grinding halt.

NIF survived the cuts. For critics of stockpile stewardship, though, it embodies everything that is wrong with the big-ticket endeavors at the labs: It's a costly science project that provides little to the stockpile. But for Livermore, it is the future of the lab and one of the best ways to attract young scientists. As one of our escorts that day glumly observed, if opponents succeeded in killing the project, Livermore would have the "world's biggest indoor soccer stadium."

Livermore traces its intellectual lineage to a 1956 Navy conference in Woods Hole, Massachusetts, where Teller promised to design a hydrogen bomb small enough to fit on a submarine-launched missile. Bruce Goodwin, who heads Livermore's nuclear weapons program, described Teller's pronouncement as a "name that tune" moment in the history of the labs. A nuclear device in those days was the size of a truck; Teller was promising a quantum leap in weapons design and, more importantly, claiming that he could do it within five years. Teller "made the whole room sort of stop," Goodwin said. "Because he had just said he could do something in between one-tenth and one-twentieth the size of what everybody else was saying could be done."

Goodwin, a mustachioed man with the earnest look of a college professor, came to the nuclear weapons labs indirectly. If James Mercer-Smith of Los Alamos joined the leagues of nuclear weapons designers out of a belief that he was engaged in a life-or-death struggle with the Soviet Union, Goodwin's admission to the elite group followed a more ambivalent story line. As a graduate student in astrophysics, he studied neutron star collapse; his adviser suggested he might be interested in working at a nuclear weapons lab—something that Goodwin, who described himself at the time as "mildly antinuclear," had never considered.

While Goodwin was studying astrophysics at the University of Illinois, the antinuclear movement was gaining serious momentum. Helen Caldicott, an Australian physician, had emerged as one of the most well-known of the movement's leaders, giving speeches at universities around the country. Goodwin heard her speak. "I was fascinated with what she said, and the irony is, you know, after having listened to her lecture when she was there and having attended other antinuclear lectures, it sort of didn't make any sense to me," he said. "So I then said, 'Well, gee, why don't I go see what they do?' and I did. And here I am today."

Goodwin, perhaps like many other scientists who entertained antinuclear leanings, eventually became convinced of the logic of nuclear deterrence. But that someone might go from being an antinuclear graduate student to the head of Livermore's nuclear weapons program was indeed ironic. Before visiting Livermore, we had spoken with Caldicott, who was still a vocal opponent of nuclear weapons. Though she admitted the antinuclear movement had largely receded into the background, she was still an influential critic. She made it clear her own views had not moderated. Weapons scientists, she told us, were engaged in a psychosexual relationship with the bombs they made, enamored of the power their devices held. "The problem is not a bomb per se, it's the psychology in these men's minds," she said.

When we asked Goodwin why Caldicott had appealed to him, he said, "She is very passionate, but not passionate in a way that's going to make you think she's not rational. She speaks very rationally and clearly and convincingly." It was, if nothing else, unexpected to have the head of the nuclear weapons program at Livermore waxing poetic about the doyenne of the 1980s antinuclear movement. Our public affairs officer suddenly cut in. "Using nuclear power to generate electricity is like cutting butter with a chain saw," he said, mimicking one of Caldicott's antinuclear pronouncements. "That's Helen." Goodwin paused for a moment and suddenly sounded slightly embarrassed. "But you know, we're not here to talk about Helen," he said, adding, "She's a very interesting lady."

We turned next to the subject of life at the lab in the era of stockpile stewardship. When U.S. nuclear testing stopped in 1992, Goodwin said, he was working on questions that were considered interesting scientifically but were not very important during the era of testing. In those days, so long as the nuke went off, most everyone was happy. "Those little interesting questions turned out to be the big questions, because now we're not going to test it and say, 'Well, we don't understand why it works, but it worked OK,'" he said. "Now we have to understand why this little fluke occurred over here, which we know, if it became really big, would cause the weapon to fail." The Livermore approach to the craft of weapons design, which focused on understanding the way the devices worked in intimate detail, came in handy, but it also changed how nuclear weapons designers themselves worked. "In 1982, I would never have gotten a good performance evaluation for studying the failure modes of a stockpile weapon," Goodwin said. "Because they didn't want them to fail—you stayed as far away from failure as you possibly could."

These days, the study of failure has become the most important thing around. "In a world where the weapons are not being replaced—they're approaching thirty years average age now—the question of when do they fail is the key question. And if they fail, what are the precursors of failure? How do you understand, if you will, the island of stability and where you fall off the cliff? And that was something that was not highly sought after in the first forty years of the nuclear era," he said. This created a rather weird inversion for the desired skills of a nuclear weapons lab, as Goodwin pointed out. "Would you buy a car from a company whose cars regularly broke down on the highway? I mean, that's not success. On the other hand, if you only have one car in the world, and you're never going to get another one, you'd better understand the precursors of when it's going to break down."

Goodwin was touching on the favorite metaphor for the Reliable Replacement Warhead. Stockpile stewardship—the upkeep of Cold War–era nuclear weaponry—is often compared to engineers maintaining a bridge. It's important to understand the tolerances, limitations, and weak points of the design. The favorite metaphor for describing the RRW is overhauling a classic car. Should you put in air bags? Antilock brakes? Perhaps a CD player? The fundamental design (the physics package) is the same, but you can trick the bomb out with new safety features and performance enhancements.

Yet the competition to build the RRW was taking the laboratories in a new direction. Depending on which lab's version you believed, either the new warhead was needed because of problems with the Los Alamos–designed W-76 nuclear warhead, whose thin uranium shell sparked concerns about its low margin of failure, or it was, as Immele told us, the brainchild of Pete Nanos, the former Los Alamos director who rallied scientists around the idea at the 2003 conference to discuss the nuclear arsenal. Whatever the truth, the plan at the time we visited was for the NNSA to hold a competition between the two labs for the design of the new warhead. The battle over the right to build the RRW had, for the first time in twenty years, rekindled the rivalry between the two labs. And the winning lab would be back in the business of design.

A stereotype persists to this day among weapons designers: Livermore designs are elegant but complex, while Los Alamos designs are crude but effective. Both labs vehemently disagree with this characterization. "Crude doesn't necessarily relate to reliable. I think that elegance, the elegant engineering in Livermore nuclear weapons gives them a longevity that's unmatched," Goodwin told us, acknowledging his prejudice. Regardless, the two facilities each take a very different approach to nuclear weapons. Goodwin understood well the difference in philosophies. He came to Livermore from Los Alamos in 1985, when he was offered the chance to work with Seymour Sack, a renowned scientist recognized as a father of modern nuclear weapons design. While at Los Alamos in the early 1980s, Goodwin participated in two nuclear tests for the W-80 warhead, a major project at the time. But when he came to Livermore to work for Sack, Goodwin said, he "learned how to do everything all over again."

When the competition was announced, critics of new nuclear weapons again expressed concern that the Bush administration was trying to undermine stockpile stewardship. After all, what was the point if indeed the labs were going to start building new nuclear weapons? Even more troubling was the question of whether replacement nuclear weapons could truly be certified as reliable, without ever having been tested. Since the RRW did not emerge from a military requirement, or even concern, regarding the nuclear weapons stockpile, one of the complaints about the proposal was that it was an idea pushed by the laboratories to keep them in business. For critics of nuclear weapons labs, this was precisely the type of conflict of interest they warned against—the labs coming up with new warheads as a way to justify their existence and funding. But Goodwin argued that the RRW, in fact, was an integral part of stockpile stewardship.

"It's an entirely different world," he said. "The enterprise that deterred the Soviet Union is enormous. It was literally capable of cranking out tens of thousands of weapons . . . If you were going to make a hundred or two hundred cars, you wouldn't build a plant that can produce millions of cars, it's a huge waste. And it's inappropriate."

Goodwin said the RRW was part of a larger objective to scale back the number of nuclear weapons to an absolute minimum for deterring war. President George W. Bush, of course, had committed the nation to the "lowest possible number of nuclear weapons consistent with our national security needs." Yet that didn't answer the question of how many nuclear weapons are necessary to meet those needs, and Goodwin's analysis, though hardly surprising, did not answer the basic question: how to determine how big the nuclear weapons complex needs to be if you don't know how many nuclear weapons you require. The issues of deterrence, which had converted Goodwin from a "mildly antinuclear" graduate student into a high-level nuclear official, seemed to have become confused, and perhaps that explained, in some small way, Goodwin's slightly embarrassed admiration for Caldicott.

In the absence of nuclear weapons work, or even amid declining nuclear weapons work, what else can a nuclear weapons lab do? According to Philip Coyle, the former Livermore associate director, the answer is the same as for any private business. Whether it's cars, toasters, or computers, if your business dries up, you look to new markets. "The labs are trying to diversify," he noted. "It hasn't been easy, because it's hard to find any other program that will fund them at half a billion or a billion dollars a year the way the nuclear weapons programs have for so many years."

Homeland security, it turns out, is one such growth area. Concerns about nuclear terrorism have come in and out of fashion over the years. In his classic 1974 book, *The Curve of Binding Energy*, author John McPhee drives around the country with nuclear weapons designer Theodore Taylor, who at that time was on a one-man mission to prevent nuclear terrorism. Taylor's concern was the then-growing nuclear power industry, which he felt lacked adequate safeguards. Many years later, with the nuclear power industry stalled, his concerns about the unchecked growth of nuclear power seem antiquated. But one of Taylor's contentions—that a crude nuclear weapon could destroy the World Trade Center—seems eerily prescient, even though the Twin Towers were felled by two airliners loaded with jet fuel.

The collapse of the Soviet Union renewed fears of nuclear terrorism, with analysts warning of the threat of Russian nuclear weapons being sold on the black market, or former Soviet scientists selling their talents to rogue nations. After 9/11, the specter of nuclear war took on a different hue. It seemed nuclear terrorism was the threat du jour.

How serious a threat is nuclear terrorism? About two months before we visited Livermore, physicist Richard Garwin painted a surprisingly stark picture. In a speech to the American Philosophical Society, he warned that a U.S. city would likely be struck by a nuclear weapon sometime in the very near future. "It's not true that we have nothing to fear but fear itself," he said. "For our country to lose a third of a million people is likely to happen."

While Garwin warned that over the next ten years, there was almost a 100 percent chance that a U.S. city would be hit by a nuclear weapon, the U.S. government was trying to prevent such a thing from ever happening. The Department of Homeland Security had opened the Domestic Nuclear Detection Office, which was investing over a billion dollars in plans to place radiation detectors at key ports. At the nuclear weapons laboratories, terrorism prevention has taken on several forms. There are, of course, worries about terrorist attacks on facilities, which led Livermore to a much-publicized move in 2006 to install Gatling guns to protect the lab's store of plutonium. But an assault on the lab, while a concern, is not the focus of antiterrorism work. Rather, the lab has become a focal point for tracking and preventing worldwide nuclear terror networks. Livermore's work on designing nuclear weapons has also given it a place in fighting nuclear proliferation and, even more importantly, nuclear terrorism. Since the 1990s, the lab has been active in an area called "nuclear forensics," which, like criminal forensics, seeks to trace the origin of nuclear materials (in the 1990s it also opened the Forensic Science Center, which actually works on criminal investigations).

In the afternoon, we sat down to speak with two scientists in the P Division, Livermore's proliferation and terrorism prevention organization (other divisions in the same directorate include the Q Division, to detect proliferation, the R Division, incident response, and the Z Division, international assessments). Mona Dreicer, the deputy P Division leader, and John Zucca, a deputy program leader, were both working on technologies and projects meant to help prevent nuclear smuggling and terrorism.

The work of the P Division was originally aimed at detecting nuclear tests under the Comprehensive Nuclear-Test-Ban Treaty, but now the focus has shifted to antiterrorism. The P Division helps secure Russian fissile materials and nuclear fuel stored in former Soviet republics; it builds radiation detection technology and explores science and technology developments "in regions of proliferation concern." Livermore is not alone in this mission. Los Alamos is also heavily involved in cooperative work with the former Soviet Union. And at Sandia, we had been given a walking tour through the lab's counterterrorism displays, which included everything from high-tech sensors the lab had installed at Russian nuclear weapons storage facilities to low-tech yet novel measures like shrink-wrapping nuclear weapons components to detect tampering. Sandia has also designed tools such as container seals and tracking devices to prevent someone from acquiring the ingredients for a dirty bomb, a conventional explosive packed with radiological materials. Such materials could be stolen, for instance, from a hospital, and even a modest explosion would contaminate a small area and create mass panic.

Yet the problem with such nuclear terrorism programs is that the threat is impossible to quantify. No one knows how much material may have been diverted to the nuclear black market—or who has purchased it there. Even worse, the targets could be anywhere and everywhere. What do you protect? "Nearly three hundred thousand cars and trucks cross the George Washington Bridge in both directions on an average day; without an efficient way to process radiation alerts, a single convoy of banana trucks could jam up traffic for hours," noted Steve Coll in a 2007 *New Yorker* article.

In their work with the former Soviet Union, Livermore scientists are not implementing a comprehensive program to secure nuclear and radiological materials; rather, they help scientists in those countries develop their own safeguards. The labs have to negotiate access to sites, and though they describe the cooperation as good, that doesn't mean they go wherever they want. "The challenge for the future is sustainability," Dreicer explained. "The U.S. is not supposed to spend the next century there protecting materials. It's to help them, to change their culture, the security culture, [so] that they will sustain it into the future."

When we asked what sort of threats concerned them most, there was a long pause. "I don't even know if it's nuclear," Dreicer replied. "I don't think either of us have been involved in an overall threat assessment, which I hope our National Security Council is doing. Weapons of mass destruction are chemical, biological, and nuclear. The radiological is a concern, too. You know, it's all part of the mix."

During the Cold War, the labs built nuclear weapons to defeat or defend against the Soviet Union's arsenal. Right or wrong, there was a clear purpose to their effort. That sense of mission attracted scientists like Mercer-Smith at Los Alamos, or converted mildly antinuclear scientists like Goodwin. The labs, of course, are not responsible for intelligence or policy making, but the threat now appears ambiguous. "To me, the threat is not saying specifically it's this site or this material," Dreicer continued. "That question is too big for us."

CHAPTER 4

Home Brew

Uncovering the Secrets of
Uranium Production in Tennessee

Every nuclear facility has a story, a tale intertwining official history and local lore. During World War II, the high secrecy surrounding the Manhattan Project required selecting sites based on isolation, but it also sometimes concealed elements of patronage. No site was ever chosen at random. It appeared on the map because someone, usually in Washington, wanted it to be there. Oak Ridge, Tennessee, was no exception.

Residents of Oak Ridge like to regale visitors with two stories of the town's origins. One involves the legend of John Hendrix, a local mystic in the early 1900s who wandered into the woods for forty days and returned to his tiny rural community with a strange prophecy. The remote valley, Hendrix said, would one day be filled with factories that would help win a great war. Less than three decades after his death, the Y-12 nuclear plant was built in Bear Creek Valley—in the exact spot foretold by Hendrix—to produce the fuel for a bomb that many hoped would win World War II.

The second story is grounded in Washington politics. Senator Kenneth McKellar, a powerful member of Tennessee's congressional delegation, agreed during World War II to help secretly channel the funds to build the facilities needed for a nuclear bomb. When asked by President Roosevelt to help conceal the secret defense project, McKellar, as legend has it, responded: "Where in Tennessee are we going to build this thing?"

The two stories—often retold in different forms—reflect some fundamental truth about Oak Ridge. The town owes its existence to government largesse, though the plentiful supply of electricity from the Tennessee Valley Authority dam—and the area's isolation—likely played the decisive role. Oak Ridge dates back to the earliest days of the Manhattan Project, when the area, described as "59,000 acres of Appalachian semiwilderness," was selected as the location of one of the original secret cities. Oak Ridge housed the factories built to separate the fissile uranium needed for the atomic bomb. The entire city was fenced off; its true purpose was concealed from most who worked there. Though its population plummeted and many of its factories went idle after the war, Oak Ridge soon found a new role as the arms race accelerated and the country needed a place to produce weapons-grade uranium.

During the Cold War, the original Manhattan Project plants evolved into a vast complex dedicated to manufacturing the exotic components for nuclear weapons. The production network stretched across the United States, from Hanford in Washington State, where plutonium was produced in huge reactors, to Rocky Flats, in Colorado, where the spherical plutonium triggers used in nuclear weapons were wrought. The complex reached south to South Carolina's Savannah River Site, which manufactured both plutonium and tritium, and to the Pantex facility in Amarillo, Texas, where the final assembly of nuclear weapons was completed. Y-12 began its life primarily as a processing center for uranium, but later expanded into the Y-12 National Security Complex, a manufacturing complex for secondaries, the components that give thermonuclear weapons their immense destructive power.

Dispersing this vast production complex across the United States protected the bomb-making infrastructure from attack. But it also offered political protection. Spreading the work across congressional districts shielded the complex from budget cuts. Times have changed, however, and the nuclear production complex has shrunk substantially, as the demand for nuclear weapons has declined. In 1989, after an FBI raid, Rocky Flats was closed down; Savannah River now only deals with tritium, an isotope of hydrogen used as an ingredient in thermonuclear weapons; and Hanford is essentially a cleanup site. Since the end of the Cold War, the production complex has shrunk by half, from fourteen sites employing around sixty thousand workers in the late

1980s to today's eight sites, which employ twenty-seven thousand people. Our trek to Y-12 was to figure out what a nuclear weapons factory does in an age when nuclear weapons aren't actually produced anymore. In other words, how do they keep busy?

Old habits die hard, and habits grounded in secrecy are even harder to kill. For most of its existence, Y-12 was one of the most closely guarded facilities of the nuclear complex, hidden behind a razor wire perimeter and closed off from public view. Those without the coveted Q clearance were not allowed on-site. Journalists couldn't even think about getting behind the fence. Frank Munger, a local reporter, described how, prior to the 1990s, he would have to relay press inquiries to Y-12 through intermediaries. In the early 1990s, a *Wall Street Journal* reporter spent a year negotiating access to Y-12, noting that the legacy of secrecy was so ingrained "that at one point even the number of rolls of toilet paper it used was classified to prevent the Soviets from figuring out how many people it employed."

It was only after the end of the Cold War that Y-12 took its first, tentative steps toward opening up to the outside world. In 1992, it held a ceremonial "fence cutting," at which it opened up sections of the plant to the public, concentrating classified work in a smaller secured area. The event was hailed as a new beginning. The Department of Energy even began offering bus tours that took tourists to visit historic sites around Oak Ridge, including parts of Y-12. Oak Ridge was playing up its nuclear heritage.

Having already visited the nuclear weapons laboratories—Los Alamos, Livermore, and Sandia—as well as the atomic test site in Nevada, we wanted to see what one of the manufacturing facilities looked like. Y-12 was one of the most active, and it dated all the way back to the Manhattan Project; it seemed like the best choice.

Yet in the fourteen years since the fence cutting, Y-12 had effectively remained a closed facility, and when we first put in our request to visit, we were unsure whether we would actually be granted access. Unlike Los Alamos, Livermore, and Sandia, which regularly host journalists and hold public tours, Y-12 experiences national press exposure infrequently at best. When we ran into Bryan Wilkes, the NNSA's chief spokesman, at a dinner in Washington, we pleaded our case and he nodded sympathetically. "Well, I think it's a possibility," he said, leaning over the cheese tray. "I mean, it's not like you're asking to visit Pantex."

A few weeks later, we received word from Y-12 that, in fact, our visit had been approved. We were on our way to the secret city of Oak Ridge.

Oak Ridge during the war was a hastily built place, where thousands of workers lived in cheap tract housing and labored in factories that were not even acknowledged to exist. While seventy-five thousand workers toiled in Oak Ridge at the height of the Manhattan Project, making it the fifth-largest city in Tennessee, today the population hovers under thirty thousand. Oak Ridge is still a small, isolated town.

The closest commercial airport is in Knoxville, but we, like many travelers, chose to fly into the bigger hub of Nashville and make the three-hour drive east. We arrived that night under heavy rain to find that what little commercial activity there was—isolated on one main strip—had ceased around nine o'clock. We drove in past a tall, white concrete blockhouse, one of the original towers guarding the approach to the town, a reminder that for the first six years of its existence, Oak Ridge was a real "secret city" that appeared on no map, surrounded by checkpoints and fenced off from the outside world. It continued to rain the full two days we stayed, shrouding the mountain landscape in a heavy mist.

Oak Ridge National Laboratory, which grew out of the Manhattan Project's X-10 Graphite Reactor, is often confused with Y-12, the nuclear production plant. The Oak Ridge lab got out of the weapons business after World War II, focusing instead on nuclear energy and basic science and technology. Yet the laboratory was linked with Y-12 by common history and proximity—and, for many years, by shared management. It was not uncommon for employees, particularly technical experts, to move between Y-12 and Oak Ridge National Laboratory. Over the years, however, commercial companies soured on running the nuclear weapon facilities. Patriotism only got you so far. "Three Mile Island, spiraling costs and fresh public calls for a nuclear arms freeze have made the nation more tentative toward nuclear power and its promise as a provider of energy and defense," the New York Times noted in 1982. "In this new and more critical period, the enthusiasm of companies for running nuclear weapons plants has diminished."

In 2000, the contract for Y-12 and Oak Ridge National Laboratory was split up. The University of Tennessee and Battelle won the management contract for the laboratory, and a consortium, going under the acronym BWXT (since renamed B&W Technical Services Y-12), took over Y-12. While the two entities still cooperate, they are, more than ever, distinct operations.

Oak Ridge National Laboratory and Y-12 are, understandably, the main employers in town, and the morning traffic heads in only one direction. The presence of the two facilities does provide some unexpected perks for a town of Oak Ridge's size. It boasts a top-notch public school system, higher-than-average salaries for the region, and, unique for this part of Tennessee, a surprisingly good bagel shop, which once hosted Henry Kissinger.

Before heading over to Y-12, we paid a visit to Oak Ridge National Laboratory, where we were given a brief overview by Frank Akers, the associate lab director for national security. Akers, a retired general, had only twenty minutes to get through thirty-seven slides, leaving him less than a minute for each. He sped through them with military efficiency. The slide show was part scientific overview, part inspirational speech. He peppered his talk with quotes from Woody Allen and adages such as "Hope is not a method." In his short presentation, Akers mixed in statistics about visitors, laboratory space, and budgets. For the laboratory, at least, business was booming. The lab's pride and joy was the sleek new Spallation Neutron Source—a massive facility that would allow scientists and researchers to play with intense pulsed neutron beams.

No gates or barriers surrounded the minimum-security complex. Unlike Y-12, the laboratory had already undergone heavy renovation. A series of spacious, modern buildings surrounded a central courtyard. Our host from the public affairs office led us into a modern glass-front building—one of the newest on-site—described to us as a model of openness and private sector cooperation. The atrium featured flags that represented past and present foreign visitors to the lab and included the Iranian flag. With an annual budget of about one billion dollars and more than four thousand employees, the laboratory had gone mainstream.

The differences between it and Y-12, a short drive away, were stark. Y-12 was heavily guarded. The nuclear weapons facility was protected by a perimeter fence and concrete obstacles that jutted menacingly out of the ground. Y-12 also had a much more blue-collar feel. As we approached the main gate of the facility, we passed a parade of cars and trucks lined up outside the entrance, as if their drivers were waiting to punch in at the factory. We drove on to the visitors' center, a small building outside the main gate. Bill Wilburn, Y-12's unfailingly polite public affairs official, was waiting for us in his pickup. He drove us through the main vehicle checkpoint, where security guards scrutinized the guest passes we'd been issued at the visitors' center, comparing them with our photo identification. As is the case with many government facilities, the security had been outsourced. Wackenhut, the private firm we had seen working the perimeter at the Nevada Test Site, provided the security here.

Like almost everyone we met at Y-12, Wilburn was a native of Tennessee and spoke with a gentle Appalachian drawl. A former newspaper reporter, Wilburn had decorated his office with a variety of knickknacks, mixing Southern culture with nuclear paraphernalia. A classic piece of Nashville poster art hung over his desk; on a shelf, a glamour shot of Emmylou Harris occupied a place of honor next to a portrait of Robert Oppenheimer. Without the highest security clearances, we could not visit the sections at Y-12 where the actual nuts-and-bolts work on nuclear weapons was done. Most of our visit would be confined to his office.

For our orientation, Wilburn arranged to take us on a driving tour with Ray Smith, a longtime maintenance worker at the facility whose exacting amateur research had eventually propelled him to the role of official Y-12 historian. His knowledge of Oak Ridge was encyclopedic. As we drove through the complex, Smith pointed out the various historical markers, including the remnants of New Hope, the small Appalachian community displaced by the bomb factory. We passed by the New Hope Cemetery—a local graveyard that, like the rest of the area, had ended up behind the massive gate. "People who have folks there can visit," Smith told us. "And people can still be buried here."

As we drove past the densely wooded hills and ridges that surrounded Y-12, Smith explained that then–brigadier general Leslie Groves acquired this vast tract of wilderness for the Manhattan Project because the land's unique topography created a natural barrier from the outside world. Only a few hundred people inhabited the valley at the time, living in rural squalor. In 1942, residents were given just a few weeks to move by the War Department, which informed them without explanation that the U.S. government would be taking over their lands.

The boundaries of Y-12 were marked—quite literally, as Wilburn pointed out—by a "blue line" on the road. To be "inside the blue line" or "over the wire" is to be within the security confines of Y-12. The boundaries may restrict the human population, but for wildlife, the blue line is a boon. The deer population has grown so much within the boundaries of the Y-12 perimeter that the Department of Energy now authorizes annual hunts—managed by the Tennessee Wildlife Resources Agency—to cull the population. (Employees organize a "deer drive" in winter, beating through the woods to push deer outside the plant boundary and toward hunters. The only catch is that deer have to be checked for radiological contamination after they are bagged.*)

Smith stopped to point to the buildings in various states of demolition. Over fifty years after its initial construction, the Y-12 complex still had a transient feel to it—owing to a combination of the hastily constructed Manhattan Project buildings and the fact that the complex had never extended far beyond its initial confines. Roads named after chemical elements like cobalt and cadmium were the only visual reminder that this was a nuclear facility. As we drove past a dead skunk splayed in the road, Smith related the story of a black bear that got inside the fence, rooting around like a spy in search of nuclear secrets. If Y-12 were ever shut down, it wouldn't take long for the weeds and wild animals to reclaim the place.

We paused at one point to look at a series of small pyramids that surrounded a large stretch of land, approximately 150 acres. The pyramids, Smith explained, were actually Perimeter Intrusion Detection and Assessment Systems (PIDAS), which monitored the area where so-called special nuclear material was stored. The hope was that by 2008 the most restricted area would shrink to just 15 acres, making it easier to secure. The consolidation would also defend Y-12 from potential vulnerability to terrorist attack.

---

* In 2001, due to post-9/11 security concerns, deer hunts on the Oak Ridge Reservation, which includes Y-12, were canceled. Having a large number of "uncleared individuals" tramping around DOE facilities with guns was considered too great of a risk.

It seemed Y-12 was in a state of both decay and renewal. We saw more than a few crumbling buildings, decorated with rusting pieces of industrial equipment. At the same time, however, we observed a tremendous amount of construction. It looked as if half of Y-12 was being torn down, while the other half was being rebuilt. And in some sense, that was precisely what was going on. Back in the confines of Wilburn's office, Tom Smith, Y-12's manager of strategic planning and modernization—a slight, mustachioed man with a broad smile—described to us how new money was pouring into a facility that had been largely starved of funds since the end of the Cold War. "It's a really exciting time around here," Smith told us. "If you go through the site now and look at all the construction that's going on, [you can tell] that modernization is really happening. And the other thing that's exciting is that NNSA is going to pursue their 2030 vision—and we're right at the heart of it."

In the early 1990s, modernization plans had been put on hold. President George H. W. Bush announced drastic cuts to the nuclear stockpile, including the elimination of all tactical nuclear weapons in Europe, and suddenly Y-12, a key nuclear weapons production facility, was given the less-glamorous job of dismantlement. Now, for the NNSA, 2030 was the magic year: It would mark the culmination of a new effort to revitalize and consolidate the nuclear complex. The idea was to build a responsive infrastructure, the official catchphrase used to describe nuclear weapons facilities that could respond quickly to future nuclear requirements. As part of Complex 2030, Y-12 was slated to become the "uranium center of excellence" of the future.

In most manufacturing facilities, the final product is shipped to a customer, never to be seen again. And this, in fact, was more or less how Y-12 operated for the first years of its existence. After the Cold War, however, it was given the dual task of rebuilding parts and components on older nuclear weapons in order to lengthen their life, perhaps indefinitely, and destroying and dismantling obsolete nuclear weapons. Y-12 was like a factory that existed for fifty years to assemble different automobiles and then spent the next ten years dismantling the cars it had built—or remanufacturing parts and components to reassemble old, long-discontinued models. The new tasks had a profound effect on the workplace culture at Y-12.

"The Cold War ended and everything was being cut back," Smith said. ". . . That was the first big shock: that we're not going to be building this number [of weapons] in the future, we're not going to be investing this money. And that kind of began the chain of some of these facilities deteriorating over time. And of course the second thing is that Y-12, for some period of time, was in pretty much a shutdown operation here, so it really shifted the emphasis from operating and production."

The shutdown was a particularly dark chapter for Y-12. After a series of safety violations, the Defense Nuclear Facilities Safety Board ordered Y-12 to "stand down," or stop work, on uranium operations. It took almost four years for these operations—the main mission of Y-12—to begin again. "I think now we're trending back to new construction, production operations and what have you, so it's kind of a shift back to running a production plant," Smith said.

During World War II, Oak Ridge was home to three central parts of the Manhattan Project: the K-25 gaseous diffusion plant, the Y-12 electromagnetic separation plant, and the X-10 Graphite Reactor, an experimental plutonium production facility that later became part of Oak Ridge National Laboratory. The Oak Ridge facilities produced the uranium that ended up in Little Boy.

By late 1943, nearly five thousand workers had arrived in Oak Ridge to operate the calutrons at Y-12. The workers intently stared at the machines without having any idea what they were for. The calutron method, which created weapons-grade uranium through electromagnetic separation, proved technically unfeasible, producing only a small amount of uranium. In 1943, work began on K-25, a two-million-square-foot, U-shaped building that, at the time, was the largest building in the world. K-25 separated uranium isotopes by pumping the uranium through a porous barrier that sifted out the heavier U-238 from the lighter U-235. Plutonium production, on the other hand, was deemed too unsafe to be done in Tennessee, so Brigadier General Groves chose a remote location in Washington State, the Hanford Site, code-named Site W.

The wartime work at Y-12 was dull, repetitive, and occasionally hazardous. Even after the war, problems continued. Complaints persisted about everything from poor housing to "vile cafeteria food." While occupational safety hazards existed across the complex, things were particularly bad at Y-12, where workers were exposed to toxic chemicals. The victim of a 1958 "criticality accident"—a chain reaction that occurs in the fissile material, bathing anyone around in dangerous neutrons—reportedly received one of the highest doses of radiation ever recorded. He died in 2002 after several bouts of cancer, including a particularly severe case that eventually required the amputation of his penis. He received just eighteen thousand dollars in compensation. A 2004 report by the Department of Energy's inspector general warned that Y-12 workers were still at risk from beryllium, a known carcinogen.

The town that grew up out of Y-12 and the other parts of the Manhattan Project did not build on a community. It supplanted it. "Oak Ridge has been a government town for its entire existence," Ray Smith, the Y-12 historian, told us. But that did not mean it was like other nuclear cities. Los Alamos was settled by big-city academics and exiled Europeans, many of whom shared a love of desert living. Livermore attracted scientists from around the country; its proximity to San Francisco and the Bay Area gave it a far more cosmopolitan feel. But in Oak Ridge, many of the staff members we interviewed— most of whom were scientists—had accents that betrayed Tennessee roots.

As we toured Y-12, we began to understand the magnitude of Complex 2030, the administration's nuclear modernization plan. Most of the activity at Y-12 revolved around two major projects: the Highly Enriched Uranium Materials Facility, a new storage center for bomb-grade uranium; and the Uranium Processing Facility, a new manufacturing center with a projected price tag of two billion dollars. There was also the U-shaped Jack Case Center, a massive office building that would sit on eight acres, and another building, called the New Hope Center. Y-12 was in the midst of a construction bonanza.

One thing about Y-12, however, would remain constant: the machine shop atmosphere. While the design laboratories—Los Alamos and Lawrence Livermore—were (for the time being) operated by the University of California, Y-12 had always been operated by industrial firms, first by Tennessee Eastman and then after the war by Carbon Chemical, which eventually became Union Carbide. The work was always focused on production. From its start, Oak Ridge was a factory town in every sense of the term. The plant struggled with unionization, strikes, and redundancies, but with the added twist of being a nuclear weapons factory. Complaints about working conditions that might become public at a car factory remained hidden behind a veil of nuclear secrecy.

Making nuclear weapons is a dangerous business. The nuclear production facilities have been beset with problems over the years, usually linked to the dangerous materials and hazards associated with making such weapons, but also because of the need for secrecy, which often hampers oversight. Some facilities fared worse than others. Rocky Flats in Colorado, for example, seemed to be a never-ending shop of atomic horrors, with incidents ranging from inhaled plutonium to alleged midnight waste incineration that eventually led to the afore-mentioned FBI raid. The raid, appropriately enough, was called Operation Desert Glow. Although the legal wrangling continued for a number of years, Rocky Flats' life as a nuclear weapons plant came to an ignominious end. Today, the area that once surrounded the complex is slated to become a national wildlife refuge.

Problems at the Y-12 plant, though less dramatic, were still rather bad. K-25, the vast gaseous diffusion plant built during the war, was a serious hazard. The original site of uranium enrichment operations was being demolished. Contamination and structural deterioration rendered the building too dangerous to salvage, although a small, tail-end portion of the monstrous structure may be preserved as a historic site. One worker at K-25 nominated his demolition work at K-25 as one of the "worst science jobs" in a contest for *Popular Science* magazine, citing his work with "asbestos, radiation, plutonium and other bad boys of the chemical realm." In 2006, a worker was seriously injured after falling through the second story of the deteriorated structure. Even in death, K-25 seemed determined to take a few more people with it.

Y-12 also had its own share of safety problems. Prolonged exposure to beryllium, for instance, left many workers with beryliosis, a chronic lung disease. And, as in any factory, accidents happened. According to the *Knoxville News Sentinel*, a 1999 explosion involving a sodium-potassium compound took place after a spill wasn't cleaned up for a week. Modern equipment that could have avoided the accident was never installed because of budgetary concerns, the newspaper reported.

Of course, the ultimate specter hanging over Y-12 is the possibility of a criticality accident. The 1958 incident led to the hospitalization of a number of workers exposed to a record level of radiation. While there hasn't been another case of uranium going critical, the safety violations have continued. In 2005, for example, eighteen hundred grams of highly enriched uranium were found in an air filter that hadn't been changed in over twenty years. It was not enough uranium to go critical, officials explained, but enough to prompt serious concerns.

Despite the atmosphere of secrecy, Y-12 struck us as having more in common with a tractor plant than a top-secret weapons facility, a fact reflected in frequent loudspeaker announcements piped into every office and work space that periodically interrupted our conversation. Reminiscent of high school loudspeaker announcements, the messages ranged from tedious to amusing. "Good morning, this is Dave Melroy of the fire protection agency," the loudspeaker boomed. "If you are thinking of using a turkey fryer during the holiday, think again. Safety experts have certified *any* turkey fryer as a fire hazard."

The speaker droned on about hot oil, grease fires, and turkey thawing before wishing everyone a safe weekend. Wilburn, the public affairs officer, explained without apology that every morning between eight fifteen and eight thirty, there was a public safety announcement. "Right now, it's kind of seasonal," he told us. "In the summertime there are announcements about, you know, being safe around lawn equipment or playing sports. It's just a way to make everybody think about being safe—not just at work, but at home."

The idea of having "safety announcements" piped into the offices of scientists at Livermore and Los Alamos would be unthinkable—not because scientists cared less about safety (although some critics of the labs might dispute that), but because the paternalism would be seen as unacceptable. But Y-12 was not focused on science; it was focused on production. It was a factory town populated with factory workers. But instead of producing toasters, cars, or toys, Y-12 was in the business of assembling parts and components for nuclear weapons.

Later that day, we interviewed Dan Linehan, a Y-12 worker dressed in a blue pinstripe button-down and Dockers—his slightly freckled face framed by rectangular glasses that gave him a look of wide-eyed innocence. He was not unfriendly, just slightly nervous. When speaking, he'd often look to the security officer in the room with us, to see which of our questions would be off-limits.

His job, to our surprise, was one of those areas.

"Can we start with your exact title?" we asked.

"OK, I'm a manager in the defense programs organization," the man replied, shifting uncomfortably in his seat. "I probably can't be more specific than that."

It's commonly said that every weapon in the U.S. nuclear arsenal contains at least some part or component fabricated at Y-12. But the fabrication of new nuclear weapons effectively ended in 1991, and the dismantlement process—the more technical term for taking apart nuclear weapons—is now the largest share of Y-12's work. The only assembly done at the complex is the refurbishment of older nuclear weapons. Thus, while Y-12 is still active in overhauling weapons, its days as a busy assembly line are long over. Refurbishment, however, keeps the plant employed. Y-12's workers build the secondaries, which are then sent to the Pantex Plant in Amarillo, Texas, for final assembly. The process also works in reverse: Retired warheads are first sent to Pantex, which does the initial dismantlement, then secondaries are sent to Oak Ridge for final disassembly. The nuclear stockpile is like a carousel, with various pieces of the inventory being added or removed for maintenance, inspection, or disposal.

When we visited Y-12 in the fall of 2006, workers at the facility were in the process of disassembling a number of warheads that had been withdrawn from the active inventory, including tactical nuclear weapons like the W48 and W79, nuclear artillery shells designed to be launched from howitzers. They were also hard at work on disassembling the W55, an antisubmarine rocket, and a warhead designed for a short-range ballistic missile, the W70.

Since Linehan would not give us his exact title, we decided to ask if he could describe the main thrust of his work. He threw a furtive glance at the security officer, who smiled and nodded his head. "I think I can do that," Linehan said tentatively. "I'm responsible for the dismantlement program here at Y-12."

So that's where Linehan came in. He was the man in charge of dismantling all these weapons. His reluctance to talk about his job—though a bit disconcerting at first—was understandable. As part of the production complex, it was still somewhat rare for staff at Y-12 to give interviews. During the Cold War, it would have been unthinkable. Dismantlement, Linehan explained, was historically a small amount of Y-12's work, though it has ramped up dramatically since the end of the Cold War. "It used to be viewed as filler work, but now definitely NNSA is making it a priority for us," he said.

Some things, however, remained classified. "I can't get into rates," he added. "I can tell you it's definitely accelerated last year and for the foreseeable future."

With the end of the Cold War, the demand for weapons-grade uranium production vanished, and weapons slated for decommissioning flowed into Oak Ridge, as did weapons-grade uranium brought in by the U.S. government from the former Soviet Union. In other words, over a few short years Y-12 had gone from being one of the world's premier uranium enrichment facilities to being something of a junkyard for used fuel and warheads.

At the end of our hour with Linehan, we asked what he found most satisfying about his job. Without hesitation, he offered an answer. "One of the big pluses is, every day—or nearly every day—you see tangible progress in what I do, because we're doing dismantlement every day," he told us. "It's like having a daytime planner where you have a list of items and you get to check them off multiple times a day. It's very gratifying."

Had we ended the interview there, we would likely have left with the mistaken impression that Linehan had found some profound satisfaction in the fact that he was helping to destroy the very nuclear arms he had once helped to build. But then we posed one final question.

"Would you have that same sense of accomplishment if you were building new nuclear weapons?" we asked.

"Oh yes!" Linehan replied, nodding enthusiastically. "Yes."

In the 1940s, thousands of workers streamed into Oak Ridge to work on the Manhattan Project. The vast majority didn't really know what they were working on. Today, workers at Y-12 know they are in the nuclear weapons business, but that doesn't necessarily mean that— prior to arriving—they have a good sense of exactly what that entails. For nearly fifty years, Y-12 was in the business of making nuclear weapons. It was a factory. Its skilled workers had to master specialized machinery and work with complex tools; they had to learn to handle specialized and possibly dangerous materials; and finally, they had to operate safely amid the usual hazards of any shop floor. And with time, the work took on a sort of normalcy.

Back in Bill Wilburn's office, we were introduced to Janice Christman, a twenty-five-year veteran of Y-12 who had risen through the ranks to become the program director of directed stockpile work. A soft-spoken woman, Christman began to tell us about her career at Y-12 somewhat tentatively. Clearly, it was not part of her normal work routine to give interviews. But as we continued, she began to speak with less hesitation. "I originally came to Y-12 not knowing much about the nuclear weapons business and not being particularly pronuclear," said Christman. "I spent a little bit of time working at the Tennessee Valley Authority in the summers between school."

It may be hard to imagine for those outside the wire, but for many employees, coming to work every day at Y-12 is just like at any job. Christman had come here in search of a better work environment, better pay, and more responsibility. Her first job at Y-12 was in the maintenance organization. She worked as a utilities engineer, a job that at first kept her away from the nuclear weapons programs. Gradually, she moved up the ladder. "The basic reason I wanted to come to Y-12 was they were the largest manufacturing facility around," she told us. "I really wanted to be in that type of environment. That was in the early eighties, and at Y-12, the manufacturing shops here were really booming in those days."

The idea of Y-12 as a booming factory may sound odd to those not intimately involved in nuclear weapons work, but that's precisely what it was. During the Cold War, the nuclear weapons complex was in a constant state of research and development, and new weapons designs were rolling off the assembly line. But those were also the years when the mission of Y-12 seemed clear to everyone. Y-12 was helping counter a Soviet nuclear threat. Christman may originally have joined Y-12 to advance her career, but she gradually found larger meaning in her work. "I was walking through a particular area of Y-12 one day, and—I still remember that day—it hit me what an amazing place this was," she said.

Having pride in the work of nuclear weapons is something quite normal for workers at Y-12—even if, as Christman conceded, it could seem strange to the outside world. Her office sported a GOT NUKES? sticker on the door, and at home she would do yard work in her NUCLEAR WEAPONS SCHOOL T-shirt.

Admittedly, however, not everyone in Oak Ridge, or the surrounding community, is completely enamored of nuclear weaponry. The week before our visit, the Department of Energy held its public hearing on Complex 2030. While Oak Ridge, like all nuclear sites, faced the possibility of downsizing, it would as likely as not be the beneficiary of centralized uranium operations within the complex, which would fortify and even expand Y-12's importance for the nuclear weapons stockpile. The hearing—like many others around the country—seemed to attract only marginal interest. It was less a discussion of practical impacts than a venue for antinuclear activism, and it bordered on theatrical. The lineup featured an impromptu skit and a series of heartfelt antinuclear denunciations by a variety of church groups, peace activists, and other nuclear opponents.

Yet some of the comments were prescient. One woman noted that the vast undertaking of Complex 2030, centered in part on building the Reliable Replacement Warhead, looked a lot more ambitious than a mere modernization program. "If we were observing another country, another government, making a proposal such as we are seeing this evening from the NNSA, how would we feel about that government and how would we enter into a relationship of trust and diplomacy?" she asked.

For the most part, however, the Oak Ridge community has been supportive. "You can't compare Rocky Flats and Oak Ridge," Christman noted, referring to the recent hearing. "I don't think the community ever accepted what was going on at Rocky Flats. It didn't matter what the benefits were. It's not exactly that way here."

Her view of the hearing's more vocal participants was similar to what we had heard from other workers at the nuclear labs. "Every time we have people who come in and approach things in terms of 'the world will never be safe until there are zero nuclear weapons,' I really wish I could feel like they were getting a better education," she said. "It's a very complex issue."

How, then, do Y-12 workers approach this complex issue? For those who work outside of the nuclear weapons industry, the fall of the Berlin Wall and the breakup of the Soviet Union marked a clear break with the past. But for the workers of Y-12, it was the beginning of a hard time on the job. Work on nuclear weapons essentially came to a grinding halt, leaving thousands of workers with an uncertain future. By 1991, when the Soviet Union broke apart, the nuclear weapons business looked like it might go bust. Christman acknowledged this period was "confusing" for employees like her.

"The closest I came to making a decision to leave Y-12 was when the Cold War ended. Not because I was a Cold War warrior and if there wasn't a Cold War to fight I was getting out," she said. "But because I wasn't sure where things were going. I made a conscious decision to stay at Y-12 because I believed we still had a role to play in national security." In fact, Y-12 soon found new purpose in dismantling and refurbishing. And over the past few years, Complex 2030 had led to fresh infusions of funds for modernization. "Now," Christman pointed out, "we have the Reliable Replacement Warhead."

What role should Y-12 play in the future? Unlike Oak Ridge National Laboratory, Y-12 has been, despite attempts to open up, confined by secrecy. Its production processes can never be competitive with those of the private sector. And unlike Los Alamos and Livermore, which have a broad scientific base to draw on, Y-12, again, was essentially designed to produce one thing: nuclear weapons.

During our tour, Wilburn stopped our vehicle at Building 9737, where he escorted us into a makeshift museum called the Hall of Success, where management had displayed some of Y-12's contributions to the commercial sector. Each of the nuclear weapons laboratories we had visited had displays meant to showcase how that particular lab had benefited the civilian economy. Livermore, for example, touted Star Wars–era technology that contributed to breast cancer detection.

But at Y-12, there was a bit more wishful thinking on display. In 1997, Congress had bestowed on the facility the designation "National Prototype Center," which was meant to attract private sector partners to commercialize Y-12 technology. Press articles, in fact, frequently cite Y-12's contribution to a naval submarine design and work on an amphibious assault vehicle, both military projects. One Hall of Success display showcased Y-12's contribution to something called a "hospital in a box," a portable surgical suite. Other products seemed destined for commercial obscurity. In one corner was a banjo. Ray Smith explained that the banjo manufacturer, who wanted pre–World War II bronze for an authentic sound, had turned to Y-12 for help in acquiring the right material. In another corner was a Coors aluminum beer can. Smith told us that Y-12—with its experience in machine tools—had helped the brewers develop a ceramic tool to make very thin cans.

Beer can technology would never be the main mission for Y-12. But Complex 2030 would give it a new lease on life. Driving through Y-12 with Wilburn and Smith, we stopped at the top of Chestnut Ridge, which provided a sweeping view of the complex below. The wind was blowing and it was starting to rain again, but from our vantage point, for the first time, we had a full sense of the scale of this secret city. Y-12 spanned the entirety of Bear Creek Valley, protected from the east by a ridge that shielded the complex from neighboring residential areas; a dense wood bounded it on the west. Smith paused for a moment to look back down at Y-12. "We were fighting wars with muskets," he said contemplatively. "And within the span of decades the world had moved to nuclear weapons."

The scenic overlook also gave us a real sense of Oak Ridge's isolation, which had served the government so well during the Manhattan Project. That was still true today. While the Knoxville newspaper and other local news outlets had done an excellent job covering the construction boom at Y-12, news of the facility's rebirth did not extend far beyond the Great Smoky Mountains, though it was clear a major news story was unfolding before our eyes. With little public debate—save a hearing or two to outline the Complex 2030 project—the government was pouring hundreds of millions of dollars into an effort to revive nuclear weapons production. According to the current schedule, it expected the first production unit of the Reliable Replacement Warhead to be made in 2012.

As we stood on the ridge overlooking Y-12—with a wind gusting so hard it began to drown out Smith's narration—it suddenly made sense to us what we were seeing. The valley below was bustling with activity. Earthmovers shuttled to and fro, flatbed trucks hauled building materials, and construction workers made their rounds. They were laying the foundations for something massive. Looking down into the valley, we were clearly witnessing the renewal of a factory that had essentially lain dormant for a decade and a half. Now it was finally coming back to life. Y-12 was preparing for the day when new nuclear weapons would once again roll off the assembly line.

Y-12 was a factory that had teetered on the brink of obsolescence, and Smith motioned to the vast complex below us, where new construction was gradually erasing the old industrial-age landscape of Manhattan Project buildings. As he pointed to the new buildings springing up at Y-12, he recalled his painstaking efforts to preserve some of its history. Through detailed interviews with surviving residents of the New Hope community, who were evacuated by the government to make way for the nuclear factory, and by overlaying pre-1942 maps with images of modern Oak Ridge, Smith had even been able to identify, he said, the exact spot where John Hendrix, the prophet of Oak Ridge, had been born.

Hendrix's prophecy shares one common thread with the narrative we heard from those we interviewed at Y-12: the idea that nuclear weapons and nuclear deterrence are inevitable, a product of some inalterable historical force.* Hendrix had said: "Bear Creek Valley some day will be filled with great buildings and factories and they will help toward winning the greatest war that will ever be." His prophecy had proved correct—even if Hendrix, who died in 1915, had not predicted the rebuilding that was going on in Bear Creek Valley today.

"It's a good story, but he missed one thing," Smith said with a chuckle. "He thought the place would be called Paradise."

---

* This sense of determinism is not unique to Oak Ridge. In the book *Blessed Assurance: At Home with the Bomb in Amarillo, Texas*, A. G. Mojtabai speaks to workers and residents in Amarillo, home of Pantex, portraying how the vision of Armageddon held by the town's Christian fundamentalists comfortably meshes with the technocratic pull of a bomb factory.

CHAPTER 5

Where's the Big Board?

Searching for Strategery in Nebraska

Nebraska carries with it certain associations. In childhood, it meant a crowded car on the flat stretch of highway between Iowa and Colorado, 450 miles of fights with siblings, with a few stops for buffalo burgers. Today, not much has changed, although big-box stores have proliferated along Interstate 80. Each exit looks the same, and with the monotonous shades of corn and soy, you get the feeling of being stuck for hours on the same two-mile stretch of road. There's little sign that Nebraska is a crucial part of the nuclear complex.

During the Cold War, the logic of nuclear deterrence was one of continued expansion, creating, as retired Air Force general George Lee Butler described it, "astronomically expensive infrastructures, monolithic bureaucracies, and complex processes that defied control or comprehension." Even the road we traveled from the Colorado border to Omaha—I-80—was a product of the Cold War, promoted to the public as an effort to ensure survival in the event of a nuclear attack. The highways traversed by long-haul truckers and retirees would also allow American cities to evacuate in the event of nuclear attack—while also enabling the U.S. military to move quickly and effectively across the country.

The one thing that never occurred to us on family car trips through the state was that during a thermonuclear war, Nebraska would have been a very bad place to be. Not only do missile fields dot the western half of the state, but the nerve center of the nuclear complex—U.S.

Strategic Command (STRATCOM), the military command-and-control post for the nation's nuclear arsenal—sits in Bellevue, a small town just south of Omaha. We came to Bellevue curious to find out how, with the Soviet Union gone, the military looked at nuclear deterrence, and to better understand how senior military leaders actually planned to wage a nuclear war.

Perhaps no state has been more intimately linked with the practice of nuclear warfare than the Cornhusker State. *Enola Gay*, the B-29 bomber used to drop Little Boy on Hiroshima, was built in a manufacturing area that is now part of Offutt Air Force Base, where STRATCOM is located. In 1948, Offutt was selected to host Strategic Air Command, better known as SAC, ensuring that the American heartland would also be the heart of nuclear strategy. Nebraska's location in the central part of the United States made it the ideal choice for a nuclear command following World War II and, later, a site for basing intercontinental ballistic missile (ICBM) silos.

Not only was Nebraska home to a growing nuclear arsenal, but it also became the center of a growing civil defense effort, beginning with the classic "duck and cover" campaign in the 1950s, which was followed later by more elaborate plans to evacuate cities in the event of nuclear attack. When the advent of ICBMs in the late 1950s shortened warning time from hours to minutes, evacuation plans were discarded, and an entirely new feature of nuclear geography appeared: a network of fallout shelters that would protect citizens (or at least those who survived the initial blast) from the poisonous effects of radiation.

By the mid-1960s, for instance, Lincoln, Nebraska, had public shelters capable of protecting one hundred thousand people, and individual citizens were told to prepare for nuclear Armageddon. The fallout shelter craze even gave rise to Nebraskits, a compressed biscuit stored in fallout shelters across the state and around the country. An old video of Val Peterson, head of the Federal Civil Defense Administration and former governor of Nebraska, lecturing Americans on civil defense planning looks suspiciously familiar; his recommendations echo the Department of Homeland Security's post-9/11 exhortations to stockpile duct tape and premeasured plastic sheeting. Then as now, disaster planning took on an absurd logic of its own.

If ICBMs made evacuation plans impractical, the growing yield of thermonuclear weapons made other aspects of civil defense sound absurd. Eventually, the campaign to build fallout shelters was largely abandoned. Years later, the shelters that survive have largely been converted to storm shelters, or put to other, more mundane uses. Tornadoes, rather than nukes, are the dominant threat. Shelters are now a running joke. As we drove to Omaha, we listened as an FM radio DJ in North Platte announced in between commercial breaks that he was "broadcasting from a fallout shelter."

But while civil defense may have receded into the background, nuclear planning has not disappeared. STRATCOM has arguably become more powerful and farther reaching than ever. When terrorists struck on September 11, 2001, President Bush flew to an "undisclosed location" later revealed to be Offutt Air Force Base. The base would have been attractive for a number of reasons: location (far from the terrorist strikes), protection (the presence of an underground command bunker), and perhaps most importantly, connectivity (STRATCOM houses the command center for an arsenal with global reach).

We pulled into Bellevue late in the evening, passing Ground Zero Comics before parking at the Best Western White House Inn, a hotel that proved much less ostentatious than its name suggested. It was situated between a Village Inn restaurant and a local barbecue joint, and its biggest selling point was that it was a mere five-minute drive from STRATCOM. The desk clerk downstairs supplied everything from phone cards to carryout menus, and the bookshelves operated on the honor system. The White House theme included hallways named after presidents and a portrait gallery of first ladies, aspirational decor that contrasted with the lived-in feel of an extended-stay hotel. Many of the residents, clearly, were military personnel on long-term assignments at the base. Everyone at the hotel was unfailingly polite and hospitable, reminding us that the heartland is an odd place to locate enough nuclear firepower to destroy the world.

Before setting off for Nebraska, we had, as every good nuclear tourist should, rented a copy of *Dr. Strangelove; or, How I Learned to Stop Worrying and Love the Bomb*, Stanley Kubrick's iconic spoof of Cold War strategy. The film begins on a fictional Strategic Air Command base, where a deranged commander convinced of a Communist plot orders his nuclear-armed bombers to strike the Soviet Union. Although the strike is called off, one bomber has deployed past a "fail-safe" point, after which it is impossible to recall.

Kubrick's movie, released in 1964, was made in the era of the "airborne alert aircraft," when SAC's nuclear-armed bomber fleet prowled the skies year-round, ready at a moment's notice to carry their payloads to the Soviet Union. The premise of the plot was imaginary—there was no "point of no return" in nuclear doctrine for bombers. Real or not, though, Kubrick's film tapped into an essential part of nuclear lore: the war machine trained to react un-thinkingly to a threat. And Hollywood did get one thing right: For decades, the United States and the Soviet Union kept their nuclear forces on hair-trigger alert.

By the time we arrived at STRATCOM in the fall of 2006, that posture had changed. The bombers—the central plot element of *Dr. Strangelove*—had been taken off alert. The Looking Glass aircraft, an airborne command-and-control center that would help direct the nuclear arsenal during war, had been grounded in 1998, though it remains on continuous alert and ready to fly. Other elements of the nuclear command were evolving as well. For years, SAC presided over the "nuclear triad," a three-pronged force that consisted of long-range bombers, submarines armed with ballistic missiles, and intercontinental ballistic missiles launched from hardened silos across the United States. This geographic dispersal of the arsenal was supposed to ensure that enough U.S. nuclear forces survived a Soviet first strike.

In 2002, the Pentagon submitted to Congress its latest Nuclear Posture Review, a document that outlines the structure of the military's nuclear forces. After portions of the classified document were leaked to the media, Defense Department officials held a press conference to discuss some of the details. Foremost, the traditional nuclear triad was dead—at least in name. In its place was a strategy combining nuclear forces with powerful new conventional weapons and ballistic missile defense.

The new posture also promised a seemingly radical change. The active nuclear forces would be reduced from about ten thousand deployed warheads to between seventeen hundred and twenty-two hundred. That number—which wouldn't count nuclear warheads in storage—was affirmed in later negotiations with Russia under the Moscow Treaty of 2002. By fall 2006, there were five hundred land-based Minuteman III ICBMs, fourteen nuclear-armed Trident submarines, twenty-one B-2 bombers, and ninety-four B-52 bombers. The total number of deployed warheads was estimated at around six thousand.

In 1992, STRATCOM subsumed SAC's old responsibilities, including the creation of the Single Integrated Operation Plan (SIOP), the war plan for nuclear weapons that has inspired many a Hollywood director. The nuclear triad didn't go away—submarines capable of firing nuclear-tipped missiles remained in the arsenal, as did air-launched nuclear missiles and ICBMs—but nuclear weapons, once SAC's sole responsibility, became just one piece of a larger STRATCOM mission. In 2002, the Pentagon folded U.S. Space Command into STRATCOM and added in new tasks as well, suddenly making the nuclear command responsible for everything from missile defense and nuclear weapons to more esoteric fields such as intelligence, surveillance and reconnaissance, and countering weapons of mass destruction. The old SAC was gone too, at least on paper, though veterans of the command printed up commemorative T-shirts and patches that warned: "SAC will be back."

In the hotel that evening, we pored over stacks of articles on STRATCOM and nuclear weapons, trying to trace the broken line between the Cold War–era SIOP and the present-day version, called the Operations Plan, or OPLAN for short. During the Cold War, reporters traveling to SAC would allude darkly to the "Doomsday Machine," the mythic computer that generated the SIOP's targets, and reflect solemnly on the military planners plotting a course for world destruction. What they usually found were military officers sitting at cubicles, which prompted an even more generous sprinkling of words like "Armageddon," "doomsday," and "apocalypse" into their writing, perhaps in the hope of making the place seem a bit more interesting.

For all that has been written about nuclear weapons strategy and theory, there is surprisingly little that describes the procedure for how nuclear weapons would actually be launched. What are the targets? How does the chain of command work? Articles on the SIOP are often devoid of any references or citations, and much of the information is out of date. When we put a question in writing to STRATCOM, asking for an explanation of nuclear command-and-control, along with any fact sheets, we received a terse, two-sentence reply: "The President of the United States has the sole authority to issue nuclear control orders.

These orders go directly from the president to the launch platform, facilitated by military channels, including U.S. Strategic Command."

In the 1970s, when journalist Ron Rosenbaum explored the mysteries of the SIOP, an answer was equally elusive. Rosenbaum's research drew him into a world of "nuke porn" as he uncovered tantalizing hints about the supposedly fail-safe launch system and other nuclear lore. At the end, Rosenbaum's response to the mysteries of the SIOP was a demand: Open it up to public view. He wrote, "But in one way or another we all have our finger on the trigger, and it's about time we knew where we're aiming, who's really giving the orders to fire, and whether we ought to obey."

What were the secrets of the SIOP? General George Lee Butler, a former SAC chief, once raised serious concerns about it. According to a 1997 profile of Butler in the *Washington Post Magazine*, he called it "Alice in Wonderland stuff" that would boggle the mind of the most experienced military planner; for the elected officials responsible for ordering an attack, the process would surely be even more mystifying. As the *Post* article noted, "The targeting data and other details of the war plan, which are written in an almost unfathomable million lines of computer software code, were typically reduced by military briefers to between 50 and 100 slides that could be presented in an hour or two to the handful of senior U.S. officials who were cleared to hear it."

And although officials at STRATCOM like to say that theirs is an entirely new command, there is no getting around the basic fact that STRATCOM does much of what SAC did during the Cold War. First and foremost, it controls nuclear forces. The major difference between 2006, when we visited STRATCOM, and 1986, still the height of the Cold War, was that STRATCOM didn't show up that much in the newspapers. As nuclear weapons receded into the background, so too did STRATCOM, reappearing briefly in 2003 when a leaked document revealed plans for an August meeting at the base to discuss the country's nuclear arsenal. That meeting reportedly would cover mini-nukes, bunker busters, and neutron bombs; the U.K. *Guardian* described it as a summit of Dr. Strangeloves on the Nebraska plains. In fact, what emerged from the meeting—as we learned at Los Alamos—was not a population-killing neutron bomb or a mini-nuke, but the Reliable Replacement Warhead, the centerpiece of Complex 2030.

For the labs, the RRW is part of the notion of responsive infra-structure—i.e., the ability of the labs to develop new weapons. "There's a deterrence aspect of that," John Immele, Los Alamos' associate director for national security, told us when we interviewed him in New Mexico. "That's deterring by capabilities. Not with the number of weapons, but by the fact that you can respond, and that the laboratories can come up with an invention or a clever response."

The labs, in that sense, seem to think the RRW is part of a much broader notion of deterrence that includes their innate ability to develop nuclear weapons. What the RRW means for the U.S. military, however, is not at all clear. Since the days when Rosenbaum investigated the SIOP, there has been very little, if any, new light shed on the U.S. military's nuclear war plans. What has changed dramatically since the end of the Cold War is the introduction of "global strike," a concept that is increasingly being used in places where politicians might have once used the phrase "nuclear strike." The idea is simple. Modern "smart" weapons are sophisticated and precise enough to hold enemy leaders at risk without blowing up their capital cities.

Longtime nuclear analyst William Arkin, however, suspects that the concept of global strike also masks the insertion of nuclear weapons into preemptive war plans. "In the secret world of military planning, global strike has become the term of art to describe a specific pre-emptive attack," Arkin wrote in 2005. "When military officials refer to global strike, they stress its conventional elements. Surprisingly, how-ever, global strike also includes a nuclear option, which runs counter to traditional U.S. notions about the defensive role of nuclear weapons."

What bothers Arkin are secret plans for a preemptive "nuclear option." Arkin raises an important point: How can anything really be a deterrent if it's kept secret? That, of course, was the fatal flaw in Dr. Strangelove. The Russians kept their Doomsday Device a secret.

The first sign that Nebraska was no longer home to nuclear stalwarts was apparent at the entrance to the General Curtis E. LeMay Building, STRATCOM's three-story headquarters. Our public affairs escort let slip that the command was planning to remove two massive monu-ments to the nuclear mission, a Trident missile and a Titan missile, which, as former symbols of SAC's might, loomed over the low-slung brick structure. The commander wanted something that might better reflect the new missions. STRATCOM, it seemed, was the base of disappearing nukes.

By the time we arrived there, the military had dispensed with the nuclear theater. More importantly, it soon became clear to us that it had no interest in even emphasizing it. Prior to the terrorist attacks of 9/11, the base provided public tours of the underground bunker located in the LeMay Building, making it something of a nuclear tourist trap. Command center tours were stopped in 2002 during renovations of the facility. We were told that the new Global Operations Center, as it's now called, was required to be "brought down" for uncleared visitors. It was doubtful we were missing much, though: We found a picture online of the commander's remodeled "situation room," which featured a few chairs seated around a semicircular table that faced an expansive map—the proverbial "big board"—and video monitor. With the exception of the map, it looked much like any other military conference room.

The underground command center, in fact, is no longer the focal point of nuclear command and control. That point was made clear when Army Major General Kevin Campbell, STRATCOM's chief of staff, told us earlier that year that the command was moving away from the Cold War–era big boards and command bunkers that made for such great sightseeing. In their place was the idea of a "distributed network" that could function, well, just about anywhere. "If you look at the architecture of nuclear command and control, there are certain fixed facilities and certain mobile facilities that have been in existence for years," he said. "What we're trying to do is get away from that architecture and put ourselves around the country at different sites."

In other words, the nuclear force no longer needs an office—it can telecommute. And true to the concept of distributed networks, our introductory briefing at STRATCOM was not in front of a big screen. Instead, we were seated in a medium-size conference room. Our morning briefer, David Thomson, an enthusiastic and youthful-looking Air Force lieutenant colonel, spent a mere thirty seconds talking about the nuclear mission.

"In SAC it was the nuclear option: the end of the story, the ultimate end," he began. "We still retain that in a deterrence role. But if you look at the span of influence across our mission sets, we can use those tool sets to just change an adversary's mind, or influence the information there. All the way from influence to thermonuclear . . . That is the span of global strike these days. All of those create a battlefield effect that is not just a burning building anymore. It might just be the changing of a mind or a mind-set."

If the main goal of SAC during the Cold War was to use nuclear weapons to avert a Soviet attack, STRATCOM now looks at anything that can, as our briefer told us, "change an adversary's mind." Thomson ran through a dizzying array of slides showing organizational charts, command authorities, and an assortment of new STRATCOM missions that ran the gamut from counterproliferation to satellites in space. Not that STRATCOM actually *controls* the surveillance aircraft, or runs the missile defense systems. Rather it delegates authority in some cases and "coordinates" resources in others. With the exception of nuclear weapons, STRATCOM is what in military parlance is referred to as a "supporting command," meaning it doesn't command or direct military operations; it merely supports them.

As the crisscrossing organizational charts showed, STRATCOM was accumulating more PowerPoint warriors, if not more real power. More significant was the appointment of a new commander, General James Cartwright, who was nominated by then defense secretary Donald Rumsfeld. Cartwright was a unique choice, particularly because he was a Marine, not a career nuclear officer.

The Marine Corps, needless to say, does not possess any nuclear weapons, and some old-time nuclear weapons officers were convinced the new commander would not value strategic nuclear forces. Equally important, a subtle prejudice was at work. Air Force officers too often view their Marine counterparts as jarheads: great at leading light infantry, but too dunderheaded for the tasks of nuclear deterrence. That stereotype can rear up in some amusing ways. In a now-famous incident at the beginning of the war in Afghanistan, Lieutenant General Gregory Newbold, a top Marine, told reporters in a Pentagon press briefing that the Taliban had been "eviscerated."

Rumsfeld made it clear the Marine general had overstepped and soon knocked down Newbold's account. The most scathing comment, however, was from Air Force general Richard Myers, the chairman of the Joint Chiefs of Staff. "I'm surprised a Marine even knows what the word 'eviscerated' means," he said.

All that raised the interesting question of how a Marine would reshape the nuclear command. But our briefer quickly moved on from our nuclear lesson. With the next slide, he described SKI-Web—pronounced "sky web," a name that sounded straight out of Hollywood. We momentarily pictured a sort of ominous computer programming doomsday scenarios, hoping to hear how SKI-Web was STRATCOM's real-life SkyNet, the mythical computer in the *Terminator* movies that takes over SAC's computers to launch a devastating nuclear strike to wipe out humankind (and sends out Arnold Schwarzenegger to exterminate the last pesky survivors).

Disappointingly, no. SKI-Web, it turned out, was merely the abbreviation for STRATCOM's Strategic Knowledge Integration–Web. It was not some newfangled system that would take over control of nuclear weapons, but Cartwright's brainchild for modernizing communications within STRATCOM by using blogs, instant messaging, and other office tools.

Other changes were afoot. When SAC, to use the parlance of our interlocutors at STRATCOM, "went away" in 2002, new names were considered. Apparently, "Global Command" was one option, but it was rejected because standard military abbreviation would have been the unsexy-sounding "GLOBCOM."

The intellectual underpinnings of the place were shifting as well. *The World Is Flat*, Thomas Friedman's globalization-for-dummies book, seemed to have become the manual for indoctrinating STRATCOM officers. Where nuclear strategists of old had once worshipped at the feet of the nuclear strategist Herman Kahn and the RAND Corporation, it now appeared that big-idea books like Malcolm Gladwell's *Blink* had replaced the copies of *On Thermonuclear War*. Jerome Martin, the command historian, explained to us that Cartwright was tapping into "a lot of business trends." By the end of the day, we'd heard enough references to Friedman's work that we suspected it had been placed on some sort of required-reading list for the command's action officers.

Despite the endless acronyms and organizational charts, there was no denying that the nuclear mission, for better or worse, was still a central part of STRATCOM's purpose. However, when we asked Martin about STRATCOM's role in developing the requirements for nuclear weapons, he politely demurred. "I'd probably get out of my depth very quickly," he said, although he did concede that STRATCOM was indeed essential to establishing those requirements. "There's the Nuclear Weapons Council," he said. "Yeah, there's a unique aspect there. But they are advisory, I think. I have to admit, I lose the bubble of how that plays through when it comes to the process."

That was all the background we got from STRATCOM staff on nuclear weapons.

After our command briefing, we were ushered into the general's office. Cartwright was standing behind a blond-wood console, wearing a flight suit with a SKI-Web shoulder patch, which read "U.S. STRAT-COM SKI-Web warrior" around the edge and featured a computer with "100 blogs" on the screen. He gestured to a long, Scandinavian-style conference table. It was unlike any general's office we had ever seen. In fact, his office looked like a conference room from a hip architectural firm. Most four-stars have interior design tastes that lean toward heavy wood paneling, overstuffed leather chairs, and lots of trophies. But the office's spare, minimalist cool seemed an aesthetic fit with the general's vision of the new command, one that was modern, lean, and wired.

Cartwright was relaxed and confident. He didn't look the part of a man who had his finger on the proverbial button. There were no pictures of nuclear weapons, no models of ballistic missiles, or any evidence at all that this was even the office of a military commander. Then again, the idea of a "red phone" connected by landlines would surely be anathema to the man who thought up SKI-Web.

We asked Cartwright about defense commentator William Arkin's provocative article about plans for nuclear preemption. According to Arkin, CONPLAN 8022, part of the current OPLAN, included a nuclear first strike option. Cartwright listened politely to the question and then proceeded to answer by recounting the history that led to the Nuclear Posture Review of 2002, which laid out U.S. nuclear strategy:

> But what came out of that first one was an acknowledgment that the world was probably changing. That we had gone through, what do you want to call it, the falling of the [Berlin] Wall, really the end of the Cold War, and some of those things,

number one. Number two, during the period between the falling of the Wall and the reviews, we had taken what most people would call the peace dividend, period, and not a lot had changed or happened from a military standpoint, but the world was changing, and so they came up with this construct called the new triad, which really envisioned that the former Soviet Union, now Russia, was not the only adversary we should worry about. That the threats in the world had both proliferated and diversified in ways that we were not yet going to be able to understand. It was moving in a direction away from, shall we call it, the status quo of the Cold War? So, how do you address that?

The monologue continued until Cartwright came around—naturally—to Thomas Friedman. The information age, he explained, had allowed nations access to military capabilities that in the past would have taken many years and perhaps tens of billions of dollars to develop. In Friedmanesque terms, the world was indeed flattening. Most people would apply that globalization analysis to business, but Cartwright saw it in terms of threats. Rather than focusing on Russia, the United States was looking at threats as far-flung as Africa and the Philippines. And those threats brought Cartwright back around to the nuclear stockpile.

"This was just kind of an acknowledgment that the strategy of, I lost the word . . . retaliating . . ." Cartwright's voice trailed off for a moment, as we realized that the man in charge of the nuclear war plan had forgotten the key phrase of the Cold War. He paused, then began again; ". . . mutual assured destruction was not going to be sufficient."

Surely Herman Kahn must have been spinning in his grave. The topic of MAD brought the general back to our question. Well, not quite our question, but the question he would have preferred us to ask—how did he envision the role of nuclear weapons? "You needed something that was able to change the calculus inside an adversary's mind, appropriate for that adversary," he continued, adding that this could be a nuclear weapon, through traditional deterrence, or it could be a conventional strike, or perhaps even psychological operations.

According to Cartwright, the size and perhaps also the importance of nuclear weapons had changed over time, and yet little had been done to reflect this in the size of the arsenal. Targets that once could only have been taken out by nuclear weapons—a country's air defenses, for instance—could now be destroyed using conventional weapons. Precision had increased; conventional firepower had increased. With precision, he continued, you didn't even need a whole lot of explosive power. "You've got precision and you've got conventional alternatives that ought to be able to offset some part of that inventory," he said.

The idea that nonnuclear, conventional weapons could somehow complement or in many cases supplant the role of nuclear weapons was an inherent part of the Nuclear Posture Review, which called for the development of new conventional weapons. Some of the Navy's Ohio-class ballistic missile submarines, for instance, would be converted to carry nonnuclear Tomahawk missiles. That concept fit with global strike, the notion that Arkin claims includes nuclear preemption. But Cartwright chose not to emphasize it in that way. His concept of global strike, which could include ICBMs tipped with nonnuclear payloads, was a logical part of deterrence. "You have conventional capabilities that are available to you, but you have people that say the only alternative is nuclear," he said. "That leaves you disconnected."

But what about the administration's earlier push to develop a nuclear bunker buster, the Robust Nuclear Earth Penetrator? Congress, unconvinced of the need for such a new weapon, had eliminated most of the funding for the bunker buster. "We rebuilt that whole activity," Cartwright said. "In the end, it actually was more about conventional capabilities and the shortfalls we had in our conventional knowledge base than it was about the nuclear side."

But if the bunker buster had failed to gain much traction, another nuclear initiative was quickly taking shape. By 2006, the more pressing issue was the Reliable Replacement Warhead, which would be used to replace older warheads in the arsenal. While early advocates of new nuclear weapons had focused on creating bombs that were possibly lower in yield and designed to take out hardened military targets rather than cities, the RRW had morphed into a different effort. The focus was now on "safety, security, and surety."

Ensuring that bombs didn't accidentally detonate was a long-standing argument for the RRW. Security—making sure that it couldn't be set off maliciously—would help reduce the forces dedicated to protecting nuclear warheads. But it was surety, Cartwright told us, that offered a significant military advantage. Reliability, he argued, would also ultimately drive down the total nuclear inventory. Why? Because you wouldn't have to use multiple warheads against a single target. "If you do RRW just on the operational side of using the warheads in the surety side of the equation, you can use less," he said. "So, again, you could start to push down the total inventory requirement, because you're not using multiples against a single target."

The four-star commander's defense of the RRW somehow struck us as uninspired. It also struck us as somewhat disconnected from the argument the labs had made about the RRW. Unlike the labs, Cartwright didn't seem concerned about a catastrophic defect across the nuclear inventory or the loss of nuclear know-how. Nor was he all that enthusiastic about other parts of the nuclear arsenal. Even the bombers—the vehicles of *Dr. Strangelove*'s road to doomsday—were being shunted aside. The B-1 bomber had already been removed from the nuclear mission; in the meantime, he noted, the B-2 and B-52 were still nuclear capable but "heavily engaged on the conventional side"—in other words, they were busy dropping conventional bombs in places like Iraq and Afghanistan.

"The value of the bomber to STRATCOM has somewhat diminished," Cartwright told us. "The likelihood of flying something like a B-52 from here to some adversary that was nuclear armed and well defended has diminished. It's not a practical way of doing business."

Bombers weren't needed anymore? We could almost see an Air Force officer shuddering. But Cartwright was not the first combatant commander to attempt sweeping changes in the nuclear forces. One of his predecessors, General George Lee Butler, attempted to reform the SIOP in the 1990s during his tenure as the commander in chief of Strategic Air Command, or CINCSAC (pronounced "sink-sack"). Convinced the war plan was complicated and antiquated, Butler scrubbed thousands of sites from the target list in Russia and created new attack options that would allow strikes against a limited number of targets. According to the *Washington Post Magazine*, "Butler proudly referred to his invention then as the 'living SIOP.'"*

---

* During his tenure as CINCSAC, Butler oversaw the transition from Strategic Air Command to STRATCOM. A military joke making the rounds at the time went: "Who killed SAC? The butler did it."

Yet Butler apparently grew frustrated with what he later decided were futile attempts to reform an unfixable SIOP. Just a few years after leaving the military, he turned around and argued that nuclear weapons should be abolished altogether, which made him the highest-ranking former general to argue for nuclear disarmament. The stance didn't win him any friends in the military. Nor did his ideas get very far.

No standing leader of STRATCOM could advocate that position and last in the job. Nor did we suspect that Cartwright shared Butler's larger antinuclear ambitions. Yet whereas military leaders had once actively advocated for new nuclear weapons, a larger stockpile, and continued improvements, we were struck by how genuinely uninterested Cartwright was in this pursuit. Despite his fondness for blogs and Thomas Friedman, his notions of deterrence underscored a larger issue. Nuclear weapons were still the most important aspect of strategic deterrence, but it was no longer clear whom they were going to deter.

As we left, we realized that Cartwright had quite artfully ducked our question about nuclear first strike.

After our interview with the general, we left Offutt Air Force Base in search of his vision of a new sort of deterrence—one that would extend beyond the realm of nuclear weapons. The new STRATCOM was supposed to be able to strike an enemy's computer networks, influence media operations, and track weapons of mass destruction. It was ambitious; it didn't sound as scary as Armageddon. But it was also confusing. STRATCOM's global mission could mean just about anything.

We drove into downtown Omaha to visit the Global Innovation and Strategy Center, known at STRATCOM as the GISC. Established by Cartwright in September 2006, it was supposed to be one of the prime examples of his vision of a military command that could abandon its narrow focus on nuclear weapons in search of a new vision of deterrence. The center was in essence a think tank.

If Cartwright's office had the minimalist look of an Ikea store, then the GISC had a more dot-com feel—or at least, it resembled what a Pentagon official might imagine a Silicon Valley firm to be like. To be honest, it looked a bit more like a Starbucks. Rather than housing it on a military base, Cartwright situated the GISC on the south campus of the University of Nebraska, inside something called the Scott Technology Center. It was a sort of research triangle that was designed to attract high-tech ventures. We entered a low, windowless building fashioned from pale concrete slabs whose lobby looked more corporate than military. The waiting area featured recessed lighting and a long, sleek counter housing the reception area. Beyond the front entrance, there were no outward signs that the GISC had anything to do with the military.

It's not particularly unusual for the military to have in-house think tanks. At the Pentagon, for example, the Office of Net Assessment dreams up scenarios and threats, looking twenty or more years out into the future (and mystifying defense officials who can barely cope with the present). At Sandia, we visited Gerold Yonas's Advanced Concepts Group, which dreamed of ways to end civilization. But neither of those entities had their own building. The online fact sheet for the GISC was surprisingly brief, no more than a few hundred words. Its core competencies were defined as "collaborative process," "creative people," and "knowledge discovery." None of those phrases really gave us any concrete idea of what, exactly, the GISC was supposed to do. Neither did its Web site.

"The terrorist attacks on New York City and Washington D.C. on September 11, 2001 clearly demonstrated that adversaries do not distinguish between America's military, commercial and civilian interests," the GISC overview read. "The logical response was to combine the Nation's diverse experience and intellect to seek answers to tough questions."

Terms like "creativity" and "knowledge discovery" don't normally show up in the military lexicon (one military officer we spoke to, in fact, invoked the "giggle factor" when referring to the GISC). One thing the GISC did have was money—roughly fifty million dollars for fiscal year 2007, a drop in the bucket for the Defense Department, but enough, presumably, to promote "creativity."

We were scheduled to meet with Kevin Williams, a civilian employee of STRATCOM who had recently been named the first director of the GISC. We were quickly ushered into the back office, and as we waited, we were offered different types of flavored water, a first for any military interview, where weak coffee or soda is usually the beverage of choice. We were asked to surrender our phones before entering Williams's secure office. Sipping our berry-flavored waters, we entered with high hopes that Williams would reveal the purpose of the new facility.

But not unlike the rest of STRATCOM, Kevin Williams struck us as a man in search of a mission, or at least a man in search of a way to define his mission. Once fully staffed, the center would house thirty-six people, he told us, of whom he had already hired twenty-four. "I look at us as a service provider," he said. "It's like, here's a nice car. Buy this car. Let's see if we can work together to get this car exactly right."

Trying to figure out exactly what the GISC was going to do with all its fancy office space wasn't easy. A good portion of the center's work—a project called Night Fist—was classified, and Williams wouldn't discuss it. The other part seemed to be a random mix of projects that had been born during a *Blink*-inspired brainstorming session. "I came in, and it was really a very early concept from General Cartwright as to what he wanted to do," Williams told us. "He basically wanted to have a place that could more or less, bottom line, tackle the tough problems. He said when we did the ribbon cutting out here, 'We need twenty-first-century solutions to twenty-first-century problems.'"

At its base, the GISC was composed of three things: a partnership group, an innovation group, and a strategy group. When we asked for an example of the GISC's work, Williams began to talk about an internship program to bring in young college students. Why? "They are on the leading edge of what I call the fully wired generation," Williams said. "They are going to be the ones who are really learning how to use information technology to its fullest. They live it. It's part of the social fabric, now . . . This whole new generation emerging is going to bring a lot of new ideas. Hopefully with our interns, we are going to see something that is jaw-dropping, a moment when they say something or offer up something as an idea, and we'll say, 'How did they think of that?'"

Still confused, we asked for another example of the GISC's work, and Williams began to talk about a flu pandemic. "What is STRATCOM doing with influenza?" he asked rhetorically. "But if you look at it, STRATCOM's mission is combating WMD. The argument is: What if they weaponized it, how would you detect something is going on in the country that is abnormal or not quite right? Why is this happening over here? You may be able to have enough of a jump on it. Maybe it would give you that little bit of time to react."

But the striking thing for us was that the twenty-first-century problems the GISC was looking at could be, well, just about anything. Like STRATCOM's proliferating PowerPoint charts, with arrows and dotted lines that connected everything in national security as if on a social networking site, the GISC was involved in everything from flu pandemics to the study of African communications. None of its projects seemed like a bad idea in theory, but we couldn't help but wonder if, in the attempt to look at everything global, it was possible to lose sight of the whole endeavor. It seemed the world of creativity could cover almost anything.

Williams wrapped up the meeting precisely at thirty minutes. As for what the GISC did, we were still in the dark. So, when his deputy, Lieutenant Colonel Jessica Meyeraan, offered us a tour of the classified sections of the GISC, we happily accepted. When we entered the back offices, red lights flashed overhead, warning employees that "un-cleared" visitors were on the premises. As we toured the work space, Meyeraan—who was dressed in civilian attire—explained how she had helped select the interior design for the GISC after visiting Silicon Valley companies. As she walked us through the different areas, she described how she had started with a "clean slate," traveling to look at how innovative companies had arranged their work spaces. She had also picked up the lingo of some of these companies: "Team room," "storytelling room," and "smart boards" were in the lexicon used to describe the various prefab areas.

We entered the main work area, divided into four-person "pods" with modular furniture that would allow people to reconfigure their own area like some sort of biological adaptation. "This is the heads-down work area," she noted, pointing to a collection of empty desks grouped around a mini-courtyard. The common environment, she continued, would facilitate "cross talking." In the middle area, soft chairs oddly decorated in 1970s oranges and reds were where workers could "plop down and do big thinking," she explained.

As we continued on past the work areas, Meyeraan pointed to a number of conference rooms. "This would be kind of a storytelling room," she said. "You'll note the absence of technology." Actually, what we noticed most was the absence of people. Plastic covering still lined the chairs near the desks, tags hung from the furniture, and the only other human being we saw was a thirtysomething with bleached hair and a goatee, who looked a bit more like a stage prop than an actual employee.

We sat entranced, listening to Meyeraan as she used words like "fluidity" to describe the decorating pattern. "I was trying to go with the color and looks you see for STRATCOM," she noted at one point.

Walking out of the classified section and back up to the front of the building, she led us past more sleek conference rooms with smoked glass. We sat down to rest for a moment in the kitchen, which we could only imagine was the military's answer to the playrooms and snack stations advertised at dot-com firms of popular lore. Conical lights—the type popular in Starbucks and trendy bars—stretched down from the ceiling, casting a gentle glow onto the brushed-aluminum kitchen-ware and sleek granite countertop. The ergonomic chairs had attached writing stations and were all laptop enabled. A worker could sit down, drink some melon-flavored water, and work on global problems—or, at least in this area, unclassified ones.

"People thinking big thoughts are more innovative when they can have spontaneous collaboration," Meyeraan noted. The room, she explained, like the rest of the work space, was about building a "fluid" collaborative environment.

It occurred to us that the GISC's opulent furnishings (at least by government standards) were almost a weird inversion of the sort found in the Pentagon, or other military buildings, where desks must occasionally be scavenged from spare offices. It wasn't that we questioned the need for nicely furnished office space—and to be honest, nothing struck us as outlandishly expensive. But we were left perplexed about the center's mission, other than "creativity." After all, the lingo they used—be it "team playing," "fluidity," "creativity," or "cross talk"—was borrowed from corporate management culture. But in business, the goal is to make money, to expand, and to dominate the market. Business can measure revenues and profits; how would the GISC measure its success?

Then again, maybe looking at STRATCOM as a corporation made sense. Rather than revenues, it wanted to expand its portfolio and stay in business. If nuclear weapons—at least as a strategic deterrent—were losing currency, then the command needed to find ways to reinvent itself, to increase its legitimacy, and to expand. General Cartwright's interest in nuclear weapons was measured in the same sort of enthusiasm a prospective spouse musters for prickly in-laws: They weren't going anywhere anytime soon, so you'd better get used to them. Cartwright accepted the nuclear mission, but it was clear that the Friedman-quoting Marine was taking a cue from the business world and looking at new areas. Nuclear weapons, at least for the military, were no longer a growth business.

We left the GISC with our half-finished bottles of flavored water and drove away from Omaha understanding that at least for Cartwright, nuclear deterrence was dead. The primary goal was no longer to deter an enemy's nuclear strike—that was just one diminishing element of U.S. strategy. In the place of nuclear deterrence and mutual assured destruction, strategic deterrence, an amorphous concept that covered everything from a public relations campaign to a bunker buster, was taking root. It had little to do with how the nuclear labs defined deterrence. And it didn't seem to provide answers to the most basic questions: How many nuclear weapons do you want? What do you use them against, and when?

The bomber forces were off alert; some of the nuclear submarines were going conventional. That left just the extensive intercontinental ballistic missile fields as the last, unreformed leg of the old Cold War stockpile of active nuclear weapons. If the ICBMs and nuclear deterrence were now an ever-smaller part of the triad, what did that mean for the men and women who sat in bunkers every day, waiting to turn the key? We left Nebraska the next morning, driving further west in search of the missile fields, and the missileers, who—according to General Cartwright—were part of a transformed vision of global strike, merely one part of a vision of global strategic deterrence, an idea that included not just a missileer sitting sixty-five feet underground but perhaps also an academic drinking melon-flavored water under the soft hue of the GISC's coned lights.

CHAPTER 6

A Cow Runs Through It

Visiting Missile Silos in the Great Plains

The order to launch arrived.

"Message incoming," announced Captain Shawn Lee.

"Alert force, alert force," Lieutenant Melanie Stricklan replied, grabbing a thick three-ring binder and flipping rapidly through the pages. A flurry of activity kicked up inside the capsule as the two young officers of the Air Force's 90th Space Wing turned intently to their task.

"Verify everyone has this message," Lee said, marking his checklist.

"Everyone in receipt," he confirmed a few seconds later. "Go to launch."

Over the next ninety seconds, the two missileers went through their checklist, calling out and affirming a series of rapid-fire commands: "Unlock codes"; "Unlock enabled"; "Go to secure storage."

At eight thirty-nine and forty seconds, the two young missileers strapped themselves into their metallic-gray chairs. The chairs were converted pilot seats, anchored to the floor on sliding rails to protect Lee and Stricklan from being thrown by the shock of a nuclear blast. Five seconds later, the two officers inserted their keys in slots—placed exactly twelve feet apart—glanced at each other, and nodded slightly. Lee began the countdown in an evenly modulated voice: "Three . . . two . . . one . . . key turn."

At eight forty A.M., Stricklan and Lee simultaneously turned their keys forty-five degrees to the right, casting a single vote to end the world.

No job is quite like that of a modern missileer—an Air Force officer whose sole purpose is to sit underground and wait for orders from the president to turn the key. Although the job requires mastering an exhaustive series of checks and procedures, the mission of the missileer is simple. "The primary duty of the ICBM crewmembers is to be prepared to launch their missiles toward enemy targets when directed by the President of the United States," a 1988 handbook states, adding with obvious understatement, "a task not to be taken lightly."

Nearly two decades after the guidebook was written, this job description remains the same—even if the world itself has changed. Two decades is a political lifetime, and the intervening years have seen the collapse of the Soviet Union, a drastic reduction in the size of the nuclear arsenal, and the advent of highly accurate conventional weapons that can, in some cases, destroy targets once penetrable only by nuclear power. Yet the mission of the missileer remains essentially unchanged. For decades during the Cold War, the missileers justified this seemingly perverse exercise in doomsday by pointing to the power of mutual assured destruction and the Soviet threat. With that threat evaporated, we wanted to see what kept them underground today.

"All wars end in tourism," observes Tom Vanderbilt in *Survival City*, his survey of the Cold War's architecture of survival. This is certainly true of the Cold War, but hundreds of intercontinental ballistic missiles are still emplaced across the northern United States. In one state, you can visit a decommissioned missile silo, and in the next, one is still active.

In 1991, when the Soviet Union collapsed, experts like Bruce Blair, a former missileer, helped jump-start informal talks with Russian counterparts about standing down the hair-trigger posture of the two sides. "I organized some conferences that then led to proposals within the foreign ministry of Russia to [President Boris] Yeltsin to de-alert. It got kind of distorted. What came out the other end was this idea of de-targeting." Under de-targeting, the weapons in the silos wouldn't be pointed at, say, Moscow. Instead, they would aim for a point in the ocean. It sounded good, but wasn't. "The weapons still have all their wartime targets in their computer file memory," Blair explained. "It doesn't take any longer to target and fire the missiles today than before the de-targeting agreement went into effect."

The change was purely symbolic, according to Blair. The two countries were still on hair-trigger alert. Worse, the move failed to eliminate the incentive for a retaliatory strike against an accidental launch. The missiles were indeed aimed at the ocean, but only the trajectory was changed, meaning a launched missile would look to the other side as if it were indeed heading to a real target. "Let's say one missile launched out of F. E. Warren [Air Force Base] that had Moscow as a wartime target. If it were launched by accident and was going to land in the ocean, it would take off on exactly the same path that it would take on its route to Moscow. The trajectory would be slightly lofted differently," he said. "It was very clever, because if you change the azimuth angle—left or right—then the missiles really have to go through a delay to recalculate the trajectory." On the Russian side, however, it was even worse, he said, because if there were a real accident, the missile would flip to its wartime target by default.

While de-alerting the ICBMs never took place, there were still important changes. Most significantly, as a result of earlier arms-limitation agreements negotiated under the Strategic Arms Reduction Treaty, the United States agreed to deactivate its Peacekeeper missiles. On September 19, 2005, the final Peacekeeper was retired, leaving the venerable Minuteman as the last of the ICBMs—and giving F. E. Warren Air Force Base a reason for continued existence. But along with the retirement of the Peacekeeper, the number of Minuteman missiles was being reduced in accordance with the 2002 Moscow Treaty, an agreement between the United States and Russia to further reduce the number of deployed nuclear warheads.

So how many ICBMs are left? The U.S. government will no longer say precisely how many nuclear weapons it has, providing fertile ground for analysts to play "guess the number" (and location) of nuclear weapons. In the fall of 2006, the respected *Bulletin of the Atomic Scientists* published what was likely the most accurate number. The article—prepared by the Natural Resources Defense Council— estimated that fifteen years after the fall of the Soviet Union, the United States still had 10,000 nuclear weapons spread across twelve states, as well as approximately 400 in Europe. The 90th Space Wing's share of that at Warren Air Force Base includes 150 Minuteman III ICBMs spread out over Wyoming, Nebraska, and South Dakota.

We came to the base in Cheyenne, Wyoming, to watch the demonstration of a launch. Since rehearsing a launch in an active capsule is— for obvious reasons—not done, missileers must practice the procedures leading up to the key turn in a mock-up facility called a Missile Procedures Trainer. A few lucky missileers will get to turn the key on a real ICBM at Vandenberg Air Force Base in California, where the Air Force fires off a missile a few times a year to make sure they work— though of course, in those tests, the ICBMs do not carry nuclear warheads. But for most missileers, the simulator is the closest they will ever get to the real thing. We came here for an answer to one question: How do missileers feel about the pivotal key turn, the one task they will perform only once, if at all?

There was a moment of silence, and then Lieutenant Stricklan and Captain Lee casually unhooked their chair restraints and turned around.

"The first several months, you get all excited, nervous, but then you get used to it," Lee told us. Stricklan disagreed.

"I've been doing this for two years," she said cheerfully, "and it makes me anxious every time."

With her shoulder-length blond hair pulled back in a businesslike ponytail, Stricklan looked more like a college student than a military officer. It was hard to believe the attractive, all-American lieutenant spent much of her time some sixty-five feet underground, living in a 162-square-foot missile launch capsule. Her fellow missileer, Lee, had a shaved head and an Air Force Academy ring, a serious look that contrasted sharply with his boyish features. They both looked terribly young.

We chatted with the two officers for a few minutes about their careers, their families, and their future plans. They struck us as serious but levelheaded—exactly the type of people you would want in control of those keys. Unlike the weapons designers at Livermore or Los Alamos, known for dark humor and mindful of their morbid power, the missileers tended not to joke about their duties in front of outsiders.

Earnestness seems to be the defining feature of the missileers, perhaps best reflected in a poem dedicated to their job (and written, naturally, by a missileer):

They feel the living throb,
of the mindless tool they run,
They hear the constant whir,
of a world that knows no sun.

Here light is ever present,
no moon's nocturnal sway.
The clock's unnatural beat,
belies not night nor day.

One online version turns "living throb" into the inadvertently porno-graphic "loving throb." But for the missileers who spend twenty-four alert shifts underground, without sunlight, the poem clearly speaks to a job that few—even in the military—appreciate. In a CNN documentary that aired in 2000, Air Force General Charles Horner, the former commander of North American Aerospace Defense Command (NORAD), described the nuclear chain of command in his typically frank and rather revealing manner: "The beauty of the system we have is: You do not have a person that cries 'The attack is coming' be the same person with their finger on the trigger. There is no doubt about it. You want your commander of NORAD, the guy who warns of attack, to err on the side of caution. On the other hand, since you want to have good deterrence, deterrence based on threat, then the commander of strategic forces has to be very aggressive, has to be a person who is out to end the world with great enthusiasm."

Each piece of the nuclear complex plays its role, from the design laboratories that draw up the bombs to the production complex that builds and maintains them. In that sense, the missileers are the last link on a very long chain that connects the development of nuclear weapons to their final—hypothetical—use. That the missileers would look at their job very differently than other members of the nuclear world is not such a surprise. But that they look at it the same way missileers looked at it twenty years ago is somewhat shocking. The world has changed; the world of the missileers has not.

That doesn't mean that missileers were out to end the world, or even that they were willing executioners of a mindless plan. During the Cold War, the justification for the missileers was the need for a credible deterrent—the promise of a swift counterattack against a nuclear first strike. The deterrent worked; the United States and the

Soviet Union averted nuclear war. Even in the intervening years, when policy makers began to discuss options for fighting winnable nuclear wars, the underlying assumption was that deterrence would ultimately work.

But without an enemy like the Soviet Union, we were curious how young Air Force officers could still justify sitting underground waiting for Armageddon. "I understand we have rogue nations that can do anything," Stricklan said. "The Soviet Union may not be the highest threat, but deterrence applies to rogue nations."

Lee agreed, with some qualifications. "The nature of the enemy has changed," he said. "We know that deterrence doesn't work with everyone."

Other small, yet not insignificant, changes have taken place in the world of the missileer. Some missileers—though not all—now have access to the Internet in the capsule, which provides them with an instant look at world events. We wondered if that might change how a missileer would react to launch orders. In the old days, the missile crews—at least in the moments leading up to a launch order—would have little or no independent "real world" information about the situation. The launch codes would come to them in an information vacuum. Access to the Web would certainly arm missileers with a lot more information in the event of a missile attack. Suppose the crews were following every update on CNN.com and had reason to doubt the validity of their orders or question the response?

Lee disagreed. The missileers had access to classified intelligence, he noted—not just what was seen on CNN. Despite the global reach of media, he said, he would feel comfortable executing a lawful order. "America is not going to be an aggressive nation," he said. "We would not just nuke someone."

Blair, the former missileer, was far more cynical when we interviewed him, calling the missileers "lost in the twilight zone." He has periodically returned to the bases, including Warren, to interview the young missileers. "You go out in the field, nothing has changed. The same kind of rationale is instilled in the crews about deterrence."

Yet both Lee and Stricklan seemed to acknowledge that deterrence—such as it was—did not have quite the unquestionable logic that it did during the Cold War and, arguably, was not such a great personal justification for sitting underground every day. "You do need some sort of personal reason," Stricklan acknowledged. "Something that is tangible."

Sixteen years after the fall of the Soviet Union, young missileers were still going to work every day, rehearsing the end of the world. What was, at least in their minds, that "tangible thing"?

These days, touring missile silos—the battlefields of the Cold War—is not really a problem. Visiting intercontinental ballistic missile sites is a great way to tour the great northern plains. The end of the Cold War and continuing negotiations with Russia led to a major reduction in active ICBM forces, and across the country, former missile silos have been auctioned off to private owners and, in some cases, reclaimed as historic sites. Decommissioned Atlas missile silos have been turned into garbage dumps, converted into luxury homes, and used as data storage facilities. The Silo House in Kimball, Nebraska—perhaps the best known of its sort—occupies a former Atlas E silo, offering fifteen thousand square feet of space (and the ability to survive a one-megaton blast). It's been valued at twenty-five million dollars.

In the Southwest, twenty miles south of Tucson, Arizona, tourists can visit a former Titan silo, which even offers the opportunity to sleep in the missile crew bunks. Elsewhere, cities and towns have attempted to turn their missile silos into tourist attractions. In 2006, the State Historical Society of North Dakota raced to raise one million dollars to turn a deactivated missile alert facility—dubbed Oscar Zero—into a museum, hoping to draw tourists to tiny Cooperstown (population: 1,100).

The federal government has also hopped on the nuclear nostalgia bandwagon; the National Park Service now advertises twice-daily tours of Delta One, a former Minuteman II silo in South Dakota. "Minuteman missiles held the destructive power to destroy civilization as we know it," the Park Service notes on its Web site. "Yet the same destructive force acted as a deterrent which kept the peace for three decades." A video features a park ranger with a South Dakota drawl standing in front of a blast door painted as a spoof of a Domino's Pizza delivery ad: "30 minutes or your next one is free."*

---

* Thirty minutes is the approximate time it would have taken for a Minuteman to reach the Soviet Union.

The Internet—and the advent of Google Earth, which uses commercial satellite imagery—has made the ICBM world somewhat less secret. Exact coordinates of active ICBMs are readily available online, although the areas around the silos and launch facilities are blurred in satellite photos to obscure visibility. And the silos and launch control facilities themselves are not barricaded behind miles of wire or enclosed in vast military reservations. Quite the opposite. They are hidden in plain sight, spread out over private land leased from farmers and ranchers. Horses and cows roam around the fences that wall off the silos; public roads go right past the facilities. In theory, an ordinary citizen can tour the silos—and some, in fact, have tried to do just that.

In 1998, for example, self-described Cold War tourist Barney Greinke decided to tour active missile silos in Montana. Armed with a map, night-vision goggles, and a GPS receiver, he found that silo spotting, although legal, attracts the attention of authorities. After driving past silos operated out of Malmstrom Air Force Base, he was detained and questioned by federal agents suspicious of his nuclear travels. It turned out the authorities were incredulous that anyone would want to visit the working silos just for the fun of it.

But Greinke's quest, however quixotic, made more sense to us than visiting empty silos of years past. We were interested in speaking to the missileers who spent their working hours manning the missile fields, waiting for a day they hoped would never come. In our case, it helped to be journalists. We simply signed up for a tour of the missile fields by ringing up the public affairs office at Warren Air Force Base and asking for one. Nuclear tourism, as long as it's officially sanctioned, is not a problem.

We made the trip to Cheyenne, driving west from Omaha, watching as the landscape altered slowly and imperceptibly, growing sparser by the mile. Back home, driving the Northeast Corridor on Interstate 95 meant navigating an interlocking network of cities, suburbs, and bumper-to-bumper traffic. Even in the Midwest, it's rare to drive for more than a few miles without seeing some sign of human habitation. But on our trip from Omaha to Cheyenne, the isolation seemed to extend for miles at a time, interrupted only by highway exits. As we approached Cheyenne late in the evening, we could see the lights of the city, a small glittering oasis amid the darkness of the plains.

Only sixty miles from Denver, Cheyenne somehow seemed far away from everything. It was also as windy as any place we'd ever been. On an average day, winds of twenty-five miles per hour whip across the prairie, launching tumbleweeds like cannonballs across the highways. On more extreme days, the high winds are a danger to traffic. When the winds reach fifty miles an hour, the interstate shuts down completely, leaving truckers and other cross-country travelers temporarily stranded.

It doesn't take much of a lesson in strategic politics to figure out why Cheyenne might have been selected to house ICBMs. Wyoming was far enough north to shorten the trip for missiles flying to Russia, yet far enough away from the coasts to ensure that a Soviet sub wouldn't pop up and launch a devastating first strike. But there was, of course, another reason. Cheyenne is at home with the military. The town was established by—and grew up with—the military, and its heritage as a frontier outpost was intimately linked with its modern incarnation as home to the 90th Space Wing. The community sees the base as a natural extension of the town.

Cheyenne, for those not from the community, seemed to inspire either a great sense of belonging or an almost unbearable feeling of isolation. Its high winds and endless winters clearly weren't for everyone. "You can only play tennis for two weeks a year," joked one of our escorts at the base. But for those who enjoyed the outdoors, the friendly community, and Cheyenne's particular brand of Western authenticity, it was a good place. The revitalized downtown has the picturesque quality of a Hollywood movie set—a frontier city dotted with steak houses, Western apparel shops, and quaint storefronts. The town's annual big event is Frontier Days, when thousands of people descend on Cheyenne for what is billed as the largest "rodeo and Western celebration" in the country. During Frontier Days, the tiny town temporarily swells to ten times its normal population of forty-three thousand.

The nuclear mission doesn't so much blend into the Wyoming landscape as it consumes it. Our stop at the official Warren Air Force Base museum underscored just how closely the worlds of pioneer kitsch and nuclear weaponry coexisted. The museum was an eclectic mix of Indian handicrafts, frontier knickknacks, and ICBM memorabilia. Unlike at the atomic museums in Los Alamos and Albuquerque, the missileers were the real heroes of the display. The museum even provided cards reminiscent of baseball cards or *Star Wars* collectibles, with different ones for "orbital analyst," "convoy commander," and "missile warning crewmember" (who must "within 60 seconds of detecting a missile launch . . . determine the direction is valid or due to computer, mechanical or personnel error").

The museum's curator, a soft-spoken woman named Paula Taylor, grew up in Cheyenne. Her sweet smile and gracious manner almost made it hard to believe that much of what she was talking about related to nuclear weapons. But for her, the history of the base was an inseparable part of the history of Cheyenne. The first ICBMs had been emplaced the year before she was born and nuclear weapons, as she reminded us more than once, were a part of her life. Cheyenne's evolution from frontier outpost to nuclear missile base was complete. "We have always been in the business of protecting people, which is what our mission is today," she said with a smile. "We've come completely full circle in deterrence— it's kind of cool that we're still maintaining it."

As with many historic sites, the story behind the naming and legacy of Warren Air Force Base is a mix of lore and fact. The base traces its roots to a different form of deterrence—not against foreign enemies but against a violent domestic threat. The fort, Taylor said, was established in 1867 to prevent conflict between Central Pacific and Union Pacific workers, who were in a race to build the first transcontinental railroad. Sabotage, it turns out, was a big problem. The fort was initially named after David Russell, a Civil War general slain in the Shenandoah Valley campaign, though it was eventually renamed for Senator Francis E. Warren, a prominent senator and Medal of Honor recipient.

Warren, Taylor explained, was an advocate of military reform. He pushed for military pay increases and diverted funding to Fort Russell. As the story went, the military repaid the senator for his largesse by offering his daughter—a dilettante who enjoyed shopping and opera— a home on the base. She found her own way into missile history by marrying John Pershing, commander of the American Expeditionary Forces in World War I, who was then just an Army captain. (During the wedding ceremony, Senator Warren—the chair of a military com- mittee—allegedly commented that his daughter could live the lifestyle she was accustomed to only if her husband were a general.) Within six months of the wedding, Captain Pershing became General

Pershing.* Years later, the Army would name a medium-range ballistic missile after him.

But perhaps the most striking part of the 90th Space Wing's legacy is the "Jolly Rogers" unit patch, a skull and crossed bombs in place of the traditional crossbones. The wing traces its lineage to the 90th Bombardment Group in World War II, a unit that flew the B-24 Liberator heavy bombers in the southwest Pacific. That unit adopted the pirate symbol as a tribute to its commanding officer, Colonel Art Rogers. When the bomber group was disbanded, the lineage was provided as a gift to Warren Air Force Base.

In the late 1950s, Warren was transformed into a strategic missile base under Strategic Air Command. The Atlas missile came to Warren in 1958, making the base home to the first operational ICBM squadron. The Atlas brought other changes to the landscape. The military would shut down local roads when moving the massive missiles; Taylor recalled having to make a twenty-five-mile detour to get to high school when the missiles were on the move. Eventually, the military paved the roads the Atlas traveled, because gravel would shred the thin skin of the missiles. The pavement would end right where the missile was emplaced.

Warren was home to twenty-four Atlas missile silos, giving birth to the first generation of missileers. They dressed in white overalls, which made them look more like lab technicians than warriors. The "white bags," as they were called, weren't worn for fashion, Taylor explained, but because the highly volatile liquid rocket fuel used in the Atlas made even the tiniest smudge of the chemical a cause for concern. The white bags may have been for safety, not looks, but missileers also traditionally donned colorful ascots. The missileer uniform went through a few more variations before the Air Force adopted standard one-piece flight suits, the modern "green bags."

Missileering in those days was a far cry from today's hair-trigger alert. It took an hour from the time the missileers got the launch order to actually send the missile on its way. Atlas, the "grandfather of ICBMs," stood seventy-five feet tall and weighed a massive 260,000 pounds. Called the "steel balloon," the Atlas missile couldn't

---

* Pershing's wife, along with his three daughters, died in a fire at the Presidio in San Francisco.

initially be launched from underground. It was stored in an above-ground "coffin" whose doors would slide open as the missile prepared to launch. A gantry would then be used to pull the missile upright, like hoisting up a stiffened corpse from its grave. One of those old gantries now decorates a bar in downtown Cheyenne.

The Atlas may have been a marvel of technological engineering, but it was also incredibly fragile. The pressurized tanks were less than a few millimeters thick, packed with a volatile liquid fuel that made minor defects potentially fatal. And even in the early days, the U.S. military was already looking for ways to place the ICBMs into hardened bunkers to ensure their survivability in the event of a Soviet first strike.

The Titan, a more sophisticated version of the Atlas, went operational in 1962, but was never deployed to Warren. Sometimes called "huge flying sewer pipes" owing to their volatile mix of liquid fuel, the Titan and the Atlas were eventually replaced with solid-rocket-fueled Minuteman missiles. As the Cold War went on, Warren again rose to prominence, this time for a "rail garrison" system based on the MX Peacekeeper. At the end of our tour, Taylor sat us down to watch a video, whose 1980s production value gave it a definite VH-1 Classic feel. The video featured a young Air Force captain speaking in a rehearsed monotone, barely blinking. We sat entranced, watching the video, a piece of Cold War nostalgia for an ICBM system that never was—mobile launchers that would camouflage themselves by riding on the civilian railway system.

The Peacekeeper could carry up to ten W87 warheads, each with a three-hundred kiloton yield. Advocates of the system argued that the Peacekeeper demonstrated the U.S. commitment to winning the arms race and thus helped drive the Soviet Union to its end. The rail garrison would have made anywhere and everywhere a target, but for the nuclear planners, it was a sensible way of ensuring the Soviets couldn't launch a debilitating first strike. The first train was expected to be operational in December 1991, but the Berlin Wall fell in 1989, and by 1991 the country that the system was meant to counter didn't even exist.

"A lot of people think the missile business is Sleepy Hollow," boomed Colonel Michael Fortney, 90th Operations Group commander. "This is a hopping place."

We were sitting that morning in the back row of an austere auditorium, listening to the briefing that the 219th squadron receives every day. A nearly identical briefing takes place at Minot Air Force Base in South Dakota and Malmstrom Air Force Base in Montana. This is the same briefing missileers get every single morning before they head off for what could, on any day, be the day they launch their missiles.

It all starts with a weather report.

Winds were gusting up to thirty-nine miles per hour (typical for the time of year). It was partly cloudy, but slightly warmer than average—snow that had fallen the week before had melted before our arrival. Most of the morning briefing covered the minutiae of maintenance that included notes on wrong bolts, vehicle incidents, reminders on security, and "duress words" (code words in the event of capture) that we weren't privy to.

Another topic for the day was the newly introduced three-day alert. Under the old system, a two-person crew would go out for twenty-four hours—spending a full shift underground in the capsule. Now three crew members would go to the facility together for three days, rotating periodically to allow one person to go "topside"—aboveground—to rest. Three-day alerts were largely a cost-saving measure, sparing the base multiple trips to change out crews. They also came with drawbacks; some missileers complained about the extended time spent at the alert facility. There was some acknowledgment in the briefing that the three-day alerts were proving—like almost all changes in workplace routine—to be a bit unpopular.

Following the fifteen-minute introduction, which covered unclassified issues, we were asked to leave the room so that the squadron could go into a classified session. We then piled into a government SUV with our traveling companions: two local television journalists, two public affairs officers—Staff Sergeant Kurt Arkenberg and Captain Nora Eyle—and another Air Force escort, Major Jared Granstrom. We headed east on Interstate 80 toward the Echo One Missile Alert Facility (MAF).

It was approximately one hundred miles from the base to Echo One—missileers cumulatively drive millions of miles each year to get from base to launch facilities—and for most of the journey we traveled on I-80, until we approached the Wyoming state line. We stopped briefly along the way at a rest station so the public affairs officers could

touch base with the MAF. At one point, we trailed a military convoy—
an armored Humvee with flashing lights driving behind a nondescript
tractor-trailer marked only with the sign WIDE LOAD.*

We exited I-80 at Pine Bluffs, a town right on the eastern edge of
Wyoming. We turned right at a Subway sandwich shop and drove
through the main drag, inevitably called Main Street. Someone more
inclined toward conspiracy theory might have thought the town had
been built there as a sort of Potemkin village, the main purpose of which
was to look so ordinary as to conceal the exit to Echo One. In fact, our
final turnoff was so easy to miss that the first time around we drove
right past it and had to circle back down Main Street. We drove a few
miles, turning on and off numbered county roads until we finally
approached a long gravel roadway.

The SUV slowed to ten miles an hour, gravel popping under the tires
as we approached what looked like an ordinary ranch house, save for
what looked like the Satellite Dish of the Gods sticking out of the top.

"Echo control, this is eight dash nine one alpha," our driver said into
the radio.

Total silence.

"Is there someone I could try to call?" Eyle asked.

"If I have to pass dispatch from the phone at the gate, no big deal,"
Granstrom said. "It sounded like somebody heard me."

"Would they otherwise know we were approaching?" one of the
television journalists asked.

"If we were just in your car, no," Eyle answered. "Obviously, they
know we're here."

Security, as we soon learned, started at the gate. In fact, we had
driven down public roads to the very end; the land surrounding the
facilities belonged to private ranchers, and the government's domain
didn't begin until twenty-five feet outside the gate.

"What would be their response if I just pulled up in my car?" one of
the television journalists inquired. "Would security just turn me
around?"

---

* Though we had no way of knowing for sure what the convoy was transporting,
"nuclear materials couriers" driving specially outfitted tractor-trailers are used to
transport warheads and drive along the regular interstate system. According to
news reports, however, they typically drive at night.

"Yeah, just turn you around," Arkenberg replied.

"It's really a judgment call," Eyle interrupted. "If you looked a little lost, obviously, this is a public road. But if you're speeding . . ."

Even though the roads are public access, local ranchers who own the adjacent land are on the lookout for those who don't belong. They are often the first, we were told, to alert security if a stranger was driving down one of the roads leading to either a missile silo or a MAF. In fact, when we stopped along the way to allow the broadcast journalists to film outside the perimeter of an actual missile silo, we could see there was just a fence protecting it from the surrounding ranch land. When doing maintenance, the military at times has to shoo away horses or cows. The proximity of the ranches to the missiles lends itself to an eerie image of what the start of a nuclear war might actually look like. Perhaps the first living thing to see the missiles flying would be a cow grazing impassively near the silo fence.

A guard finally appeared and stuck his head in the window to ask for identification; for the second time that day, we handed over our documents. We entered the MAF, beginning with a tour topside to get a sense of how the crew spent its time. From the inside, the building looked something akin to a college dormitory with all the usual trappings, meaning the largest and most modern item was a large-screen TV set up in the common room. A dining area adjacent to the living quarters offered cafeteria-style seats; farther down, a narrow hall led to a series of bedrooms where the security staff and others slept in shifts, along with a cramped office for the facility manager, a sort of superintendent of the missile world. The facility manager on duty at Echo One that day was Greg Hansen, a friendly, ruddy-faced tech sergeant who seemed to know every bolt, knob, and wire that filled the MAF.

War, as the saying has it, is hours of boredom punctuated by moments of sheer terror; sitting topside in a MAF is an exercise in the former. The focus here was clearly on finding diversions. The closet was filled with standard-issue games like Yahtzee and a special edition of Monopoly dedicated to U.S. Space Command. Not surprisingly, we also spotted Risk ("the game of strategy"). Videos, magazines, and books were all in high demand. There were few personal effects. Since the crews swapped out every three days, the troops never stuck around long enough to get comfortable.

The first order of business was lunch, or at least ordering lunch. The MAF cook came out and explained apologetically that there had been a logistics mix-up, so there was a somewhat limited selection of food—a subtle reminder that the MAF was not designed to last very long after a nuclear war. The choices for the day: cheeseburgers, french fries, and tater tots. "I also have chicken tenders," the chef added helpfully. "Unfortunately, if anyone is a vegetarian . . . anybody vegetarian? I don't have lettuce or anything to make a salad. Or vegetables, or anything like that."

Almost everyone ordered hamburgers.

Our descent into the capsule started with a quick overview of the facility's security. A line of young enlisted men blazed through a recitation of their responsibilities and weaponry.

"My post is within security patrol center unless properly relieved. I'm armed with an M4 rifle, a lightweight, gas-operated, shoulder-fired weapon with 180 rounds of 5.56, four-to-one ratio of ball/tracer ammunition," one guard rattled off. "Communications available to me are commercial landlines, station, whistles, hand and arm signals— and as last resort, my personal weapon fired in rapid succession three times. We are currently Protection Condition Alpha due to a general terrorist threat. We are also deadly force authorized on this post in accordance with AFI 31–207, warning shots are not authorized."

Security duty at the silos and launch facilities is generally an uneventful job. Protesters, when they come, are usually peaceful. One notable exception was in 2006, when a trio of antinuke protesters dressed as clowns spawned such cute headlines as KRUSTY VERSUS MINUTEMAN III. The clown attack was spearheaded by a Roman Catholic priest in his 70s; he and two veterans cut their way through the chain-link fence and managed, at least according to their claims, to smash the lock to the entry hatch using a "sledgehammer and household hammers."

The security detail suggested that most protests at the silos and launch facilities weren't a big deal. "We basically go and make sure they don't get on-site," one of the security guards told us. "We don't interfere with them, as long as they are not disturbing our resources."

For a third time that day, security checked our identification, and after they had keyed in a code to a yellow authenticator—a portable keyboard that looked more Cold War than high-tech—we were finally allowed to enter the underground part of the facilities. As the elevator descended, we were given rules to follow: Keep your hands off the equipment; don't touch switches or valves; stay away from high-pressure hoses; and watch your heads. With those words of wisdom, we entered the subterranean world of the missileers.

We arrived at the bottom—not at the capsule but inside a sepulchral cavern that housed a cluster of pipes, machinery, and tanks. An aging environmental system kept cool, fresh air flowing into the capsule, and diesel generators—tested once a month—allowed the capsule to operate off the power grid if necessary. The industrial equipment, like everything else in the MAF, dated back to the Cold War. Hansen, the facilities manager, noted that the companies who had produced the environmental control system had long been out of business, making it all the more important that the system be maintained.

To our right out of the elevator was the missile capsule, separated by a set of twelve-ton blast doors. The capsule is often compared to a yolk suspended in an egg, an apt analogy. Four twelve-hundred-pound cylindrical shock absorbers sat under the capsule, which was also suspended from the ceiling. In the event of a nuclear blast, the capsule might shake up and down like a yolk in an egg, but the shell would remain intact. Or so goes the theory.

As we stepped inside the capsule, there was something strangely familiar about the scene. It was the image of the iconic 1980s Cold War–era thriller *WarGames*. The movie opens with two missileers being given the order to launch the missiles; one of them hesitates, the other pulls a gun. The scene is pure Hollywood. The idea of officers casually tossing the launch keys to the incoming shift, or shooting a rogue pacifist, is fantasy. The officers on duty wore no holstered sidearms. But the set was nearly identical—perhaps because the capsules had not been updated since the 1980s. Manuals marked "secret" were stored neatly on upper shelves, and above that was the gray metal box that held the keys. Most people imagine the world of the missileer only in the moment of the key turn—a flurry of intense activity. In fact, quarters are cramped and the day-to-day routine is pretty boring. The toilet made airplane lavatories look spacious, and there was only one small bed—one missileer can nap while the other keeps watch.

Once inside, we were introduced to Captains Joseph Reveteriano and Jason Martin, the missileers on alert that day at Echo One. They were seated in front of a console with an array of incomprehensible push buttons, hardwired telephones, and flickering computer screens. A collection of black and red binders—some marked "Secret," others "Top Secret," and yet others "FOUO" (For Official Use Only)—was parked atop the console. Perhaps the most prominent reminder of what the missileers were doing was not even the simple lockbox that held the keys, but the digital clock lit up in red against a black background and flashing Zulu time (the military designation for Greenwich mean time)—a seeming miniature version of a doomsday clock.

We listened politely as the captains ran down a list of their responsibilities, which included endless procedural checklists. The missileers are constantly on watch for anything that trips the sensors around the facility or silo. Even innocuous visits—like ours—take place only through a series of carefully orchestrated checks.

Each MAF is connected to ten Minuteman III missiles. Multiple MAFs are linked to the same missile field—part of a redundant system meant to protect against a disabling first strike. Launching a missile requires the consent of two MAFs, or "votes," in missileer parlance. Essentially, each missile capsule has a vote that is cast when the two missileers simultaneously turn their keys. It requires two votes—i.e., four people in two separate capsules—to initiate a missile launch. The missileers do not know which of their colleagues in the MAFs are set to cast the second vote. Everything in the nuclear world goes in pairs: two people to vote, two capsules to launch a missile, and so forth.

"What if me and Captain Martin joined the dark side?" Captain Reveteriano asked us rhetorically. The answer, he explained, was obvious. That wouldn't be enough—they would have to conspire with another missile crew, but they wouldn't know which one to conspire with. Even that wouldn't be enough: The missileers can only launch the missiles with the correct codes—codes that come directly from the president. The testament to the success of this system, they told us, was that in over four decades, there had never been an incident that could have led to an illicit launch.

Inside the capsule, we chatted with the captains about their lives and jobs. Reveteriano became a missileer because it was part of Air Force Space Command. Before going into the Air Force, he, like most Americans, didn't realize there were people sitting underground manning the country's nuclear forces. Nor did he know anything about the life or work of the missileers when he signed up for the career. But space and missiles, he surmised, were the "way of the future." That, plus he was working on his master's degree at night.

Space may indeed be the way of the future, but there is no getting around the fact that the missileer corps is shrinking in size—and arguably, importance—at least in the eyes of senior military officials, who have deferred funding upgrades and replacement systems. When we asked the missileers about their thoughts on pulling alert in the post–Cold War era, we suddenly got a jumble of explanations.

"The reason we're doing what we're doing is because of deterrence," Reveteriano told us. "Are we doing anything different? No."

Did they feel, we asked, that their job was any less important or urgent?

"You know, we could get a message at any time," Reveteriano answered. "Look at 9/11, just when you think things are going smoothly, well . . ."

Reveteriano continued, talking a bit about history, World War II, and how the United States was in a very different, perhaps more frightening world of rogue nations and terrorist threats. "It's different, yes, the threat is different," he agreed, offering no explanation of why or how 9/11 would lead to a full-scale nuclear attack (or even the seemingly inverse logic—that terrorism perhaps now posed a bigger threat to the United States than nuclear annihilation).

We realized that at least for the two missileers at Echo One that day, thinking about the job didn't extend very much beyond the day-to-day duties. And those duties, over the years since the end of the Cold War, have changed very little. Perhaps the biggest change in missileering over the past few decades has been the introduction of women, followed later by coed missileer teams. While such mixed teams are now commonplace, there were a few bumps along the way. The dimensions of the launch capsule, which measures just six feet wide and twenty-seven feet long, make for extremely close—and isolated—quarters. The addition of a door to the toilet is a relative novelty; in years past, just a curtain separated it from the rest of the capsule. On our visit, we noticed that the missileers had piled up their personal belongings, mostly backpacks and magazines, on the single cot for lack of storage space.

Women began training to serve as missileers starting in the late 1970s. In 1988, they were allowed to serve with men, a decision that didn't prove particularly controversial until 1998, when twenty-five-year-old Lieutenant Ryan Berry, a devout Roman Catholic, asked for a religious exemption to avoid coed duties, in order, as one religious publication described it, "to protect his family from the vagaries of his own heart."

Initially, the young lieutenant was granted an exemption from a mixed-sex alert duty, but when he switched squadrons and attempted to renew the exemption, the Air Force balked and Berry was given a poor review.* And for the first time, perhaps, the missileers' dirty laundry was aired in public. Editorials described a debauched missileer force that spent its time perusing contraband pornography; mixed missileer teams were fraternizing off duty (with the presumption being that a little hanky-panky might perhaps be taking place on duty as well). Suddenly, the concern was not just the lustful heart of one Catholic officer, but rather, the safety of the nuclear deterrent being compromised by missileer teams hooking up underground. The argument, according to Berry's defenders, was simple: "Mixing men and women in potentially compromising settings creates sexual tensions that can distract from the mission," according to one opinion piece that ran in the *Baltimore Sun*.

Nowadays, however, Berry's concerns sound anachronistic. Not only are coed teams common at Warren, but we were told there were currently seven or eight married couples pulling alert together.

The world has changed, even if the missileers have not. Bob Wyckoff, the retired Air Force officer who authored the missileer poem, is still writing, though he has adapted his verse to the post–Cold War era:

---

* Berry's defense rested on the fact that he claimed he never refused to serve with women and was punished merely for asking for the religious exemption. He switched career tracks and went on to be promoted within the Air Force. Berry sued and the Air Force later agreed to remove his poor performance review from his record.

We raised the ante by fielding MX,
Then Star Wars Projects stacked the decks.
With technical progress that they couldn't follow,
The Soviet threat was revealed to be hollow . . .

Taurus, Pegasus, Athena, Minotaur,
Now Atlas V and Delta IV.
Threats from abroad remain and increase,
Our duty now is to keep space for peace.

But keeping space for peace may not always require missileers sitting deep underground. The Navy has already moved to convert some of its nuclear-armed submarines to ones that launch cruise missiles. Nuclear-armed Air Force bombers are passé, at least according to General Cartwright of STRATCOM. Unless the ICBM fields are converted into conventional fields—something that would presumably not have to be manned around the clock, or even require the same elegant set of checks and balances that nuclear weapons require—what will be the role of missileers?

The concern for missileers is that they will become relics of the past. Dressed in their flight suits and sitting in front of vintage control equipment, the missileers are sometimes reminiscent of the wax figures installed in the civil defense shelter in the Las Vegas atomic museum. Looking at photos of the decommissioned silos turned museums, one is struck by how closely they resemble the still-active silos. And despite the sunny view of missileering we got from our interviews on base—with public affairs and a senior officer ever present—there is grumbling in the field. Missileers maintain an active online forum, where signs of discontent are clear and morale appears to be at an all-time low. In one post, a missileer calling himself "Spank" celebrates the fact that he will get to retire with his missileer badge, rather than a recently adopted space patch. "Woo-Hoo! I never have to wear the Gay Space Wings! La-la-la-la. I get to retire a MISSILEER!"

Without the ICBMs there would be no missileers—and no F. E. Warren Air Force Base. Over one hundred years of history would disappear, likely leaving just Paula Taylor and the museum. Sitting inside their capsules, the missileers had to find ways to imagine that deterrence worked, and that it was justified; otherwise, not only wouldn't they be there, but quite sanely, the country wouldn't want them there. The military is not set up to wish itself away, and though we heard missileers say they hoped they would never have to turn the key, certainly none of them expressed the desire to have their jobs go away. Quite the opposite, the stated presumption was that their jobs would always be necessary, because there was always someone who needed to be deterred.

The hair-trigger alert, of course, is the main reason for having the missileers. In the fall of 1991, as the Soviet Union slid into chaos, the United States wanted to make a show of goodwill. Among the steps the U.S. government took was to de-alert all the Minuteman II missiles, Blair, the former missileer, told us. "That's almost half our Minuteman [missiles] de-alerted overnight," he said. "The step they took included taking the launch keys away from the crews." The missileers, minus their keys, still had to pull alert in the capsule. "They were very upset," Blair acknowledged. "They felt, what's the word? Emasculated."

Back in 2005, General Lance Lord, then the head of U.S. Air Force Space Command, boasted that there were nine thousand Air Force personnel who were safeguarding an ever-shrinking stockpile of nuclear weapons. "As the wing commander at F. E. Warren," he said, "routinely I was asked, 'How does winning the Cold War change your mission?' It doesn't." As Fred Kaplan, author of *The Wizards of Armageddon*, points out, "It may well be that the Air Force missile men are simply, desperately, looking for something to do."

It was hard to imagine that keeping young, educated, and highly trained Air Force personnel locked underground was really the best use of resources. If nothing else, it struck us as terribly unimaginative. Nuclear deterrence did not always exist, and it seemed somehow odd to think that it always would.

On our second day at Warren, we went to meet with Colonel Michael Morgan, the squadron's wing commander. We asked him what life was like for the missileers compared with during the Cold War. Morgan recalled life as a missileer during that period in Minot, North Dakota. His memories were of a beach party. He described how he and his friends hauled sand to a fellow missileer's basement and set up beach umbrellas and drank mai tais in the middle of winter.

"Nobody wanted to clean up the sand, so we left it until next year, then we had 'son of beach party,' and then we had 'grandson of beach party' the following year," he said.

Life was different at Warren, he noted, but perhaps not so much because of the era, but because the community was not as isolated. Denver, after all, was less than two hours away. However, time has changed at least how the public thinks—or more to the point, doesn't think—about the silent community of missileers. According to at least one poll, most Americans now believe the chances of an all-out nuclear war are remote.

But for Morgan, the fact that the missileers were not really at the forefront of most Americans' minds was, if anything, a good thing. "These are strategic nuclear weapons," he said. "I think it's absolutely imperative that our citizens, our nation, doesn't worry about us. They are not concerned about our ability to respond; they are not concerned about the safety and security of our weapons systems. The message that we have is not for the American people; the message that we have is for our potential adversaries. And what we do speaks loud and clear to the folks overseas, if you will. And I think, by and large, the missile community, the strategic nuclear community, is just fine with being in the background and not out in front in the minds of the American public."

For Morgan, as for the missileers, deterrence was a philosophical question best left to Washington and the politicians. "It's our job as professional military officers to salute smartly and carry out the desires of our duly elected civilian officials," he told us.

Superficially, it would be easy to consider the missileers mindless robots who simply follow orders to turn the switch. But the missileers we spoke with were striving for a way to make sense of their job—that "tangible thing" that Lieutenant Stricklan had expressed to us in the mock-up capsule. What is it that would actually make a missileer turn the key?

It was clear to us that the missileers were all trying to hang onto deterrence as the rationale to do their jobs. It was no wonder the focus of their training was on mastering the rote procedures that led to the key turn—the idea, after all, was to make sure that they didn't need or want to grope for abstract ideas or questions. What would happen, we asked Lee and Stricklan, after the missiles launched? That, after all, was something that couldn't really be rehearsed.

"After?" Lee replied, looking a bit perplexed.

As we had learned the day before, the MAFs were meant to survive a nuclear attack—at least long enough for the missileers to turn the key. They were not intended for any sort of long-term survival. There was just a few days' worth of food at the MAF and no medical care, let alone long-term life support. As Bruce Blair recalled of his days as a missileer, the post-Armageddon plan was for him and his fellow missileers to report to a local National Guard bureau. "Our instructions were you hang out till you've launched the last missile. Then you dig yourself out and you walk to Helena, Montana," he told us. Blair was stationed at Great Falls, some two hundred miles away from Helena. In other words, he was ordered to walk "through smoking, irradiated ruins of a state, where you would basically die of radiation poisoning within an hour after leaving the silo."

Those were his post-Armageddon orders. It was, as he put it, "a joke."

Yet the missileers belowground had at least a better chance than the crew topside. So what, we asked, would the crew do? The facilities were built to withstand a nuclear blast (though even that was somewhat doubtful); so, presuming they survived the initial thermonuclear onslaught, what would come next? Very little thought had been given to that. Like the bomber pilots who were presumed to be flying their nuclear payloads to a certain death over the Soviet Union, few had really thought about the "day after" for a missileer. Their duties ended with the key turn.

Lee's answer, perhaps not surprisingly, was not really about himself, it was about the men and women topside, who would be completely unprotected in the event of a nuclear strike. "As an officer, I would make the choice to bring my men down," he said solemnly.

But Granstrom, who was standing behind Lee, frowned slightly and shook his head. The cook and the facility manager could come down, but not the security crew, he insisted. "Security forces would stay up to the bitter end," he said, "to protect any unlaunched missiles."

That is the paradox of deterrence. For deterrence to work, the missileer must be able to follow orders that seem absurd. What sort of officer, knowing the end was near, would leave the men and women under his command aboveground, condemned to a certain death in the name of a principle—deterrence—that hadn't worked? The logic of

Granstrom's answer was clear; it was the same logic that guided deterrence, which meant following the prescribed steps to the very end, however pointless they might be at the moment of execution.

Our gaze shifted back to Lee for his response. A simple calculation would support Granstrom's view. If you were willing to turn the key after deterrence had failed, why concern yourself with enlisted military personnel who had signed up to sacrifice their lives in the name of deterrence?

It was quiet, and for a moment, as we waited for Lee to concur with his senior officer, we forgot that we were in the training capsule and not back underground like the day before. Lee merely shifted uncomfortably in his seat and stared straight ahead, neither contradicting nor affirming the major's position.

It occurred to us that perhaps the reason Lee would bring his people down was that "tangible thing" that would lead him to turn the key. It wasn't abstract notions of deterrence or a warped sense of patriotism— or even avenging his possibly dead family. It was simply a sense of duty and loyalty to the people with whom he served.

In that instant, we knew that if the missiles were flying, and Armageddon was on its way, Captain Lee, without doubt, would bring his people down.

CHAPTER 7

How We Learned to Stop Worrying About the Bomb in Pennsylvania

The Rebirth of Site R, the Government's Secret Nuclear Bunker

For a place that's supposed to be secret, Site R is easy to find.

Just drive north on the Catoctin Mountain Highway to Maryland Route 140, make a left at the stop sign, and head straight on through the picturesque main square of Emmitsburg. Eventually, you'll reach the Pennsylvania state line, where MD-140 becomes PA-16. Travel another six miles or so, turn left onto Harbaugh Valley Road, and about three quarters of a mile up the road, there's an old stone chapel. On the other side of the road is a double fence topped with tightly looped concertina wire. It adds a touch of menace to the scenic patch of Pennsylvania farmland dotted with modest wood-frame houses and weathered barns.

The only official acknowledgment of the military facility is a sign marked WARNING. In small letters, the text reads: "This installation has been declared a restricted area according to a Secretary of Defense directive issued 20 August 1954 under the provisions of section 31, Internal Security Act of 1950. Unauthorized entry is prohibited." The fine print is explicit: "Photographing or making notes, drawings, maps, or graphic representations of this area or its activities is prohibited unless specifically authorized by the commander."

Officially known as the National Military Command Center–Raven Rock Mountain Complex (NMCC-RRMC), Site R lies about sixty miles northwest of the Capital Beltway. Established after the Soviets detonated their first atomic bomb in 1949, Site R became the bunker where commanders could be whisked away in the event of a nuclear attack on Washington. It housed command-and-control and communications equipment that would allow the Department of Defense and other federal agencies to keep the government running in the event of an emergency. Over the years, the complex became a part of a much larger "continuity of government" scheme, designed to ensure its survival even after a massive nuclear strike.

During the Cold War, the United States and, in some cases, other countries sought salvation from nuclear paranoia deep underground, hoping to protect key leaders from the scorched earth that would be left behind by an atomic weapon. Over the course of several decades, the U.S. government carved out a series of tunnels, bunkers, and caverns, the extent of which is still unknown.

Major bunkers, such as those at Cheyenne Mountain and U.S. Strategic Command, are well known. Others, like Raven Rock and the Mount Weather facility in Virginia—believed to be a nuclear bunker for civil government—are acknowledged, though their exact functions remain obscured. Then there are those bunkers that are unacknowledged but exist in the realm of reliable rumor, like the ones presumed to be at the Camp David presidential retreat in Maryland and beneath the White House in Washington.

Bunkers weren't just for sheltering VIPs. There were also bunkers to protect nuclear weapons, like the cavernous facility carved out of Manzano Mountain in New Mexico. Beginning in mid-1947 under the code name Operation Water Supply, the military tunneled into the mountain, creating a steel and concrete crypt for nuclear weapons. Inside the vaulted storage cases were "birdcages" that protected the weapons' plutonium trigger, separate from the nuclear weapon. (At one point, Manzano was also home to President Dwight Eisenhower's emergency relocation center, though the development of thermonuclear weapons made the command facility obsolete.) There was even an underground bunker for cold hard cash: the Federal Reserve's Mount Pony, a 140,000-square-foot bunker in Culpeper, Virginia, opened in 1969 to keep money safe from a nuclear holocaust. Today, the Library of Congress uses the bunker to house movies and music.

Prior to the terrorist attacks of September 11, 2001, Site R was almost obsolete. As a 2000 profile of the facility in the *New York Times Magazine* reported, "By the 70's, the Soviets had warheads capable of pounding Raven Rock to rubble (assuming they had found it)." The facility went "from bunker to garage, used in part to house the mobile communications units (trucks) that are supposed to fan out to remote areas in case of war or other disaster to ensure the continuity of government operations." The end of the Cold War made the mountain hideaway even less important, and in 1992, after the collapse of the Soviet Union, the Pentagon announced that it had done away with twenty-four-hour alerts there; the facility would be preserved in "care-taker" status.

September 11 put Site R back in business. Within hours of the attack, a motorcade of SUVs with black-tinted windows was seen blazing down Route 140, taking the left turn up Harbaugh Valley Road. News reports speculated that Site R was, in fact, Vice President Dick Cheney's undisclosed location. Not that anyone in the White House or the Pentagon would talk about it. An information page hosted by the Defense Information Systems Agency was scrubbed; the only official reference we could find online to Raven Rock was on the less-than-informative home page of the 114th Signal Battalion. Media tours, it seemed, were out of the question.

In 2002, the facility briefly reemerged into public view when the Pentagon placed a seventy-four-million-dollar line item for Site R in its voluminous annual budget request. Asked about the site and its role in continuity-of-government operations, then–Pentagon spokeswoman Victoria Clarke said the money would be spent on "communications" upgrades, but gave few other details about plans for the facility, which she noted predated September 11. "It is part of an overall plan to make sure that the military, the Pentagon, can be up and operating," she said. "And I'll just leave it at that."

In the years since, the Pentagon has not been any more forthcoming on details of what the millions of dollars have gone toward at Site R. After a number of fruitless phone calls, a helpful public affairs officer at the Pentagon directed us to U.S. Northern Command's National Capital Region press office at Fort Leslie J. McNair in Washington, D.C. A desk officer directed us to Barbara Owens, a civilian public affairs officer at the National Capital Region headquarters. "Barb, I had a telephonic inquiry this morning from this gentleman," the officer wrote in an e-mail copied to us. "I wasn't sure what exactly he was talking about, so I asked him to provide his request via email. Ron suggested I send it to you since you have experience with the referenced site."

"Thanks," replied Owens. "We occasionally receive Site R queries. I will coordinate with OSD [the Office of the Secretary of Defense] and Raven Rock."

That was the last we heard from them.

With the threat of all-out nuclear warfare receding into the background, what was the reason for Site R's secrecy, and why was such a facility expanding? Unperturbed, we mapped out our own itinerary for a U.S. bunker tour, determined to find out why, after so many years, nuclear planners were still digging deep underground.

A persistent trait of bureaucracies is the instinct for survival and a penchant for expansion. Organizations, like people, want to survive and grow richer. So it is with continuity of government. In theory, continuity of government is built into the Constitution and elaborated in national law. If the heads of government are wiped out in some catastrophe, rules of succession ensure a smooth and legal transition. But in the nuclear era, the U.S. government needed to hedge its bets. During the Cold War, it spent billions of dollars to build a network of bunkers—in bureaucratic parlance, "hardened facilities"—designed to ensure that the apparatus of government and the military would survive a first strike.

Protected beneath two thousand feet of granite in Colorado Springs, Colorado, and immortalized by Hollywood, the Cheyenne Mountain Air Force Station complex is the world's most famous bunker. Originally built to house the North American Aerospace Defense Command Combat Operations Center, the mountain command post became the archetypal Cold War bunker—and is accordingly the fictional home of the rogue mainframe computer in Cold War–era movies like *WarGames* and *The Terminator*. Hollywood's fascination with Cheyenne Mountain embodied public fears that the government's plans for "nuclear survivability" would place the survival of institutions over the survival of people.

Cold War intellectuals like Herman Kahn and his cohorts at the RAND Corporation spent years wrestling with these problems. "Thinking the unthinkable" was Kahn's shorthand for ensuring that the American side would be prepared to go on, in some form, after a devastating nuclear exchange with the Soviet Union. "Reconstruction will begin," Kahn famously wrote, "life will continue, and most survivors will not envy the dead."

Kahn's arguments horrified disarmament advocates, who worried that talk about the "survivability" of nuclear war—versus the certainties of mutual assured destruction—would make a nuclear exchange more likely. But the evangelizers of civil defense were possessed of a sort of unassailable, if morbid, optimism. They noted, for instance, the bombing campaigns against German cities during World War II. Despite the best efforts of the U.S. and British air forces to cripple German industry, its output actually rose over the course of the war. With the right combination of shelters and the hardening of strategic sites, they surmised, some segment of society could survive. It was a "mine-shaft gap" theory that was easily parodied, especially when presented in a dumbed-down form by Reagan-era defense officials. In 1981, Deputy Under Secretary of Defense T. K. Jones famously told a reporter over an after-dinner cordial, "If there are enough shovels to go around, everybody's going to make it."

The history of government advice on civil defense—from the 1950s "duck and cover" campaign to the 1980s focus on continuity of government—was less than reassuring. In the laissez-faire 1980s, civil defense never seemed much more than a do-it-yourself affair. Government-issued publications such as Oak Ridge National Laboratory's *Nuclear War Survival Skills* offered helpful tips on stockpiling food, building shelters, and measuring fallout; sturdy public buildings were marked with FALLOUT SHELTER signs. As *Time* noted in 1982, "Unlike the fallout-shelter mania that followed the Berlin crisis of 1961, when the Kennedy Administration spent $257 million . . . for civil defense, the Reagan program is focused on 'crisis relocation' to evacuate probable target areas, and on contingency plans for resuming normal operations after a nuclear attack." Bureaucratic preparations suggested the government's plans for protecting its citizenry, which included postage-free emergency-change-of-address forms, were irrational at best.

Still, the government's focus on preserving government was enthusiastic, well organized, and generously resourced. James Mann, author of the book *Rise of the Vulcans*, describes how Dick Cheney and

Donald Rumsfeld, as former executive branch officials, took part in a series of exercises in the 1980s designed to test the U.S. government's ability to survive a nuclear attack: "A core element of the Reagan Administration's strategy for fighting a nuclear war would be to decapitate the Soviet leadership by striking at top political and military officials and their communications lines; the Administration wanted to make sure that the Soviets couldn't do to America what U.S. nuclear strategists were planning to do to the Soviet Union."

After September 11, plans for continuity of operations were dusted off and updated, though not necessarily improved. A 2004 General Accounting Office report criticized government agencies for, in many cases, having made little progress in ensuring vital government functions. One problem appeared to be that government agencies weren't particularly aware of which of their functions were vital. As the GAO pointed out, one wayward agency's continuity plans omitted "9 of 10 high-impact programs for which it was responsible," though they included such frivolous items as "provide speeches and articles for the Secretary and Deputy Secretary."

The idea of visiting Site R as part of a nuclear vacation is by no means far-fetched; Fodor's even includes the bunker at Raven Rock on its list of atomic tourism sites, although it notes that visitors shouldn't expect to get that close to the actual facility.

In the fall of 2006, as we waited for an answer to our request to visit Site R, we found a notice posted on the Web site of the Defense Threat Reduction Agency for a Hardened Facilities Manager Conference to be held that week at Raven Rock. The conference, the notice read, "will focus on priority issues of both countering enemy underground facilities (UGF) and protecting friendly underground facilities." It promised detailed presentations by managers of the underground facilities. "In addition," the notice stated, "technical and vulnerability issues will be discussed and site tours will be provided."

It was unusual to publicize a conference about underground facilities, particularly at a place like Site R, which exists in a quasi-secret status. It was even more unusual to see the notice out of DTRA—a unique Pentagon bureaucracy that indirectly descends from the old Defense Nuclear Agency. It focuses these days on tracking WMD threats, and much of its work is classified. DTRA also funds much of the Pentagon research into destroying enemy bunkers. Intrigued, we sent an e-mail to the contact person, providing our affiliation and politely inquiring if we could receive an agenda or further information on the conference; we sent a separate note to DTRA's public affairs office.

That, at last, got the attention of someone in the Pentagon bureaucracy. The DTRA spokesperson informed us that the conference was most definitely not open to the press, expressing surprise that the notice had ended up on the public Web site of the agency. The contractor running the conference, in the meantime, promptly sent us an agenda and accompanying information. We quickly perused the documents, which began with an "information package for Raven Rock Mountain Complex SITE R" that featured an almost childlike drawing of a mountain with two satellite dishes perched on top and a road leading inside the mountain. At the bottom was a note from Colonel Daniel Roper, the installation commander, welcoming conference attendees to Raven Rock Mountain Complex—Site R.

The doors to Site R may have been closed, but bureaucratic bungling had secured us a copy of a wealth of unclassified information. The basic agenda of the professional conference offered some very definite clues as to what was going on inside this network of top-secret facilities. In attendance were representatives of hardened facilities across the United States: the Kirtland Underground Munitions Storage Center, a nuclear weapons depot at Kirtland Air Force Base, in New Mexico; the Cheyenne Mountain complex, in Colorado Springs; and U.S. Strategic Command, in Omaha, Nebraska. Also present was a facility representative from CP Tango, a command post facility for U.S. forces in South Korea. Engineers were hosting afternoon sessions on the practical matters of providing internal and external power—and alternatives such as solar power—as well as mining issues and security and blast-door designs. Renovations and upgrades were also topics of discussion. Reading through the information packet and agenda, we realized this was the military equivalent of a Las Vegas convention, only instead of plastics salesmen, it was a gathering of bunker managers.

Surviving nuclear war was once the chief focus for bunkers. But absent the threat from the Soviet Union, the "hardened facilities managers" had found fresh purpose. A glance at the agenda suggested that flu pandemic now ranked up with a nuclear exchange on the spectrum of threats for which the government was preparing. One of the conference sessions focused on pandemic influenza screening, another on "Extending Post Attack Endurance at Underground Facilities." The end of the Cold War, it seemed, had produced a new rationale for maintaining a costly network of fortified underground facilities like Site R. As we waited in vain for the Pentagon to respond to our Site R visit request, we decided to travel to Colorado for a better glimpse of this subterranean world.

On September 11, 2001, as top defense officials were being whisked to Site R, Air Force general Ralph Eberhart, the four-star chief of U.S. Space Command and NORAD, was stuck in traffic.

Eberhart had been in his headquarters at Peterson Air Force Base in Colorado Springs when airliners struck the North and South towers of the World Trade Center. NORAD, the joint U.S.-Canadian command that monitors North American airspace, had been scheduled to conduct an exercise called Vigilant Guardian, which would have simulated a bomber attack from the former Soviet Union. The command post inside Cheyenne Mountain was well staffed; Eberhart headed for the bunker. But on the way there, he got caught up in Colorado Springs' congested roadways.

NORAD Road, marked for "authorized traffic only," winds up Cheyenne Mountain, past cookie-cutter housing that abuts the military reservation. Colorado Springs may bill itself as a mountain resort town, but it has quietly grown into the state's second-largest city. A military contracting boom—and an influx of high-tech companies—has fueled new suburban development. The underground complex is only about a dozen miles from Peterson, but as local newspapers would later reveal, it took the general three quarters of an hour to make the journey up the mountain. A missile from Russia, by contrast, would reach Colorado in just thirty minutes. Cheyenne Mountain might have survived the Soviet Union, but it looked like it might be put out of business by unchecked urban sprawl.

After Eberhart reached the NORAD operations center inside Cheyenne Mountain on 9/11, the twenty-five-ton blast doors were finally sealed. It was the first time the mountain complex had "buttoned up" since the end of the Cold War.

Five years later, the place was still plagued by the same traffic. Construction had slowed everything on Interstate 25 to a maddening crawl. After a frustrating wait in traffic, we finally found the exit to Highway 115—Nevada Avenue within Colorado Springs city limits— and headed south. The exit to Cheyenne Mountain was clearly labeled, one exit past South Academy. Unlike the bunkers housed secretly amid close-knit rural communities, Cheyenne Mountain sits outside Colorado Springs, a city that is also home to Peterson Air Force Base, the Air Force Academy, and Fort Carson.

Arriving early for our tour, we waited in the visitors' center while a contractor argued with a private security guard about whether he could present his duplicate driver's license or needed his Department of Defense common access card. Judge Mathis held forth on the television as a junior airman vacuumed the floor. While perusing copies of *Space Guardian*, the base newspaper, we noted the main headline, which described a recent buttoning-up exercise inside the mountain, the first time the blast doors had been closed since September 11, 2001.

Built as a command-and-control center in the days of the Soviet bomber threat, Cheyenne Mountain was once the ultimate symbol of the national will to survive a nuclear strike. The Rocky Mountains are low in seismic activity, making them ideal for a blast-proof facility, and the mountain was reckoned as North America's geographic dead center, providing the most advance warning of an incoming bomber attack. Equally important, Colorado Springs already had an established military community. Construction workers moved nearly seven hundred thousand tons of granite to excavate the North Portal, eventually carving out a facility that covered 412 acres and was buried two thousand feet underground. Building the complex cost $142 million—an enormous sum for the mid-1960s.

Today, Cheyenne Mountain hosts four separate commands: NORAD, U.S. Northern Command (NORTHCOM, a Department of Defense "unified command" that was established after September 11 to oversee homeland security), STRATCOM, and Air Force Space Command. In military parlance, Space Command has "ownership" of the facility—most of the personnel who maintain the place work for the Air Force. One of Cheyenne Mountain's main missions is strategic missile warning—early detection of missiles launched against the United States. There is also a theater missile warning system that uses a network of satellites and sensors on the ground to detect the heat signatures from shorter-range missiles that might threaten U.S. forces overseas. The Air Warning Center is also housed within the complex. It monitors the airspace over North America, tracking thousands of aircraft flying over Canada and the United States.

A heightened security regime—put in place before the Y2K clock-turning scare—meant that the Cheyenne Mountain Directorate had stopped conducting tours for the general public. Nonetheless, nuclear vacationers could still get a chance to see the iconic North Portal. After contacting the public affairs office, we were able to tag along with a tour group from the University of Denver, professors and students enrolled in a graduate degree homeland security course. Eventually our tour group arrived on a government bus, escorted by our uniformed chaperones. The bus took us through a checkpoint and drove up to the top of the access road, where our group was dropped off at the James E. Hill Technical Support Facility, Building 101. U.S. and Canadian flags fluttered in the breeze. Welcome to Cheyenne Mountain.

As we entered Building 101, the group fanned out over the lobby to look at the signed photos of celebrities who had visited Cheyenne Mountain, all posing in front of the North Portal entrance: a dapper-looking Peter Jennings, the late ABC anchorman, and CNN's Kyra Phillips, who had signed her photo: "To all my *friends* at NORAD and US Northern Command! Not only do you make me feel *secure* but *so* proud! Love, Kyra Phillips, CNN." There were other VIPs, some of more questionable acclaim, including the Colorado Crush arena football team, the Denver Nuggets cheerleaders, "adult contemporary" singer Alison Krauss, and B movie actress Linda Purl, star of the made-for-TV movies *Frozen Impact* and *Born Free: A New Adventure*. Clad in a fur coat, Purl mugged for the camera. And of course there was a framed portrait of Clifford the Big Red Dog, who visited Cheyenne Mountain in December 2004. We had the sense that long before we got there, Cheyenne had morphed into something that resembled a Disney resort.

Lieutenant Cheryl King, a Canadian Navy officer who had embellished her pixilated camouflage uniform with a poppy for Remembrance Day, received our tour group. "First off, we want to dispel a rumor: The antennas on top of the mountain are local TV; they have nothing to do with NORAD," she said, walking us through a Power-

Point briefing that listed all the different commands housed inside the mountain. She also explained the system of five watch commands (Alpha, Bravo, Charlie, Delta, and Echo, of course) and the shift system inside the mountain (six days on and four days off, in eight-hour shifts). Charlie watch, she noted with pride, was overseen by a Canadian Navy captain or colonel. Before we began our escorted tour, she offered a piece of advice: "Cheyenne Mountain was designed as an all-male facility, so ladies, please go to the bathroom in the visitors' center."

Our bus rolled up to the main entrance, an exhaust-pipe-shaped portal crowned with concertina wire and block letters: CHEYENNE MOUNTAIN COMPLEX. Entering the tunnel, we passed a smaller sign: INSIDE THE MOUNTAIN IS A NO HAT NO SALUTE AREA. Our bus continued down the two-lane passageway leading into the heart of the complex, obeying the posted speed limit of fifteen miles per hour, creeping along like a ride at an amusement park. Inside the mountain, the heads of STRATCOM and NORTHCOM have their own parking spaces—each neatly marked with four stars—but rank and file must be ferried into the complex on a shuttle bus. The bus deposited us beneath two thousand feet of granite near an enormous vault: one of the three blast doors in Cheyenne Mountain.

During the confrontation with the Soviets, the military always kept one blast door at Cheyenne Mountain sealed, just in case of a sneak attack. During a shift change, an outer blast door would close off the connecting passageway before the inner door could be unsealed. The underground bunker is not airtight; the facility uses overpressure to keep air flowing out, preventing contamination from seeping into the mountain. Tunnel builders used smooth-face blasting to carve out the tunnels—walls studded with rock bolts to fortify against a collapse. The doors were built to withstand a multimegaton blast. Without any natural light, the interior is bathed in a weird fluorescent glow; the air is oddly damp. Tarps fixed to the ceiling of the tunnel catch water that seeps into the bunker—it takes as long as two weeks for rainwater to seep through the rock above. When the water reaches the carved-out interior, it rains inside the mountain.

After the Cold War ended, Cheyenne Mountain's blast doors were propped open, exposing the interior of the bunker, which was, well, a bit disappointing. Blame Hollywood. Rather than a single, vast cavernous auditorium packed with billboard-size television screens and flickering electronic maps, there were fifteen steel buildings arrayed inside a warren of tunnels, each structure resting on enormous springs to withstand the seismic tremors from a multimegaton nuclear blast. From the exterior, they looked like orphaned pieces of naval architecture or stacked double-wide trailers. The buildings were, in fact, deliberately designed like a Navy ship, built out of continuously welded three-eighths-inch steel to protect against an electromagnetic pulse and connected by catwalks.

Almost from the start, Cheyenne Mountain raised a fundamental dilemma that still plagues all of the Cold War shelters. They were carved out when leaders thought they would have time to evacuate to a safe location. The advent of ICBMs, however, made that goal quixotic, while the increasing firepower and accuracy of thermonuclear weapons meant that even if leaders did reach their hideouts, it was increasingly less likely they would survive. Almost as soon as shelters were built, they became obsolete. As a spokesman for Cheyenne Mountain acknowledged years later, "One great irony is that the yield and accuracy of nuclear weapons systems improved quickly enough to render the facility potentially vulnerable the day it was completed in 1965."

Yet military officials continued to operate as if that reality did not exist, and Cheyenne Mountain pressed on with its operations for several more decades. Ironically, it was the terrorist attacks of September 11 that finally proved that a bunker was an anachronism in an age when communications could be run from almost anywhere. It wasn't just the location of Cheyenne that was problematic, either. It turned out that the military wasn't even looking in the right direction. Radar facing out to detect a Soviet attack was useless against hijacked aircraft attacking from within, and Federal Aviation Administration (FAA) radars that could have detected those aircraft weren't hooked up to the computers at Cheyenne. Isolation and fortification—once the cornerstone of the mountain's raison d'être—now appeared to be a liability.

Some procedures changed inside the mountain following September 11. NORAD began sharing radar information with the FAA, and representatives from the FAA and the newly established NORTH-COM moved inside the mountain. The command center doubled in size. But as it turned out, putting the Cold War bunker on a proper post-9/11 footing was not easy. Upgrading computers and electronics inside a hardened facility is costly and time-consuming; so is finding extra space to accommodate extra personnel and equipment. A post-9/11 modernization plan—originally supposed to cost around half a billion dollars—went more than four hundred million dollars over budget. In mid-2006, it was still incomplete.*

Even little things like local commute times proved problematic for the mountain fortress. During an exercise in 2005, Admiral Timothy Keating, the head of NORTHCOM, became frustrated while shuttling between Peterson Air Force Base and the mountain. "I can't be in two places at one time," the admiral complained. In the summer of 2006, Keating ordered the Cheyenne Mountain complex to be put on "warm standby," moving most of the surveillance crews—and an undisclosed number of support personnel—out of the mountain. All of the STRAT-COM personnel would relocate to Peterson. So would the Air Warning Center and all the NORAD functions.

Major General Kevin Campbell, STRATCOM chief of staff, explained the problem to us quite succinctly at a conference in Huntsville, Alabama, in 2006. "Cheyenne Mountain is a good operation; it has executed the mission it was given. But we felt that if we didn't move that mission set out of the mountain, or at least some of it, then some of the technologies stay tied to some legacy technologies. You really have to 'dumb down' new systems when you bring them in and you marry them with these legacy systems in Cheyenne Mountain."

Touring Cheyenne Mountain, we would hear the same observation. We climbed a set of stairs and were ushered inside an operations room parked square in the middle of the second floor of one of the steel buildings. It looked like a down-market news bureau, with watch officers crowded into small cubicles, staring at flat-panel screens. Disappointingly, none of the officers had red telephones for passing threat assessments up to the White House. A perky Navy lieutenant in a flight suit gave us a briefing on the Air Warning Center, charged with watching the skies over North America. "Prior to 9/11, the work stations were not really organized in here; it was kind of a cluster," she said, politely truncating the military's catchall expletive for a disorganized situation. "Now everyone faces the same way."

---

* As a GAO report noted, "The Air Force, which has overall responsibility for the program, currently estimates program costs will total about $707 million through fiscal year 2006—about a 51 percent increase over initial estimates."

After September 11, new procedures were put in place. The North American air defense network uses a series of ground-based and airborne radar to track aircraft flying inside U.S. and Canadian airspace. In addition, aerostats—tethered blimps—monitor the southern border with Mexico. Around seven thousand aircraft enter North American airspace each day; a small number are tracked as "unknown," usually because they have strayed from their flight plan or have not followed procedure. If they cannot be positively identified, NORAD will scramble fighter aircraft to establish visual identification. Some high-profile locations, particularly around Washington, are off-limits to civil aviation.

What, then, is the future of this nuclear bunker? Cheyenne Mountain, the ultimate Cold War retreat, would not be completely mothballed. Admiral Keating wanted it maintained in a state of readiness so that operations could be up and running within one hour. The mountain bunker still has its advantages: It is hardened against all conventional attacks. As one of our Air Force escorts put it, "If the enemy's at the gates, I guarantee that they are going up the hill."

Lieutenant King, the Canadian public affairs officer, preferred to describe the status of the facility as "hot standby," although she acknowledged that the place would pretty much empty out over the next year or so. When we asked what future visitors to the mountain could expect, she replied, "Eighteen months from now, you'll see a whole lot of empty desks and flashing computers." The military would keep the computer stations updated, as part of Keating's plan to keep Cheyenne Mountain as an alternate site. But the place might otherwise be a relic—a museum of the Cold War. Asked what would become of it, King shrugged.

"Will we become Disneyland? Who knows?"

Not all the facilities designed to protect leaders from nuclear war have proved as enduring as Cheyenne Mountain.

For decades, people living in White Sulphur Springs, West Virginia, heard rumors about a mysterious bunker hidden beneath the Greenbrier, the town's posh, five-star hotel and historic landmark. The whispering started in 1957, when drill rigs appeared on the property's Copeland Hill. Management quickly moved to dispel the rumor, explaining in the employee newsletter that the Greenbrier was considering whether to build a new wing that would feature an exhibit hall and indoor recreation area. And sure enough, in late 1958, the Chesapeake and Ohio Railway, which owned the resort, began construction work on the new West Virginia Wing at the Greenbrier.

Every now and then, locals would trade stories. So-and-so knew someone else who claimed to have knowledge of a secret hideaway at the Greenbrier. Whenever someone new moved to town—which was not often—they would gleefully pass on the rumor. It was small-town gossip, mostly, but the rumor persisted. The bunker, some said, was built for the president.

A few months after his appointment as the official historian of the Greenbrier, Robert Conte was summoned to his supervisor's office. The stately Greenbrier had a rich history dating back to the eighteenth century, and Conte, who held a Ph.D. in American studies, had joined the resort in 1978 after a stint at the National Archives in Washington. One of his first assignments was to provide some historical background to an Associated Press reporter, who was researching a feature story. A few days after the visit, the reporter phoned back with an unusual follow-up question: "Is there really a bomb shelter at the Greenbrier?"

Conte, as it happens, had heard that same rumor. He even mentioned it once to the chief engineer, who quickly dismissed it as a "silly story." When he got the follow-up call from the reporter, he repeated the engineer's answer: "Silly rumor, can't get rid of it." The AP then published a story—mainly about the history of the Greenbrier but also quoting Conte denying the existence of a bomb shelter.

Nearly thirty years later, Conte still had a vivid memory of what happened next. "Well, the boss calls me in and sits me down," he told us. "And I think he's going to pat me on the back for getting this nice coverage." Instead, the boss banged his hand on the desk. "There's no goddamn bunker at the Greenbrier!" he barked. "And that," Conte continued, "was my first indication there's *got* to be a bunker in the Greenbrier."

Newcomers like Conte quickly caught on that the topic of the bunker was taboo. They heard rumors, but they quickly learned to dismiss them. Among employees, at least, the subject was not discussed. "You know, we all sort of knew there was the eight-hundred-pound gorilla in the room that we didn't talk about," Conte said. "And we tiptoed around the whole thing ... I guess we were all like codependent children of alcoholics, right? We didn't talk about it."

That changed in early 1992, when another reporter paid a visit to the Greenbrier. The journalist, Ted Gup, seemed to have unusual confidence in his story. He came into Conte's office, put a tape recorder on the desk, and, as Conte recalled, said: "I'm here to talk about what's under the West Virginia Wing." And of course, Conte repeated the line that there was nothing underneath the West Virginia Wing.

Conte told him everything he knew. By then, he'd worked at the Greenbrier for years, and he recited all the reasons for the rumors. During World War II, the U.S. government had interned diplomats from the Axis powers; Eisenhower had played golf there a lot; construction on the West Virginia Wing had been completed just in time for the Cuban Missile Crisis. According to Conte, Gup just sat silently while the tape recorder kept rolling, clearly not persuaded by the denials. So, as a final gesture, Conte offered to open all his archives. He gave Gup an hour to peruse the entire collection, promising the journalist he would find no indication of a bunker. "And he took me up on it," Conte recalled. "He must have spent an hour looking through all of this stuff. And I'm thinking, 'Boy, I've outfoxed this guy.'"

But Conte's attempt to debunk Gup's bunker theory actually provided the reporter with a new opening. According to Conte, Gup found old employee newsletters, and by focusing on the bulletins from 1960 and 1961, he compiled a list of names. He then went to the phone book—many retired Greenbrier employees lived in the area—and called everyone. Most people were probably reluctant to talk, but he was able to piece together information here and there. Conte recalled Gup later thanking him for providing good information. On May 31, 1992, a story headlined LAST RESORT appeared in the *Washington Post Magazine*. "At the height of the Cold War, the U.S. government built a relocation facility for Congress at this West Virginia luxury hotel," the story began. "Three decades passed, the Cold War ended—but inside the Greenbrier, time stood still."

The story blew the lid on a three-decade-old secret at the Greenbrier. There was indeed a bunker—not for the president, but for Congress. (The rival *Washington Times* actually got the scoop, but only because someone purloined a copy of the magazine section before it was actually distributed.) News broke on a Friday. That morning, a group of employees was summoned to a meeting in the office of Ted Kleisner, the Greenbrier president and managing director. It was an unusual gathering. Kleisner stood up and announced that the Greenbrier was going to acknowledge a thirty-five-year secret. He inserted a tape in a VCR and hit play.

On-screen, a man stood at a lectern that bore an impressive-looking seal on it. "Greetings," the man said. "If you are watching this video, something has happened to breach national security." The man in the video went on to explain a secret leasing arrangement between the government and the Greenbrier. In the event of a national emergency, Congress would relocate to a bunker under the West Virginia Wing; the government would take over the entire Greenbrier facility. The video had been prepared for the board of directors of CSX, now the parent company of the Greenbrier. They had no idea about the bunker.

Then Paul "Fritz" Bugas stood up. Everyone at the Greenbrier knew him as the regional manager for Forsythe Associates, the company that was responsible for repairing telephones and televisions at the hotel. Forsythe Associates was a front. Bugas was the bunker manager.

We arrived early one Saturday morning in October for the Greenbrier tour, hoping to find a nuclear shelter that finally lived up to our Hollywood-inspired vision of secret passageways and masked blast doors. It didn't disappoint.

The hotel caters not just to the wealthy elite, but also to the type of people who still believe in taking extended family vacations in a single resort. The people drifting in and out could easily have been extras from the film *Dirty Dancing*. The elegant resort itself looks straight off a movie set, a sort of faux White House, with large white columns and elegantly manicured lawns. Beyond the main hotel are smaller buildings that cater to the resort's leisure activities, such as swimming and golf. A shuttle service takes guests around the expansive grounds. Inside the main lobby, we were taken through a series of multicolored rooms with gilded edges, fancy floral wall tapestries, and life-size portraits. With its enforced dress codes and mid-twentieth-century decor, the Greenbrier seemed strangely out of time and place, stuck perpetually in the 1950s. Even the understated bar in the lobby, we were told, was an accommodation to modernity.

The old congressional shelter is located beneath a wing of the hotel that was added in the late 1950s specifically at the government's request. The government subsidized the construction of the entire West Virginia Wing—including the secret annex—at a cost of about fourteen million dollars, a tidy sum at the time. The hotel got a new wing, and Congress got a bunker. Construction wrapped up on the complex in October 1962—just days before the Cuban Missile Crisis. It was the closest the Greenbrier bunker ever came to being activated.

The key to preserving the Greenbrier's secret was its ingenious design. The bunker was hidden in plain sight. A lower level of the West Virginia Wing, which included a giant exhibit hall and two meeting rooms, was actually part of the bunker, and open to the public. Some people logically speculated there was a secret elevator that went down, believing there was a fortified nuclear bunker deep underground. In fact, to reach the shelter, one took the elevator up to the exhibit hall and meeting rooms. An eighteen-ton blast door was cleverly concealed behind a false door; a screen masked the hinges. And if someone noticed there was a gap between the fake door and the wall, it would be explained away as a storage area for tables and chairs. In other words, the bunker was partially open—the secret was the hidden blast doors.

Lynn Swann, the hotel's spokeswoman, and Linda Walls, a twenty-eight-year employee of the Greenbrier and now the director of bunker tours, escorted us down a corridor at the far end of the exhibit hall to a pair of double doors marked off by a sign: RESTRICTED AREA, DO NOT ENTER. An electronic alarm droned on the other side of the door. Walls pushed the doors wide, leading us deeper into the hillside—a point about forty feet underground. A twenty-five-ton blast door concealed the entrance to a concrete passageway, the main portal to the bunker's interior living quarters. During the Cold War, a ledge along the tunnel wall was stacked with freeze-dried rations. Enough food was stored to sustain the entire Congress for sixty days.

During the three decades the bunker was kept secret, the Greenbrier exhibit hall was used for trade shows, pharmaceutical conventions, and the occasional theme party. On the fall day when we visited, an insurance association had rented out the hall. The spacious room was cluttered with potted palm trees and party costumes and was filled with the strong odor of glue being used to assemble the decor for the elaborate jungle-themed event. In the event of war, this hall would have been converted into a sprawling underground office space; the bunker was designed for eleven hundred people—enough room for each member of Congress and one staffer.

With the power of hindsight, some features of the open area provided seemingly easy clues to its purpose. For example, there were two meeting rooms, ostensibly for events. "That was one of the things that nobody really noticed," Swann told us as we peered into the room that would have been the House floor post–nuclear strike. Next door would have been the Senate gallery. "Gee, you've got four hundred and forty seats in it, and that one has a little over a hundred, imagine that," she said. "What an odd number to do, right?"

If Congress had relocated to the Greenbrier, the evacuees would have processed through the tunnel, filtering in through a small decontamination area with a shower room that could hose off about 120 people per hour. Their clothes would have been discarded in a burn bag, and they would then have been issued light clothing—fatigues, underwear, and sneakers—and a ration of toiletries and soap. Inside the eighteen dormitory rooms, the accommodations were quite spartan. Legislators and select aides would have been housed on thin metal bunk beds. Walls, our guide, pointedly informed us that members of Congress had not created some plush bomb shelter. "Their dorms were *filled* with those beds," she said as she showed us around the cramped living quarters. "And they would have shared those tall lockers, and they would have shared those community showers."

That wasn't quite the whole story. If the bunker had been used as an emergency relocation facility, the government would have taken over the entire Greenbrier resort. All sixty-five hundred acres—not to mention the deluxe hotel rooms, tennis courts, swimming pools, and three world championship golf courses—would have become government property. Once the fallout had drifted away, every room in the five-star hotel would have been assigned to a member of Congress, while the bunker would have been reserved for secure meetings and emergency communications. The shelter's designers had even built a television studio, complete with a backdrop of the U.S. Capitol, to serve as a place to broadcast postapocalyptic messages.

Planners had also designed for other contingencies. Walls led us down into the engine room in the lowest recesses of the bunker ("the basement of the basement of the basement," she called it), past the three twenty-five-thousand-gallon tanks that would have kept the facility supplied with fresh water and the fourteen-thousand-gallon diesel tanks that would have fueled the generators. "You're welcome to step in there; just don't go down the stairs, because they are . . . so steep and treacherous," she said, ushering us into a small room. "And this," she continued in a lighthearted voice, "is an *incinerator*."

We paused in front of the black iron furnace. "It was very important to burn up government papers—*couldn't have any government papers here!*" Walls chirped. As we stared at the oven doors, she intuited what was on our minds. In shape and size, the doors to the furnace looked more like the entry to a crematorium than a run-of-the-mill incinerator. Her tone softened: "To be real honest, in the event of emergency, this would have been very necessary if someone had passed away. It could burn hot enough to consume pathological waste." She paused. "And on that happy note, we'll go upstairs!"

While the bunker remained on standby for over three decades, it very quickly outlived its purpose. The advent of the ICBM, which could reach the continental United States within a matter of minutes, meant that the bunker—some five hours' drive from Washington—was too far away for a hasty evacuation. Like Cheyenne Mountain, the secret nuclear bunker was obsolete on day one.

"Just how Congress was expected to reach the Greenbrier is unclear," Gup wrote. ". . . The installation only made sense if the planners anticipated evacuating Congress many hours, if not days, before a crisis turned from rhetoric to attack. Yet mobilizing 535 members of Congress and evacuating them to a resort area 250 miles away in the middle of a crisis would almost certainly draw unwanted attention to the site." The *Washington Post Magazine* article quoted former speaker of the House Tip O'Neill, who recalled being briefed on evacuation plans. "Jesus, you don't think I am going to run away and leave my wife?" O'Neill said. "That's the craziest thing I ever heard of."

For the Greenbrier, the end of the government relationship was difficult. The bunker attracts tourists, but not enough to make up for the loss of government income.* And after all, in the absence of an immediate threat, who really needs a nuclear bunker? It turns out,

---

* The government made annual payments to the Greenbrier for use of the facility.

however, that some people do. With fears of terrorism and natural disaster, the bunker has found a new client: private companies. On our tour, Walls firmly instructed us not to take pictures in the tunnel—her explanation was that the Greenbrier's bunker was now a storage site for private companies seeking to house documents and records. She also barred us, without explanation, from taking pictures of the engine room. From critical elected leaders to critical paperwork, Greenbrier's role in national security was still alive.

While the Greenbrier bunker went dark, Site R in Pennsylvania experienced something of a rebirth. These days, Pentagon bureaucrats routinely disappear from their desks and tell their families they're "going TDY" (on temporary duty) in Pennsylvania. They are, in fact, probably no more than an hour's drive from home. But while on duty at Site R—or staying at a designated hotel in nearby Gettysburg—they are standing by in case of Armageddon. Life for the bureaucrats is far from luxurious. According to military analyst William Arkin, a government handbook on bunker life directs those heading out to Site R to bring two changes of clothing, "combination lock, flashlight, two towels and a small box of washing powder." Living quarters may also be tight, he notes. "In the event of an emergency, officials expect Site R to be so crowded that the dormitory's three-tiered bunk beds will be assigned in 12-hour shifts."

After several months of silence from the Pentagon, we realized that if we wanted to visit Site R, we were going to have to go on our own—without any sort of official sanction. A few months after receiving our helpful information packet on the site, we headed out on what would be the final leg of our bunker tour. Armed with exact directions (and even the shuttle schedule from local hotels in case we cared to stay overnight), we packed camera equipment, notebooks, and some water in the car and headed north to visit Site R.

In winter, the foliage on Raven Rock Mountain is sparse, which made it easier to catch a glimpse of the complex through the trees. Raven Rock Mountain itself is hard to miss: A communications mast, painted red and white, is perched atop the peak. The Army's 114th Signal Battalion (the "Signal Masters of the Rock"), a unit based out of nearby Fort Detrick, ran Site R until 2001, when it was transferred to the Military District of Washington.

"We call it the underground Pentagon," said the bartender at the Ott House, an unpretentious, wood-paneled bar in Emmitsburg, just a few miles down the road from Site R. "Everyone knows where it is." In fact, everyone knew someone who had been inside, she told us. Her father, for instance, worked as a construction contractor there. And on weekends, federal employees assigned to staff Site R frequently come down the road to Emmitsburg for burgers and beer. Sometimes tourists looking for Camp David, the nearby presidential retreat, stumble upon the place as well.

The existence of Site R is not classified. According to the security guidance issued to federal employees—and sent to us as part of the conference information package—the existence, location, and basic mission of Site R is "unclassified/FOUO" (for official use only), a designation that is used to suggest a level of official secrecy but is merely a handling designation. Things like specific functions, design details, and a listing of the agencies housed inside, however, are marked "confidential." The most sensitive information concerning Site R— actual planning assumptions, vulnerabilities, and continuity-of-operations plans—is classified as "secret."

From the intersection of Route 16 and Harbaugh Valley Road, we could see several pickup trucks parked next to an array of satellite dishes. A bit further on was the low-slung concrete facade of the tunnel entrance. A compact, pale-brick structure—what appeared to be the facility security building—sat just past the main entrance. Further along, and beyond view, were the main portals to the bunker.

We stopped across from the main entrance, pulling into the stone chapel parking lot. We debated briefly the meaning and interpretation of the warning signs posted on the fence surrounding the installation, and whether the federal government could really prevent us from standing on the side of a public road, taking notes and pictures of the outer perimeter. Other reporters, who have made it as far as the guard post, have been warned that describing security or other details could result in fines or jail time. According to the Reporters Committee for Freedom of the Press, in 2000 two photographers on assignment for the *New York Times Magazine* were arrested for trespassing after taking pictures of Site R from private property. After debating the pros and cons, we decided to give it a try, for no other reason than to see what would happen. So long as we stayed on the public road, we could argue we were on the right side of the law. For the next fifteen minutes, we stood outside, taking notes and snapping pictures. Cars passed by, but no one stopped.

According to the conference materials we were sent, visitors spending a night inside the bunker pass the main checkpoint, where Pentagon Police Department officers look them up on the access roster and issue a temporary visitor badge. They proceed to the security building, where they are provided instructions on where to go for billeting. Inside the mountain complex, all cameras, cell phones, laptops, pagers, and PDAs are prohibited. Those items must be left at the hotel. Bringing approved government equipment in or out of the complex requires a sheaf of paperwork. Luckily, not everything at Site R is about restrictions and security. First on the conference agenda were cocktails.

The conference agenda also promised participants a tour of a HEMP construction site (a significant amount of seminar discussion was devoted to "HEMP technologies"). It sounded like a hydroponic growing scheme going on deep underground, but HEMP, in this case, stood for "high-altitude electromagnetic pulse": a nuclear burst high in the atmosphere that would destroy vulnerable electronic equipment. The phenomenon was first observed during the era of atmospheric testing, when a high-altitude nuclear test in the South Pacific—code-named Starfish Prime—short-circuited electrical equipment, set off burglar alarms, and interrupted radio and television transmissions in Hawaii, over eight hundred miles away. The notion that some enemy could launch an attack that would zero out electronics, instantly crippling the high-tech U.S. military, became a fixation for military planners. During the Cold War, major weapons had to be hardened against EMP. In recent years, military planners have expressed concern about EMP weapons—devices specifically built to destroy electronics.*

---

* Long a fixture of science fiction, EMP has become a favorite threat discussed among national security circles and by Republican defense hawks like former Pennsylvania representative Curt Weldon and Maryland representative Roscoe Bartlett. A congressionally funded EMP commission in 2004 named EMP strikes as "one of a small number of threats that can hold our society at risk of catastrophic consequences." It warned that "rogue states" such as North Korea or Iran could develop the capability to deliver a crippling EMP strike against the United States that would destroy the electrical grid and leave the country defenseless.

We got back in the car and decided to see how easy it would be to find another entrance to the facility. Operating without a map, we drove along the main road, following the outer perimeter fence to the opposite side of the mountain; guided by the terrain, we headed up a winding rural road lined with modest, well-maintained houses, most flying the American flag. Within a few minutes, we came upon the rear entrance to the facility, a chain-link gate fortified by a concrete pillbox. Here the security was more visible, and a resident working in his front yard looked up at our car as we circled through the dead-end road, pausing this time only for a minute or two to snap pictures.

Few details were available about what lay beyond those gates and, more importantly, inside the mountain. A *Pittsburgh Post-Gazette* article describes "six-stories of underground offices, subterranean water reservoir, and banks of mysterious antennas, dishes and massive, steel doors." Author James Bamford writes of "a secret world of five buildings, each three stories tall, computer filled caverns and a sub-terranean water reservoir." From our conference materials we knew more about what the mountain contained, but even the best telephoto lens could provide no picture of the interior. Our conference program offered intriguing hints of additional construction. A panel titled "Mining & Roof Bolts—Gorilla Rock Update" had been led by two miners, hinting that new excavation might be taking place deep inside the mountain. Site R, once on the edge of closure, might now even be expanding.

Underground worlds, once created, take on a life of their own, something that writer Tom Vanderbilt describes as the "architecture of conspiracy," an enduring legacy of the Cold War: "The subterranean state and the black budget created a world without walls and without boundaries . . . and, in the absence of visible lines of power, the paranoid draftsman steps in, sketching an Escher-like world of inter-locking secret tunnels and furtive conduits of power." We imagined, somewhere inside the mountain, the lively debates of the bunker managers plotting out new underground worlds, discussing the best ways to filter air, carve tunnels, and stockpile food. William Arkin, a longtime follower of nuclear battle plans, calls many of these plans inane, and yet, the government feels compelled, even now, to keep digging. "On a philosophical level, that's the point," he told us. "It doesn't end."

When Ted Gup first revealed the existence of the Greenbrier bunker, it was clear that some in government had begun questioning the practicality of the bunker—and the cost to the taxpayer of maintaining it. The bunker existed for as long as it did because of the secrecy that protected it, not just from the Soviet Union (which had dissolved by the time Gup exposed it), but also from public scrutiny, which would have undoubtedly raised questions about the sense of maintaining a luxury bunker for occupants who would have been vaporized long before they could have reached its doors. By the end, the secrecy was an end unto itself, protecting the bunker for the bunker's sake.

What, then, is the future of these netherworlds? The United States largely abandoned its systems of civil defense shelters in 1992. The Greenbrier bunker is now primarily a nostalgia trip, and Cheyenne Mountain is weighing its future as a nuclear version of Disney. Yet continuity-of-operations plans move forward, and not just in Pennsylvania. After the terrorist attack of September 11, the Department of Homeland Security began offering grants to cities for projects to protect populations against weapons of mass destruction. Some cities took this as carte blanche to reinvigorate their Cold War shelters; Huntsville, Alabama, added a massive cave to its plans for civil defense. "Unlike the fallout shelters set up during the Cold War, the new ones will not be stocked with water, food or other supplies," an Associated Press article on the plan noted. "For survivors of a nuclear attack, it would be strictly 'BYOE'—bring your own everything."

Touring the subterranean worlds of nuclear survival, it became clear to us that ordinary civilians were left out of the equation during the Cold War. And so it goes in the post–September 11 era. Beyond some lackluster advice (stock up on bottled water and duct tape) and a few public relations gimmicks ("September is National Preparedness Month!"), the U.S. government has committed few resources to ensuring the survival of the general population in case of some doomsday scenario. If the images of mayhem and panic in post–Hurricane Katrina New Orleans taught us anything, it's that evacuation in time of nuclear crisis would be chaotic at best, and government-designated shelter perhaps even worse. And even for government VIPs, it's not likely to be any better. "If something really happens, it doesn't matter how many facilities there are, [the government] won't be in control of what people do," Arkin told us. "That's the bottom line."

We paused for one last look at the outline of Site R. The security instructions given to the attendees of the bunker conference summed up the government's view. "Remember: The more the public knows about this facility, the more our adversaries do, and the more vulnerable we become." As we snapped our final pictures, we realized that a permanent government bureaucracy would always find a reason for digging. Standing by the tightly guarded entrance to the mountain complex, the true purpose of which is obscured from the public it is designed to protect, we couldn't help but think that perhaps the only thing Site R protected was its own existence.

CHAPTER 8

Rocket City, USA

Huntsville's Space Odyssey

On the morning of December 13, 2001, President George W. Bush made a short appearance in the Rose Garden to announce the United States' withdrawal from the Anti-Ballistic Missile Treaty with Russia. "Today, as the events of September the 11th made all too clear, the greatest threats to both our countries come not from each other, or other big powers in the world, but from terrorists who strike without warning, or rogue states who seek weapons of mass destruction," he said. "We know that the terrorists, and some of those who support them, seek the ability to deliver death and destruction to our doorstep via missile. And we must have the freedom and the flexibility to develop effective defenses against those attacks."

Initially, nuclear weapons were delivered by bombers lumbering through the skies and, like any aircraft, could be shot down. The advent of the ballistic missile changed the entire calculus: A nuclear attack with intercontinental ballistic missiles was nearly unstoppable. The ABM Treaty, adopted in 1972, helped preserve the Cold War's nuclear balance of terror by ensuring that neither the United States nor the Soviet Union would (with certain exceptions) deploy active defenses against ICBMs, thus guaranteeing mutual assured destruction. The treaty was seen as a landmark of arms control, limiting the need for new offensive nuclear weapons and reinforcing a key point of nuclear deterrence: The only defense against nuclear attack was massive retaliation.

The United States had tested and developed a number of ballistic missile defense systems, and the remnants of some of these Cold War programs still litter the landscape of North America. In the 1950s and 1960s, many U.S. cities were ringed by Nike missile emplacements, originally designed to shoot down Soviet bombers. After the Soviets tested the first ICBM in 1957, the Gaither Committee, an independent U.S. government panel, warned of an impending "missile gap" with the Soviet Union. Among other things, the Gaither Committee recommended more fallout shelters, accelerated work on ICBMs, and the development of an antiballistic missile system to protect Strategic Air Command bases. In due course this led to the Army's Nike Zeus program.

Nike Zeus didn't work particularly well. It was dangerous (each Nike Zeus interceptor carried a four-hundred-pound nuclear warhead that would go off near U.S. territory) and it was expensive. But congressional support kept the program going. By 1963, Nike Zeus had morphed into Nike-X, and a few years later Nike-X evolved into the Safeguard missile defense system, with its nuclear-armed Spartan and Sprint interceptors. One Safeguard system—designed to protect ICBM fields, not cities—was deployed in Grand Forks, North Dakota, in the late 1960s and early 1970s. While sanctioned by the ABM Treaty, the site was decommissioned in 1975. The Soviet Union, meanwhile, maintained a missile defense system around Moscow that was armed with nuclear-tipped interceptors.

By the late 1990s, the limits the ABM Treaty placed on the development and deployment of new missile defenses had become a rallying point for defense hawks. By scrapping the ABM Treaty, Bush signaled a major new commitment to pursuing ballistic missile defense technology and placed himself squarely behind the legacy of President Ronald Reagan, who in a 1983 speech had called for an ambitious national effort that would make nuclear weapons "impotent and obsolete."

However, the Bush administration would also have to find a way to disassociate itself from Reagan's Strategic Defense Initiative (SDI), mockingly dubbed Star Wars by its critics. Under President George H. W. Bush, SDI had foundered, as research efforts shifted away from defending against a massive Soviet missile attack to a less-ambitious program that would shield the United States from limited strikes.

President Bill Clinton was even less of a fan. After he took office, the Reagan-era Strategic Defense Initiative Organization (SDIO) underwent something of a shake-up. SDIO was rebranded as the Ballistic Missile Defense Organization (BMDO) in April 1993; more importantly, funding was slashed.

Still, missile defense never really went away. Clinton, who reluctantly agreed to continue funding the system his administration had inherited, spent around one billion dollars per year on national missile defense research. In the late 1990s, missile defense experienced something of a renaissance. Driven by Republican proponents in Congress, funding for national missile defense was revived.

Missile defense was given another boost in 1998, when Congress ordered Director of Central Intelligence George Tenet to appoint a Commission to Assess the Ballistic Missile Threat to the United States. The commission—better known as the Rumsfeld Commission, after its chairman, Donald Rumsfeld, a former secretary of defense under President Gerald Ford—raised the alarm over the threat posed to the United States by "rogue regimes" armed with ballistic missiles. "Ballistic missiles armed with WMD payloads pose a strategic threat to the United States," the commission wrote. "This is not a distant threat." Six weeks later—as if on cue—North Korea tested a three-stage Taepodong intermediate-range missile that passed over Japan, alarming the U.S. intelligence community. In 1999, Congress passed the National Missile Defense Act, which committed the government to fielding missile defense as soon as it was technologically feasible.

Before George W. Bush took office, Republicans realized they would have to present missile defense a bit differently, shedding the old Star Wars associations of ill-conceived technology. Missile defense was easily lampooned as Reagan's naïve dream, a technologically immature system. The Bush administration's strategy was to develop a "layered" ballistic missile defense system focused on ground-based interceptors, rather than space-based weapons. Other elements included Navy ships reconfigured as missile shooters and sophisticated new sensors, along with a futuristic laser weapon that could shoot down a missile in the vulnerable first phase of flight.

Some of the old Reagan-era Star Wars concepts—such as space-based interceptors known as Brilliant Pebbles—were still in circulation, but they had no real funding. The X-ray laser—which would have been pumped by a thermonuclear weapon—was not even discussed. The old SDI vision of space-based weapons was discarded, and the newly reminted Missile Defense Agency (MDA) would give new life to a community of rocket scientists and find a new purpose for the missile business. What was it about missile defense that, after all the years, failed tests, and canceled systems, kept the idea alive? We hoped to find the answer in Huntsville.

Like the atomic bomb, the ballistic missile traces its origins back to World War II, when a team of German scientists led a crash research-and-development effort to build the V-2 rocket. Rocketry developed in parallel with the nuclear complex, and much as Los Alamos was the birthplace of nuclear weapons, Huntsville, Alabama, where the German rocket scientists were brought to work after World War II, was the locus of U.S. efforts to develop the ICBM—and, later, to build a missile shield to defend against ICBMs. Huntsville, home to the Army's Redstone Arsenal, would be one of the main beneficiaries of new investment in missile defense. Though the city likes to emphasize its civilian space program, Huntsville's military researchers have been heavily involved in the development of missile defense, such as the Patriot air defense missile system.*

In preparing for our trip to Huntsville, however, we had been warned that the surviving German rocket scientists could be a bit press-shy. Of the original group of 118 German rocketry experts brought to the United States after World War II, only a handful were still alive. We were planning to attend the Space and Missile Defense Conference and Exhibition held annually in the city, but we also wanted to understand how a Southern cotton town had become synonymous with rocket science. In its early days, when the Germans were most influential, Huntsville was all about building rockets that would allow the United States to deliver a nuclear warhead anywhere in the world. German scientists had literally put Huntsville on the map, transforming the

---

* The effectiveness of the Patriot system in the 1991 Persian Gulf War may have been overstated. While the military claimed success in shooting down Scud missiles launched by Iraq, later analysis showed that the system's performance was less than spectacular.

sleepy town—once known as the "watercress capital of the world"—into Rocket City, a hub of missile and space technology.*

We planned our trip for August 2006, to correspond with the conference, which was held at the aptly named Von Braun Center (after the renowned rocket scientist Wernher von Braun). The onslaught of military contractors had already begun when we arrived. Local hotels were booked up, and the rental car agencies were turning away anxious customers. That influx of cash from defense contracts—Huntsville is also home to Army helicopter research—was on display the moment we stepped into the arrivals hall of Huntsville International Airport. We passed through a long arcade illuminated by advertisements for defense contractors ("Booz Allen Hamilton: complex issues, clear solutions"; "Honeywell: a tradition of commitment to the Army"; "I fly Sikorsky, because this is war"). In an era of declining NASA budgets, Huntsville had found new direction, and once again Rocket City was humming with activity.

On our first morning, we drove early to the U.S. Space and Rocket Center, located between downtown Huntsville and the airport, seeking relief from the wilting northern Alabama heat. Konrad Dannenberg arrived at the reception desk soon after, pushed in a wheelchair by Al Whitaker, the amiable head of public relations for the Space and Rocket Center. Despite assistance from Whitaker, Dannenberg looked quite fit, dressed in a smart white golf shirt embroidered with a patch that commemorated the first space shuttle flight. He removed a pair of oversize wraparound shades, revealing alert blue eyes, and introduced himself with a still-thick German accent.

Dannenberg was one of the last surviving veterans of Operation Paperclip, the top-secret postwar military effort that rounded up an elite group of German rocket scientists and sent them to the United States to prevent them from falling into Soviet hands. The prize catch was von Braun, who had designed the world's first ballistic missile. His maniacal belief in space travel would propel Huntsville to the front lines of rocket research, while his expertise would help the United States reach the moon less than a quarter century later.

---

* It was also known by the name "Hunsville," a less-than-polite reference to the German rocket scientists.

Our first contact with one of the aging scientists had not been encouraging. "I will be ninety-three years old this year, and age is taking its toll," Ernst Stuhlinger, a rocket scientist originally from Niederrimbach, Germany, told us, when we called him from Washington. Mid-August was not the best time, he explained. His children were visiting that week. He politely suggested we contact him again in a few months. He left us, however, with a bit of wisdom: "Von Braun said, 'We talk all the time about space, but our real problem is time.'"

Von Braun died in 1977, and Huntsville is protective of its dwindling community of elderly scientists. Whitaker had told us the Germans were becoming more reluctant to do interviews; too many journalists had asked uncomfortable questions about World War II. Von Braun, after all, had been Hitler's top rocket scientist, designing the A-4 ballistic missile—better known as the V-2 or Vergeltungswaffen-2 (Vengeance Weapon 2)—at the Peenemünde research center on the Baltic Sea. While his admirers liked to highlight von Braun's heroic contribution to the Apollo space program, they could never quite shake questions about his SS commission or the role of slave labor at the V-2 production facility.

But Dannenberg, who had just turned ninety-four, had said he would be happy to meet with us. His wife, Jackie—an avid equestrian—would be out at the blacksmith's on the morning before the conference, and Dannenberg could give us a personal tour of the U.S. Space and Rocket Center.

The teenager manning the reception desk sprang up to greet Dannenberg, who occasionally came to the museum to read stories to children. Before leaving us alone, Whitaker laid down Jackie's deadline: "I promised his wife we'd wrap this up no later than two o'clock." We wheeled Dannenberg out the back entrance of the museum to a pavilion overlooking the rocket garden, the center's panoramic display of missiles.

It was a brilliant August morning, and Dannenberg put his shades back on to give us our guided tour. Pointing with his cane, he traced the parallel evolution of military rocket design and civilian space exploration. The Space and Rocket Center had an impressive collection, from the U.S. Army's Redstone and Jupiter-C rockets to the massive Saturn launch vehicles used to send astronauts to the moon. A full-size replica of the *Apollo 11* Saturn V rocket towered over the collection; further back was an actual Saturn V launch vehicle, cut into sections and lying ignominiously on its side. The Saturn V was never designed to withstand outdoor storage in Huntsville's harsh, muggy climate, and a family of raccoons had taken up residence inside the fuselage. The center had embarked on construction of a new exhibition space on the other side of the park to house and preserve the rocket, selling bags of "Saturn V Coffee" as part of its fund-raising campaign.

Born in 1912 in Weissenfels, south of Leipzig, Dannenberg joined an amateur rocket society in Hanover during his youth. His early interest in rocketry probably saved his life. He was drafted into the German army in 1939, serving in an antitank unit until 1940, when he was released from military service to work at von Braun's Peenemünde design bureau. His company was subsequently sent to the eastern front—but Dannenberg, by virtue of his rocket hobby, was saved from a veritable death sentence. "Rocketry managed to get me out of the army and get me to Peenemünde, because they had the high priority," he said. "And without that priority . . . I probably would not have made it. My company went eventually to Moscow, and I know of only one person who came back . . . they were all decimated."

At Peenemünde, Dannenberg worked under Walter Thiel, a rocket engine specialist. Dannenberg concentrated on developing a simplified engine intended for V-2 production. The V-2 was Hitler's second "vengeance weapon," preceded by the V-1 flying bomb, a pulse-jet-powered missile dubbed the "buzz bomb" or "doodlebug." Dannenberg showed us a V-1 fuselage, painted the bright yellow of a Marshmallow Peep and mounted on a pedestal. The diminutive aircraft—a sort of early cruise missile—was dwarfed by the rocket collection in the park. The V-1 had a small propeller mounted on its front, not to power its flight but to serve as a measuring instrument. After a certain number of rotations, the power plant would switch off and the V-1 would dive to its target.* "Of course, it was a very inaccurate vehicle, also as the V-2 was at that time," Dannenberg explained. "Von Braun had not had a chance to make all the changes that we had originally planned."

---

* Hanna Reitsch, a renowned German aviator, resolved some of the guidance and control problems in the V-1 by actually piloting a version of the aircraft in a daring test flight.

Von Braun's chance to make those changes to the V-2 design would come after the war, when the German scientists were brought to the United States as part of Operation Paperclip. Dannenberg was first sent to work at Fort Bliss, Texas; he later moved to Alabama to work on the Redstone and Jupiter missiles for the Army. The Redstone, a direct descendant of the V-2 design, incorporated all the design advances von Braun and his team had originally planned for the V-2 but were not able to realize in the wartime rush to production.

More than just the follow-on to the V-2, the Redstone proved a much more lethal weapon. The V-2 carried a one-ton (one-thousand-kilogram) high-explosive payload; the Redstone was designed to carry a thermonuclear warhead. As we wheeled him past the static display of a Redstone in its olive-drab paint, Dannenberg recalled another interesting historical footnote. "You know that von Braun had the idea to use the Redstone vehicle with some solid propellant stages on top of it to launch a satellite—and he proposed it even before the Russians launched the Sputnik," Dannenberg said. "But Eisenhower, the at-the-time president, was not really in favor—particularly of the Redstone, knowing that it was designed by a German team, and he wanted the Americans to make their own."

The United States would pay for slighting German rocket expertise. The Navy had been tasked with building the Vanguard missile, which, as Dannenberg noted with some professional pride, failed several times. Von Braun finally received permission to do what the German rocketeers had proposed earlier, using a modified Redstone with solid propellants on top (a rocket designated the Juno-I) to launch the Explorer-I satellite. The first U.S. manned space flight—a suborbital flight by Alan Shepard—was also launched atop a modified Redstone.*

Dannenberg, in essence, was repeating the official narrative. Von Braun wanted to use his rockets for peaceful space exploration. And sure, the Redstone could be adapted to loft an astronaut or a satellite

---

* In parallel, another group of German scientists was working in the Soviet Union. They had also been whisked out of Germany, to help the Soviets get a jump start on the nuclear arms race. In Russia, the Germans also worked from a V-2 design, an effort that would yield a modern weapon known as the Scud missile. The use of the Scud ballistic missile by Iraq in the 1991 Persian Gulf War would later spur renewed calls for missile defense, and once again Huntsville would owe its future—and its funding—to the Germans.

into space. But the multiple-stage rocket designs that grew out of the V-2 program also paved the way for the weapon that would ultimately transform the nuclear arsenal, the intercontinental ballistic missile. Von Braun's designers at Peenemünde, in fact, had worked out a paper design for a long-range, multiple-stage missile late in the war. While the Peenemünders later insisted the rocket was designed for space transportation, the design was dubbed the Amerika rocket—because it would have had sufficient range to reach the United States.

But ICBMs and missile defense are not subjects the German rocket scientists like to discuss. Our few attempts to bring up weapons with Dannenberg were politely but hastily dismissed. Journalist Ken Silverstein experienced a similar reticence when he interviewed Ernst Stuhlinger a few years prior. "Stuhlinger spoke proudly of helping send men to the moon and predicted that the United States will one day succeed in landing astronauts on Mars," Silverstein wrote in *Mother Jones*. "But when I asked him for his opinion of missile-defense programs, the garrulous old scientist suddenly clammed up." Stuhlinger eventually told Silverstein that he was skeptical of the administration's missile defense plans.

While missile defense and nuclear weapons were of little interest to him, Dannenberg talked at length about the space program. He joined NASA's Marshall Space Flight Center as deputy manager of the Saturn program, eventually receiving a NASA medal for his work on the rockets that successfully reached the moon. But he also took great pride in the breakthroughs achieved on the V-2 engine design. After our tour of the rocket park, Dannenberg brought us inside the museum, where he got up from his wheelchair to show us the inner workings of the V-2 engine in loving detail. Afterward, we took a break in the cafeteria. Over coffee, Dannenberg recalled the first successful V-2 launch, in 1942, his most memorable moment as a rocketeer. "I was still a designer at that time, and for that reason I was really personally involved with the V-2 engine," he said. "So the first successful V-2 launch is still my highlight—although I have seen many Redstone launches, Jupiter launches, Saturn launches, and shuttle launches."

More recently, Dannenberg had watched space entrepreneur Bert Rutan launch his suborbital rocket plane, *SpaceShipOne*. That, he conceded, had been quite impressive. But, he added, "again, I was not directly involved in building it, so it was not as good as the first V-2 launch—the first successful V-2 launch." In many ways, Dannenberg's memories reflected the same pride nuclear weapons designers had when recalling the successful test of a bomb they had helped build. But there had also been much more at stake for the V-2 team. The Peenemünde designers had seen two launch failures. A third failure would have meant cancellation of the whole project. And if the V-2 had been canceled, history would have been much different. Dannenberg believed there would have been no space program, no conquest of the moon, no satellites—and no ICBMs. "I think it would not even have happened," he said. "I don't think amateur groups are in the situation to build something like the V-2 or even-bigger vehicles like we build today."

Rocketry, in other words, might have remained the province of cranks and hobbyists, dreaming up schemes to fire rockets to deliver the mail or take aerial snapshots. Dannenberg's amateur rocket society would have been confined to dreams of space travel. There would have been no technological base from which to loft nuclear weapons across the globe. In Dannenberg's view, credit went to von Braun—not just for his scientific and organizational talent, but for his genius in getting money from the military. "In a way, it takes a special talent like von Braun to use the idea to not continue as an amateur—but to use the big funding that he could get from the government and to join the army," he said. "Particularly in the war in Germany, when power was scarce, when materials were scarce."

Von Braun maintained that his true goal was space flight. Reaching space, however, meant striking a few bargains along the way. Dannenberg said that von Braun and his army counterpart, Walter Dornberger, were able to "sell the program, to go to Berlin, to get the money, to negotiate with the air force." Working first for Hitler, then for the Americans, von Braun believed the military was only a means to an ultimate end of space travel.

It was well past noon, and we had promised Al Whitaker that we would drive Dannenberg home before his wife returned from the blacksmith. But Dannenberg clearly wasn't ready to go home. "Shall we go for lunch?" he suggested, pointing to a nearby Marriott hotel. "You've probably noticed I still like to talk about these things," he said. "[It's] a lot of fun."

Over lunch, we turned to more terrestrial matters. That same day, following a month of intense fighting, Israel and Hezbollah had concluded a cease-fire. During the conflict, Hezbollah had fired salvos of short-range Katyusha rockets into northern Israel; the militia had also struck with longer-range missiles, hitting the port city of Haifa. Israel had retaliated with air and artillery strikes, a naval blockade, and a ground invasion of southern Lebanon. News reports had featured graphic images of civilian casualties on both sides. Dannenberg expressed sympathy for the Lebanese. "You can't understand what a horrible thing war is unless you experience it," he said, pausing to take a bite of his grilled-chicken sandwich.

That Dannenberg would sympathize with the Lebanese was perhaps not surprising. Israel was retaliating for rocket strikes on its territory. During World War II, German rocket scientists had been targeted by Britain. A British bombing raid on Peenemünde in 1943 had killed his boss, Walter Thiel, along with Thiel's family.

Dannenberg seemed happy to continue on, but it was already well past the time we had promised to return him home. After a brief stop at a research park that was named after von Braun, where Dannenberg showed us a few historic photographs from Operation Paperclip, we drove him home through a development of new luxury houses just outside of Huntsville. This had been farm country, he told us. Only more recently had Huntsville seen a housing boom, and their rural life was being encroached upon by McMansions. At his house, he invited us to come in and visit. Jackie had not returned from the blacksmith's, so he gave us a tour.

Inside the Dannenberg home, there was no tribute to ICBMs or missile defense, just space memorabilia and NASA portraits. Their living room was a shrine to space travel. Dannenberg showed us a photograph of himself and his wife that had been carried aboard the space shuttle *Columbia* on a mission from April 4 to April 8, 1997. An astronaut had snapped a picture of the photo, which was placed against the porthole of the orbiter. Framed with a certificate of authenticity from NASA, it showed Dannenberg, medal around his neck, with Jackie, an attractive woman several decades his junior, in a sleeveless black dress.

For von Braun and the veterans of Paperclip, life had been a series of compromises in pursuit of the singular goal of space travel. Those compromises had meant working for the fascist regime in Germany and working for the U.S. military to develop missiles to counter the Soviet threat. Yet Huntsville's resident Germans maintained that it had always been peaceful space travel, not weapons, that had motivated them. Had it been worth it, we wondered? "We didn't just want to go to the moon; that's a part of the Earth's system," Dannenberg had told us earlier that day. "We might have stopped there on our way, but our plan was to go to Mars."

Dannenberg seemed reluctant for us to leave. There was more NASA memorabilia he could show us, more stories of von Braun to tell. But we suspected Jackie would be back soon, and it would be best if we were gone before she returned. We bid our good-byes and left Konrad and Jackie, floating in space.

The rocketry work—both military and civil—has long made Huntsville unique. The city boasts more engineers and Ph.D.s per capita than any other American city. Thanks in part to the Germans, it also has a decent symphony. Yet Huntsville's fortunes have always been linked to the whims of Washington, and periods of boom and bust have depended on the program du jour. In the 1960s it was Apollo; in the 1980s it was Star Wars. In the 1990s, when the "peace dividend" meant massive military cutbacks around the country, Huntsville scrambled to maintain its economic base. These days, however, Huntsville is experiencing a renaissance, most of it due to missile defense. Boeing, the prime contractor for the ground-based missile defense system, is expanding rapidly, hiring hundreds of engineers to fill positions for its burgeoning Huntsville operations. New businesses have sprung up in and around Huntsville to support the Missile Defense Agency (MDA), and even downtown Huntsville is reemerging from years of urban decay, with fusion restaurants opening next to hip coffee shops.

We stayed with family in nearby Decatur, part of the Huntsville metropolitan area and sometimes referred to as a "twin city." The mix of Southern values, military culture, and a driven engineering community made for some unique contrasts. TEAM JESUS bumper stickers adorned pickup trucks parked next to sleek European sedans sporting NASA decals. Driving to the missile defense conference, we listened to a local radio station, which featured an advertisement for the *Forward*, promising the best coverage of the Israel-Hezbollah conflict. It seemed a bit odd to hear a New York–based Jewish newspaper advertised in the

South, but in fact, Alabama has always boasted strong ties to Israel, and U.S.-Israeli missile defense cooperation is particularly close. The United States, for instance, provided significant funds for Israel's own missile defense program, called Arrow.

On the first morning of the conference, we drove to the Von Braun Center, a convention hall that had hosted many big events in the past, from performances of *Annie* and the "world famous" Lipizzaner stallions to concert appearances by Hank Williams Jr. and Hootie and the Blowfish. But for the 2006 Space and Missile Defense Conference and Exhibition, the place seemed to be at capacity; we had to park our rental car in an overflow lot several blocks away from the center. At the entrance to the main exhibit hall and auditorium, Huntsville police inspected our bags; a sign warned attendees that no weapons would be allowed in the facility. Security, even for a military conference, seemed unusually tight.*

The conference theme for the year was "Global Missions—Meeting the Challenge." The top speakers on the agenda included Lieutenant General Henry "Trey" Obering, the director of MDA, and Jeff Sessions, a Republican senator from Alabama and a staunch advocate of missile defense spending. Obering received a particularly warm round of applause as he took the podium. The agency was relocating the majority of its positions to Huntsville, while keeping its headquarters in Washington. That would mean over twenty-two hundred new jobs for the city, not counting all the defense contractors that would arrive to provide services for the agency.

The huge auditorium was brimming with attendees—a mix of men in their fifties dressed in dark suits and somewhat younger men and women in military uniform. We settled down in seats in the back to hear Obering, a trim, graying Air Force general, set the tone for the conference with a speech that outlined the urgent need for building new missile defenses. The pulsating background music and crowded room gave the place the intense feeling of a megachurch. Only instead of fire and brimstone, it was rockets and missiles. "We are facing a real threat," he said in a grave, measured monotone. "It is one that is growing."

---

* Security the following year would be even more restrictive. At the 2007 conference, a zealous FBI agent would confiscate a Dictaphone from an *Aviation Week & Space Technology* reporter.

As proof, Obering pointed to recent headlines. On July 5, 2006, North Korea had conducted a series of missile tests, including the launch of a long-range Taepodong-2. That missile had failed after less than a minute, but the North Korean flight tests had alarmed defense officials. Some analysts believed the Taepodong-2 had the potential range to reach Alaska. "Millions of Americans woke up to the fact that missile threats are real and we have to do something about those," said Obering as he clicked briskly through his PowerPoint presentation. Luckily, there was salvation.

Obering then cued up a video, an arresting three-minute trailer for a slick, thirty-minute film called *A Day in the Life of the Missile Defense System*. The short film had a pulsating *Top Gun*–style sound track, with a professional voice-over artist who intoned lines about "saving lives and protecting freedom." To a casual observer, *A Day in the Life of the Missile Defense System* lent the impression that the United States had already achieved the extraordinary, shielding Alaska, Hawaii, and the Lower 48 with an interlocking and layered series of missile defenses: missiles buried in silos in Alaska and California; Aegis ships equipped with ballistic missile interceptors in the Pacific; and Patriot batteries on standby, ready to shoot down any short-range missile threat. It seemed, at least according to the video, that Ronald Reagan's vision of shielding the United States from nuclear attack was now closer than ever.

The reality was a bit less impressive. Following President Bush's directive to begin deployment of a layered missile defense system, MDA began actual fielding of a limited system in 2004 with the emplacement of a handful of ground-based interceptors at Fort Greely, Alaska. Missile defense capabilities would be added in two-year increments, or "blocks." Block 2004 included early versions of the ground-based interceptors, Aegis ballistic missile defense ships, Patriot PAC-3 missiles, and some command-and-control equipment; Block 2006 would build upon the existing system by adding improved interceptors, deploying a powerful new X-band radar, and upgrading the system's software. But the system was a long way from the stated goal of defending the United States and its allies against enemy ballistic missiles launched from any point on the globe and in any phase of a missile's trajectory. At the time, the actual ground-based interceptors had a spotty record of hitting incoming missiles.

Years of problems (or in Pentagonese, "challenges") had left their mark. Instead of making grandiose promises of a leak-proof shield, as SDI once had, MDA advertised that it sought a "limited" defense against a "rogue" nation; i.e., North Korea or Iran. Countering the thousands of ICBMs owned by Russia was unthinkable. "It was to be a start," Obering said. "It's not to be an end-all."

In addition to the ground-based interceptors, MDA was also testing a sea-based system, Aegis Ballistic Missile Defense, that was supposed to be able to counter short- and medium-range ballistic missiles. The Navy planned to equip eighteen ships with the interceptors; MDA had tested the system with somewhat better results than the Army's ground-based missiles. Both the ground- and sea-based interceptors were "hit to kill" systems. Their missiles carried no explosive payload; rather, sophisticated sensors guided the interceptor's "kill vehicle" to the target, destroying the incoming warhead by force of impact. It was, as often described, like a bullet hitting a bullet.

MDA had claimed a number of successful hit-to-kill intercepts in tests, but there had also been costly test snafus, such as a flight test from Fort Greely in February 2005, when an interceptor missile failed to take off after the machinery that held the missile in place wouldn't retract. Critics claimed even the successes proved little, pointing to the scripted nature of the ballistic missile defense tests, which included a GPS "beacon" that signaled the location of the target missile to the interceptor.* Perhaps an even bigger problem was decoys; they were easy and cheap to build, and it wasn't clear whether the defensive system would ever be able to reliably distinguish real warheads from fakes.

Adding to the controversy, MDA was planning even more ambitious upgrades to the missile defense shield. Ground-based interceptors were designed primarily to hit targets in the "midcourse" phase of flight, when the enemy missile has already exited the atmosphere, but MDA also sought weapons that could hit a threat missile in the "boost" phase, shortly after launch, when an enemy missile is most vulnerable. MDA had funded two futuristic boost-phase efforts, the Airborne Laser (an enormous chemical laser mounted on a modified Boeing 747) and

---

* While testers insisted the beacon was not used to guide the actual kill vehicle— the "bullet" that would strike the incoming warhead—they had a hard time explaining how the test reflected real-world conditions.

Kinetic Energy Interceptors (high-speed missile launchers) that would be deployed to a region of potential conflict in the event of impending attack. The costs of both systems were quickly mounting.

During the conference, John Rood, a boyish-looking official from the National Security Council, articulated the president's vision of missile defense, delivering an upbeat message. Rood, described by *Washington Post* reporter Dafna Linzer as part of the National Security Council's "Sesame Street Generation," belonged to a coterie of young Republicans who had grown up in an era of unquestioned U.S. supremacy. The United States, in their view, didn't need to be encumbered by treaties and arms control. Missile defense, for this group, was a symbol of unilateral defense and a measure of progress. Rood, in fact, had spent much of his time in the White House helping dismantle the 1972 ABM Treaty.

Just a few short years ago, Rood told the audience, Fort Greely had been on the base closure list; no interceptors were on alert at Vandenberg Air Force Base; the sea-based X-band radar was just a concept; and Aegis ships were not equipped to serve as missile defense shooters. And where there was not a single ground-based interceptor site five years ago, the U.S. government was now beginning discussions over a third interceptor site in Europe. Perhaps the biggest change, he continued, was the United States' withdrawal from the ABM Treaty. "We had all sorts of quotes from critics that the sky would fall if we left the ABM Treaty, and no one even mentions this anymore because nothing happened—it went away with a whimper," Rood told Linzer. "Not being encumbered with all this baggage from the Cold War is a huge advantage."

Russia, in fact, had initially responded to the scrapping of the ABM Treaty with a shrug. But the United States' near-messianic belief in missile defense was gradually pushing it toward greater confrontation with Russia as the Bush administration pursued the third interceptor site, in Eastern Europe. In early 2007, the administration announced plans to base missile defense assets in Poland and the Czech Republic. If agreement with the two countries was reached, the United States would station up to ten ground-based interceptors in Poland and place a radar system in the Czech Republic. The interceptors, MDA officials explained, were intended to counter rogue regimes in the Middle East—in other words, Iran.

Public opinion, however, was deeply divided in both Eastern European countries over the presence of U.S. missile defense sites. Even in strongly pro-American Poland, there was a growing sense that the United States was dictating the terms on missile defense, rather than making a concerted effort to explain why the sites would be in Poland's national interest. And Russian officials were strongly opposed to the positioning of U.S. missile defense assets in the former Warsaw Pact countries; Colonel General Vladimir Popovkin, the commander of Russia's space forces, described the U.S. plans for Eastern Europe as an "obvious threat" to Russia.

The Russian argument was a bit of a stretch. The Russians had enough ballistic missiles to easily overwhelm the nascent ballistic missile defenses. And MDA pointed out that Poland was the wrong place to station interceptors if you wanted to take down Russian ICBMs, which were programmed to take the shortest route to the United States—over the North Pole. But the United States' casual disregard for the "Cold War baggage" of treaties and arms control agreements in pursuit of missile defense had pushed Russia to a more aggressive military posture in Europe. In April 2007, Russian president Vladimir Putin announced a moratorium on Russian participation in the 1990 Treaty on Conventional Armed Forces in Europe, an agreement that kept caps on nonnuclear forces in Europe. It seemed the United States was taking a major strategic gamble: antagonizing Russia (which was a major nuclear power) by deploying nascent missile defenses (which had not been fully tested) to defend against Iranian nuclear weapons (which had not yet been built).

North Korea had not perfected a missile that could even reach Alaska; Iran was further from developing a ballistic missile even remotely capable of striking the continental United States. And yet the United States was investing in missile defense at a rate of almost ten billion dollars a year.

By 2006, missile defense was more than just a multibillion-dollar investment in interceptors; it was an outward expression of a particular type of politics. President Bush's push for national missile defense appealed to a certain kind of conservative, particularly those with a deep belief in Fortress America. It was a vision that favored military power and unilateral action over treaties and international consensus. For true believers in this vision, missile defense was more than just a military technology or weapon; it was an article of faith.

On the final day of the conference in Huntsville, we sat down to talk with Riki Ellison in a small bar behind the auditorium. The space, which had been set up as a pressroom, had an odd, psychedelic decor, with the added touch of overflowing bowls of candy and drinks supplied by the defense companies. Ellison was the head of the Missile Defense Advocacy Alliance (MDAA), a nonprofit group whose mission was to educate the public on the need for missile defense. Like Huntsville, Ellison had an unusual history. While playing football at the University of Southern California in the early 1980s, he blew out his knees several times and didn't expect to get picked up for the National Football League. So he started taking classes in international affairs and Soviet politics.

In March 1983, Ronald Reagan made his famous "Star Wars" speech, and Ellison got hooked on missile defense. He became a protégé of William Van Cleave, a professor of international relations at the University of Southern California and a onetime arms control negotiator who had worked as a defense adviser to Reagan during his presidential campaign. A member of the Committee on the Present Danger, a hardline group that had formed in the 1970s to alert the public to what it saw as a growing Soviet threat to the United States, Van Cleave had been an early enthusiast of missile defense technologies and had helped drive through Reagan's massive defense spending increase. So Ellison was groomed early on for his missile defense advocacy.

But much to his surprise, Ellison was drafted by the San Francisco 49ers in the fifth round of the NFL draft. He still didn't expect his professional football career to last, so he interned with various aerospace and defense firms in the off season, helping Lockheed Martin market its Exo-atmospheric Re-entry Interceptor Subsystem, a ground-based interceptor developed for SDI. After winning three Super Bowl rings, Ellison made missile defense his life.

The broad-shouldered ex-athlete was a bit tired from the conference—his knees weren't so good these days, he complained—but he was upbeat after several days of optimistic news on the missile defense front. He greeted us cordially—for a former linebacker, he had a surprisingly delicate handshake—and we settled into one of the plush, leather-upholstered booths.

Ellison wasn't the first celebrity to enter the missile defense arena. Jeff "Skunk" Baxter, a former member of the Doobie Brothers, actually made an even stranger career transition, to working on classified studies for MDA. Ellison, on the other hand, was focused on public support. As head of MDAA, he was well connected to the missile defense establishment. He was given access to the heavily restricted missile defense tests and would know details of their successes or failures long before MDA publicly released them to the press or to Congress. But his main job was as an evangelizer working to convince the public that the country needed missile defense. Ironically, his polls consistently found that most Americans believed the United States already had a working system in place to protect them from nuclear attack.*

Not everything was rosy, however. The newest concern for missile defense was establishing an interceptor site in Europe. If MDA didn't get around to spending the money on stationing interceptors overseas, Ellison said, it would be "very difficult" to convince Congress to part with that money at a later date. And convincing Europeans to host missile defense sites would not be easy. While the United States said that the missiles in Poland would protect continental Europe, most Europeans did not see the same threat from rogue states armed with ballistic missiles as the United States envisioned. Ellison hoped they might still come around. Like General James Cartwright, the head of U.S. Strategic Command, he had been reading Thomas Friedman. Ellison said, "Because the world is flat—the global economy—any strike on any city, whether it's here or there, will hurt everybody."

Friedman's globalization theories, it seemed, were becoming the guide for nuclear strategy in the twenty-first century. But there was another reason for Ellison's urgent evangelizing. President Bush would eventually leave office, and by mid-2007 negotiations were only just getting under way with the Czech Republic and Poland. Missile defense enthusiasts were privately concerned that if no deal were reached on new interceptor sites in Eastern Europe before the end of his term, they would never happen.

---

* In a 2005 survey of Arizona voters, for instance, MDAA found that 61 percent of respondents believed the United States already had a missile defense—versus 33 percent who correctly answered that there was not yet such a system.

Ellison was careful to avoid partisanship. After all, the "burn rate" at the time in Iraq and Afghanistan was around eight billion dollars per month and climbing; cutting missile defense would be an easy way to pay the bills. He knew that for missile defense to survive beyond one administration, it would have to have at least some support from both parties. He noted, for example, that he had recently briefed Senator Hillary Clinton's staff. He had also sought meetings with powerful critics of missile defense funding, such as Senator Dianne Feinstein. If the next administration were Democratic, he said, he was confident that missile defense would have enough inertia to sustain itself. "It's here to stay," he said with assurance.

But would Ellison be happy with a limited missile defense? Back in the 1980s, Reagan had called on scientists to develop new technology that would make nuclear weapons irrelevant. But the soaring rhetoric had given way to less-ambitious plans of developing a small, limited— but expensive—system that could counter a threat from terrorists or rogue nations. "It's been a transformation," he said, "because for all the old boys—the old-school 'beat the Russians'—missile defense was primarily to take on the Russians and defeat their missiles. This was really the core of the Reagan system, [and] now it's a small, limited system to take out terrorist attacks."

But Ellison was unperturbed that missile defense had quite literally fallen to earth. "The fact is that if we have a deployed system that functionally works, [it's] going to deter the proliferation of these systems," he continued, referring to the countries that sought to enter the ballistic missile club. "And I think the key thing for everybody is that these countries are not going to invest in a system that's going to be defeated. So that's a pretty big deal if you can do that."

The timing was good, too, he pointed out. North Korea's launch of a ballistic missile the month before the conference helped demonstrate the importance of missile defense. Just a few years ago, this was a small, rather poorly attended event of missile defense officials reminiscing about the Reagan-era peace shield. But the dramatic growth in missile defense spending—and President Bush's renewed focus on the issue— had revived the conference, and arguably, the city of Huntsville. The conference, Ellison noted, had been a great success. "I think it has a lot to do with the Alabama delegation and the support here in Huntsville," he said.

That the missile defense system had not yet proved it could hit even a single missile under realistic conditions did not seem to bother Ellison. And after all, Rocket City had always been a city of dreams and believers. There were those, like Wernher von Braun, who believed that man's destiny was Mars and those, like Ellison and others at the conference, who believed that rockets—both offensive and defensive—could somehow guarantee U.S. security. The Paperclip veterans had tied their space dreams to the Pentagon's goals. The rocket men might have reached the moon, but Mars was still far away. The adherents of missile defense, who once dreamed of a space-based peace shield, had to settle for a few dozen interceptors in the ground. We wondered what von Braun, had he been alive, would have thought about his end of the bargain. For Ellison, it had worked out quite well.

"It's been a great ride," Ellison said, reflecting on his professional evolution from football star to missile defense cheerleader. "I've actually been there from the beginning, from where it was just dreams and the SDI program—which was just space based—and now it's got some reality."

With the unshaken faith of a believer, he added, "It's got to work."

CHAPTER 9

Fantasy Island

Vacationing in the Marshall Islands

Like many U.S. initiatives in the Marshall Islands, the plan began with the best of intentions. In April 2006, a small group of volunteers—many of them employees of the U.S. Army—released four endangered sea turtles into the waters off Kwajalein Atoll, an isolated military base in the remote western Pacific.

They and a handful of other turtles had grown up in captivity in a carefully tended man-made pond on the island of Kwajalein. People found some of them on the beach as hatchlings and raised them in aquariums and then, when they grew too large to be pets, placed them in the small turtle pond. Others were found injured and brought to the pond for rehabilitation.

Some might argue that the turtles' problems—even prior to their release—could be blamed on the Americans, who put them in captivity in the first place (a large sign over the turtle pond warned, in English and Marshallese, against feeding hot dogs to the turtles). On the other hand, the Americans cared deeply for the sea creatures. In case of a turtle emergency, residents were instructed to page Kwajalein Range Services (KRS), the government contractor that operates the base on behalf of the Army.

In either case, a local lobby to free the sea creatures got its way, and about half the turtles were to be released. Before they were returned to their ocean habitat, two of the turtles were fitted with GPS transmitters so conservationists could track their movements; each turtle also had a number placed on its carapace for identification purposes. The U.S. Embassy in the Marshall Islands, which put out a press release praising the volunteer effort as an example of U.S.-Marshallese cooperation, politely urged citizens of the Marshall Islands to let the four turtles swim unmolested. The government of the Republic of the Marshall Islands (RMI) also did its part. "These turtles would best serve the RMI by remaining free to live and reproduce in the ocean," its news release said. "The RMI/EPA requests any citizen catching one of these turtles to please release it."

The plan—despite the noble intentions—suffered one major flaw. What were beloved pets for Americans were also a traditional food of the Marshall Islanders. Shortly after their release, the GPS signals disappeared. The numbered turtles were never sighted. It was presumed, at least by the Americans, that the captive turtles—used to being fed and cared for by people—had been particularly vulnerable to capture and were more likely than not turned into someone's dinner.

In a sense, the turtles were emblematic of the troubled relationship that has tied the United States to the Marshall Islands for over sixty years. Good intentions (and sometimes not-so-good intentions) have left the islands in what local politicians sometimes call a "bad marriage" with the United States. After capturing the islands from Japan, the United States turned much of the area into a giant atomic proving ground, touching off a total of sixty-seven nuclear devices, including the first true hydrogen bomb, the Mike device, in 1952. The device—hundreds of times more powerful than the bombs that leveled Hiroshima and Nagasaki—vaporized the small island of Elugelab on Eniwetok Atoll.

The magnitude of nuclear testing in the Marshall Islands is astounding. The combined explosive power of the tests was over one hundred thousand kilotons, seventy-five times more than the total yield of all the nuclear tests in Nevada. The 1954 Castle Bravo test, involving the most powerful nuclear device detonated by the United States, had a yield of fifteen megatons, a thousand times greater than the Trinity test. Castle Bravo was also a radiological disaster, dispersing radioactive ash over the inhabited atolls of Rongerik, Rongelap, Utirik, and Ailinginae. A Japanese tuna boat, the *Daigo Fukuryu Maru*, had the bad fortune of sailing downwind from the test, and its crew members fell victim to radiation sickness; the boat's chief radio operator died a year later.

Hundreds of Marshallese had to be evacuated to Kwajalein. They had received no prior warning of the test.

For the people of the Marshall Islands, the consequences of atomic testing in the Pacific were extraordinary. Traditional communities were displaced by the tests; prolonged exposure to radiation created a legacy of illness and disease. The U.S. government acknowledged the impact of testing only belatedly. Decades later, mistrust still lingers and many Marshallese remain convinced they were little more than human guinea pigs in a U.S. government experiment.

The people of Bikini and Eniwetok atolls have continued to pursue compensation in U.S. courts, but the U.S. government is trying to get their case dismissed. The chances that the Marshall Islands will receive just compensation seem increasingly remote. But there is one card left to play, and that is Kwajalein. The Marshall Islands' only bargaining chip is the small—but essential—role Kwajalein continues to play in the U.S. nuclear arsenal. In the summer of 2007, we set off to see exactly what this outpost, once a key part of our nuclear complex, does today.

"Heading to Kwaj?" asked the burly man in the baseball cap. He spotted us lining up at Honolulu International Airport for the flight to the Marshall Islands. He extended a hand and introduced his wife, a petite blonde with tight curls. "You must be new—it's a small place, typically you know first-timers," he said. "What do you do?"

When we replied that we were journalists, the reaction was telling. "Oh," he said, taking a step back, as if a snake had crossed his path. "You're going to *Kwaj*?"

Kwajalein Atoll is in the flyover waters of the western Pacific, some twenty-one hundred miles southwest of Hawaii. The last series of nuclear tests in the Marshall Islands was conducted in 1958, but the U.S. military continues to use Kwajalein for nuclear target practice, lobbing intercontinental ballistic missiles—minus their live warheads—at the Kwajalein range, where a sophisticated array of radars, telemetry instruments, and optical sensors can track the missiles with great accuracy. The classified radars on the atoll form a critical link in the U.S. military's space surveillance network, and U.S. Army Kwajalein Atoll (referred to by everyone on the island by the acronym USAKA, pronounced "you sock-a") plays an important role in the development of missile defense.

Visitors to USAKA are unusual—for many years even family and friends of those living on Kwajalein weren't allowed to visit. Today, such visitors are still restricted and must be cleared on an individual basis. And journalists, well, they are almost unheard of. When we first called Bill Congo, the head of public affairs at the U.S. Army Space and Missile Defense Command, to request permission to visit Kwajalein, we thought we were asking for a standard tour of a military base. Instead, we got a long silence on the phone. "Yes, so, the nuclear issue, well . . . it's a rather sensitive topic," Congo said.

But after several more phone calls, we were told that we had been cleared to go.

Kwajalein is what is referred to in Army-speak as a GOCO—a government-owned, contractor-operated facility. And the departure lounge was packed with perfect specimens of those civilians who visit or work at such facilities. There was the bespectacled man in a button-down shirt, poring over a Government Accountability Office report; the engineer from Huntsville, Alabama, home of the U.S. Army Space and Missile Defense Command, in his Kwajalein baseball hat; and, boarding in first class, the man with a walrus mustache wearing a white T-shirt emblazoned with green letters in Arabic and English that read, JEDDAH SAUDI ARABIA. The lounge was a microcosm of the world of Pentagon contracting.

The rest of the passengers on the flight were Pacific Islanders, en route to various destinations in Micronesia. Kwajalein can be reached by military aircraft or by the regular Continental Micronesia flight, a Boeing 737 that flies from Honolulu and makes stops in remote destinations like Kosrae and Chuuk en route to Guam. Our outbound flight from Hawaii stopped on Majuro, the capital of the Marshall Islands, where we were asked to disembark for a security check before flying onward to Kwajalein. Escorted into a damp transit lounge, we waited with a group of men in the tropical uniform of the U.S. government contractor (baseball cap, wraparound shades, and Hawaiian shirt). One lonely, sunburned young Mormon missionary, dressed in a white shirt, tie, and name tag, sat clutching a handwoven Marshallese bag and nervously rubbing his hands. The Marshall Islands, despite the tropical climate, are not a tourist destination, making Mormons and Peace Corps workers the primary American visitors.

After forty-five minutes, we reboarded the plane and completed the last leg of our trip. The island of Kwajalein lies at the southern tip of Kwajalein Atoll, a necklace of coral islands. On the approach to Bucholz Army Airfield, Kwajalein's military airport, our Continental Micronesia flight skimmed over the southern edge of the island, passing the Ground Based Radar Prototype, a tracking device developed for the national missile defense system. Enclosed in a bulbous white radome, it looked like a giant golf ball, teed up on its concrete platform and ready to be driven into the Pacific Ocean. Looking down from our seats on the plane, we couldn't imagine anything landing on such a tiny sliver of land.

Kwajalein is a boomerang-shaped atoll of just 749 square acres and, strictly in terms of the environment, one of the worst places in the world to conduct any sort of military work. Supplying the tiny atoll, either from Guam or Hawaii, is a logistics nightmare. The salt water will begin to erode anything in a matter of days, and the ocean hammers relentlessly at the island. Even the land itself isn't safe: It must be periodically bolstered with landfill to prevent the inevitable erosion. Nothing on the atoll really belongs there. Coconut palms—not indigenous—sway languidly in the northeasterly trade wind, while white radomes of various shapes and sizes decorate the tiny island like Christmas ornaments.

But the island does have two saving graces as a military installation. First, its location places it outside of the range of hurricanes, and typhoons are few and far between. But most important, its location far away from major population centers makes it ideal for activities that are secret, dangerous, or both.

We arrived in mid-June, at the height of the rainy season, and were greeted by a blast of humid air and the distinctive scent of jet fuel. The airfield is bounded on one side by the "fuel farm," a strategic reserve of aircraft fuel parked in storage tanks, off limits to photography. This was unmistakably a military installation. Baggage was lined up for inspection by a K-9 team (anyone caught sneaking drugs onto Kwajalein faces immediate arrest and eviction). The doors to the arrival hall were sealed, and a Kwajalein police officer in shorts and a high-and-tight military haircut barked instructions, ordering us to fill in arrival sheets on a clipboard. After handing over copies of our travel orders—

essential for entering Kwajalein—we were issued photo ID cards and copies of the local safety guide.

The Army's 7th Infantry Division captured Kwajalein from the Japanese in three days of fierce fighting in early February 1944. In the run-up to the amphibious assault, the Navy lobbed tons of ordnance onto the island, where Japanese defenders had built a series of re-inforced concrete bunkers and gun emplacements. After the shocking losses on Tarawa in November 1943, the U.S. military learned its lesson. It avoided a frontal assault by sailing into the lagoon and attacking the Japanese defensive perimeter from the rear, saturating the island with high explosives. The campaign was a major success, but the collateral damage continues. Our safety pamphlet warned against picking up unexploded ordnance.

Anne Greene and Tamara Ward, civilian employees of the Army and our hosts on Kwajalein, were waiting for us in the arrivals hall. With her short graying hair and tanned skin, Greene had the look of a longtime Kwaj resident. They had brought an Army golf cart to give us the guided tour. Greene had been on the island for twenty-seven years, and as we drove along the perimeter, she explained the Kwajalein experience with the weary authority of a Kwaj vet. "Things don't last long here," she observed as someone clattered past on an old single-speed beach bike. The main mode of transportation on Kwajalein is bicycle, but the fine saltwater mist that blows across the island has a tendency to corrode new bikes in less than a year.

With Greene at the wheel, we circled the island. Over the years, Kwajalein has served a number of roles in the world of nuclear weapons: as a target for intercontinental ballistic missiles, as a test range for missile defense systems, and as part of the U.S. system for tracking foreign ballistic missiles. Much as a tour of the Nevada Test Site is a crash course in atomic testing, a golf cart excursion around Kwajalein offers a condensed version of U.S. nuclear history. In 1962, a Nike Zeus missile fired from the Kwajalein range successfully "inter-cepted" an Atlas D ICBM in flight. Back then, the only hope of destroying an incoming ICBM was to launch a nuclear-tipped inter-ceptor at it; the Nike Zeus passed within two kilometers of the Atlas D reentry vehicle, so that counted as a successful "hit." (Nike Zeus was later canceled after it became clear the system would not be able to distinguish decoys from a real missile.)

A drive around Kwajalein is also a tour of military detritus. At the southern end of the island, at the elbow of the boomerang, is the "shark pit," where abandoned ship boilers, tractor engines, and bilge tanks, rusting away in the ocean spray, fortify the shoreline. Further on, we drove past a large concrete dome built to house a giant phased-array radar for Safeguard, a missile defense program abandoned in the 1970s. The massive structure is now a dumping ground for used equipment. Along the lagoon side of the island, we also spied modern-day missile defense equipment, such as the USS *Worthy*, an Army vessel now used in support of tests of the Terminal High Altitude Area Defense system, a medium-range missile defense system. Just down the road was the Ground Based Radar Prototype, an X-band radar that had been developed by the Missile Defense Agency as part of the new U.S. ballistic missile defense shield. It was supposed to move to the Czech Republic as part of the Bush administration's plan to build a missile defense site in Eastern Europe, but for the time being, it remained mothballed.

A delegation of Poles and Czechs recently visited, and the reaction to the massive radar was, according to Greene, rather negative. A media frenzy in the Czech Republic was focusing on the health effects of being so close to a massive radar, despite assurances from the U.S. government that it posed no risk. The Missile Defense Agency had even issued a publication showing that the Kwajalein school was in direct proximity to the radar (presumably to emphasize that the U.S. government wouldn't put the children of its own citizens at risk). But seeing is believing, and the foreign reporters wanted to visit the local school, Greene explained, to make sure the children weren't mutated.

It was not the first time Kwajalein had suffered from bad press. A reporter visiting the Marshall Islands for *Outside* magazine recounted his reception on Kwajalein, where an Army public affairs officer curtly informed him that he would be denied entry to the base. After he was escorted off the island, the journalist described Kwajalein as "a strange, Strangeloveian place, whose inhabitants spend their days tracking death machines." A 1990 documentary called *Home on the Range* played on the rather stark contrast between the suburban lifestyle of American workers on Kwajalein and the squalid living conditions of the Marshallese on neighboring islands. But perhaps most memorable for current residents was a stinging *Harper's Magazine* article that painted a less-than-flattering portrait of Kwajalein residents. The article quoted one employee responsible for "host nation" activities describing the Marshallese as "the laziest, most wasteful people."

"When people found out there were reporters coming, they were about to have a stroke," Greene said, exhaling on her cigarette. Media relations have never been Kwajalein's strong point. Just a few weeks before we arrived, Kwajalein's lone public affairs officer, whose main job was to write the *Kwajalein Hourglass*—the community newsletter—returned to the United States, leaving Greene, an administrative assistant, to care for journalists. Greene's penchant for frank, expletive-laced language and knowledge of the island ironically made her the ideal host.

We stopped at the turtle pond, where the surviving four turtles, now permanently in captivity, paddled around. Greene placed the blame for the fate of their comrades—presumed dead—squarely on what she saw as the misguided actions of the "environmentalists." Environmentalists, so far as Greene was concerned, had done nothing particularly good for the atolls. There was the turtle lobby, which had killed the local pets, and then, she noted, there was Greenpeace, which had transported Marshallese from Rongelap Atoll, contaminated by nuclear tests, to different islands where they had no means of support. (The residents of Rongelap asked to be moved after the U.S. government unexpectedly gave new, more alarming information about their radiation exposure; a U.S. Department of Energy memo called the government's failure a "substantial indictment," blaming the agency's own missteps for the inhabitants' decision to leave.)

After a couple of hours driving around, we had pretty much seen everything on the island. Kwajalein is sometimes described as a wealthy American suburb transplanted to the middle of the Pacific. That is something of an exaggeration. Kwajalein's housing area looks more like a downscale subdivision of an underfunded military base. Families live in cookie-cutter concrete duplexes ("old housing") and generic two-story town houses ("new housing"). Unmarried residents have their pick of worn-looking aluminum-sided trailers. A contractor recently installed a series of "bubble" houses, three-bedroom prefabs shaped like Tylenol capsules. Perhaps the most extravagant residence on Kwajalein belongs to the USAKA commander, an Army colonel who occupies an oceanfront house that once served as the officers' club.

"Downtown" Kwajalein is a single tiny intersection with a post office, a coffee shop, and a DVD rental place. A convenience mart we visited, the Ten-Ten, was stocked with canned soups, frozen chicken wings, and Hamburger Helper; the Ten-Ten liquor store offered cold beer, chips, and a few porno magazines. Macy's (no relation to the stateside department store) featured baseball hats and T-shirts embroidered with the USAKA logo, and Surfway (once known as Safeway, until the grocery chain threatened litigation) had a delivery service. We picked up a copy of the *Kwajalein Hourglass*, which featured the television schedule for the Armed Forces Network channels, classified ads for boating equipment, and the cafeteria menu (Thursday: Ham Steak Hawaiian). It also listed the scholarships awarded to graduating high school seniors (Class of 2007: twenty-three students). Armed Forces Entertainment would occasionally fly in entertainers to perform on Kwajalein; during our stay, we passed on the chance to watch the Maynard Triplets ("Three Times the Charm"), a blonde trio from Omaha who had failed to make the cut on *American Idol*.

While housing and amenities on Kwajalein are fairly basic, recreation on the island is without parallel. Residents enjoy spearfishing, scuba diving, and deep-sea fishing year-round. A marina offers motorboat rentals; the Yacht Club organizes sailing lessons and an annual regatta. It's a great place for raising children: no traffic lights, no violent crime, and no requests for the car keys. The worst thing a "Kwaj kid" has to worry about is falling off their bike. Still, the place wasn't all it's cracked up to be. We quickly found out, after leafing through the Army welcome packet, that a family can be sent home for the conduct of a child. According to the brochure's description, "Standards of conduct and behavior tolerable in areas where anonymity is the rule may not be acceptable in the small-town environment of Kwajalein." Essentially, not unlike on an episode of *Survivor*, the Army can vote you off the island at any time.

During our visit, the official population of USAKA stood at 1,852—though during the summer vacation months, it had dwindled to around 1,300 or 1,400. Of that number, only nineteen were uniformed Army personnel; fifty-two were civilian employees of the military; and the remaining numbers were civilian contractors and their families. At the height of the Cold War, the population here was as high as 4,000. Living on an isolated tropical island, however, was not for everyone. As

Kwajalein lore had it, every so often, a newcomer would step off the airplane, take one look at the island, and immediately demand to go home.

Missile reentries are something of a spectator sport for Kwajalein residents, who gather at the island's North Point to watch the show. The operations team, however, watches the reentry from the control center, fixed on the data streaming in from the Super RADOTs, optical sensors that can track objects beyond the edge of the atmosphere.

We were originally scheduled to fly out to Kwajalein to watch GT-194, a Minuteman III launch and reentry mission scheduled for April, but the test schedule slipped—without explanation—to June. Less than two weeks before we were scheduled to depart, we were informed by Army Space and Missile Defense Command in Huntsville that the GT-194 test had been postponed again, to August, and that date was tentative. We decided that we couldn't wait for the launch and would visit the island anyway.

The downside of that decision, however, was that instead of watching mock warheads fall into the lagoon, we learned about the launch in a PowerPoint briefing. Lieutenant Colonel Justin Hirniak, the commander of the Reagan Test Site, and Merrie Beth Schad, one of the test directors at the site, explained the ins and outs of the test range in their office's conference room. Hirniak, a veteran of several tours in Iraq and Afghanistan, seemed to be relishing the chance to spend a two-year assignment with his family on Kwajalein.

Hirniak's job was to oversee the "mission ops" side of Kwajalein. His personnel ran the ballistic missile tests, space surveillance operations, and tests of the Ground-Based Midcourse Defense system. While welcoming us, Hirniak was quick to add, "It is a DOD installation, and there are certain areas and certain things that we do, for national security, that we just kinda have to keep quiet [about]. I apologize for that, so don't take it like we're trying to hide something—we're not a nuclear dump site. I guarantee you that; otherwise I wouldn't be here. We're not hiding UFOs."

Schad, Hirniak's deputy, had the taut, tan look of a surfer. She had been on Kwajalein for seventeen years ("At one point I decided I wanted to make a change in my life and came over," she explained). She had a background in industrial security and communications security, but she started at the bottom of the ladder, learning every task involved in planning the ICBM missions. She began as a data editor, then worked her way up to project engineer, and was now a test director. But what kept her—like many—on Kwajalein was the lifestyle. "There's two different types of people out here, those who love the water and those who don't," she said exuberantly. "I love the water."

The staff was busy with planning and preparation for the missions rescheduled for August. The next fiscal year's schedule was going to be packed, and Schad walked us through the planning stages for an ICBM test. Schad described the process as "getting with the customer," in this case, the Air Force. The Navy also uses Kwajalein as a target range for submarine-launched ballistic missiles.

Around three times a year, a Minuteman III intercontinental ballistic missile is selected at random from a base in Wyoming, North Dakota, or Montana. It is packed up and trucked across the western United States to Vandenberg Air Force Base, a launch facility in Santa Barbara County, California. The missile's crew then goes on alert, rehearsing the same steps it would take in its underground capsule if it received launch orders from the president. The nuclear warhead is, of course, removed before the test: The test flight is a "health check" for the ICBM, not the nuclear warhead itself.

After the Air Force crew turns the launch keys, the missile is lofted skyward. The three-stage ICBM arcs over the central Pacific; the first- and second-stage engines burn out north of the Hawaiian Islands, dropping away to impact points in the ocean. West of the International Date Line, technicians on Kwajalein can observe the third stage of the ICBM as it hurtles over the horizon. Thrust terminates and the post-boost vehicle (or "bus," because it carries the warheads) separates from the rocket. There is a flash of high-explosive charge as the bus discharges its payload, and the cone-shaped reentry vehicles come hurtling down to their preprogrammed destinations at supersonic speed. The flight from Vandenberg Air Force Base to the Reagan Test Site, some forty-five hundred miles away, takes just under thirty minutes.

ICBM reentry vehicles are aimed at one of several target areas around Kwajalein Atoll. One impact point is in the waters north of Roi-Namur

Island; another is near the East Reef of the atoll. The waters beyond the coral reef are thousands of feet deep, so the missile payload will settle on the ocean floor, beyond recovery. The Air Force can also target the relatively shallow waters of the lagoon—between 120 and 180 feet deep—allowing recovery of the reentry vehicle for further tests. Seen from Kwajalein, the final stage of an ICBM test can be quite dramatic. White-hot reentry vehicles streak through the clouds toward their impact point. M-X Peacekeeper ICBM tests—discontinued after the Air Force retired the missile in 2005—were the most stunning. Photos of these shots adorn posters, calendars, and information booklets about the island. Each Peacekeeper carried a payload of up to ten independently targeted warheads, yielding the ultimate images of ICBM tests: the incandescent trails of the reentry vehicles reaching down like the fingers of an angry god.

The reason for these tests is to make sure the ICBMs still work, and even more important—and part of what makes the Marshall Islands such an attractive target—is to ensure that, after traveling halfway around the world, the missiles are still pinpoint accurate. One of the ways to calculate the accuracy of a missile is to aim for the Kwajalein Missile Impact Scoring System (which has the unfortunate acronym KMISS), an underwater range located off the coast of Gagan Island. KMISS is a series of underwater hydrophones that detect the sound of a reentry vehicle striking the water. It measures the time it takes for the sound of impact to reach different depths and distances to provide an accurate score that is calculated within a few hours of a launch-and-reentry mission.

For an even more precise measurement of missile accuracy, the Air Force can also aim for solid earth, targeting a "land impact" site on Illeginni Island. While the reentry vehicle used in an ICBM test is essentially a dummy warhead with no nuclear payload, it strikes home with terrific force. The sheer kinetic energy of the dunce cap–shaped reentry vehicle hitting the small island gouges out a crater thirty feet wide and eight feet deep. After a test, the Air Force sends someone out with a GPS unit; they stand at the bottom of the impact crater and measure the accuracy of the shot. The ICBM reentry vehicles are very accurate, but not perfect. On one occasion, Schad told us, the reentry vehicle struck the helicopter landing pad on the small island instead of the planned target area, leaving a huge crater.

Kwajalein Atoll, in essence, is a giant bull's-eye for ballistic missiles. The Reagan Test Site operates a network of range instrumentation: radar, telemetry, optics, weather, and communications equipment, linked by an underwater fiber-optic line that rings the inside of the lagoon. Instrumentation is stationed on six islands around the atoll, allowing the range operators to provide their military customers with highly accurate measurements of their missile shots. It's a sophisticated—setup. Radars on Kwajalein and Roi-Namur can precisely track the deployment of reentry vehicles, while fixed ballistic cameras capture incoming missile trajectories as they pass through the field of view.

Conducting a test on Kwajalein is not cheap. In military-speak, the island poses a "major challenge of geography." It depends on a twice-weekly barge from Guam for basic resupply. Everything else, from perishable goods to critical spare parts, must be ferried in by airplane. Supporting just one ICBM mission, for instance, means flying in a group of technicians from the United States, housing them, paying them per diem, and flying in their equipment. Adding to the cost is the physical environment of the Marshall Islands. Everything requires constant upkeep and protection from the corrosive salt mist. The Pentagon estimates the cost of a single missile defense test involving Kwajalein to be between eighty and one hundred million dollars.

Rather than being a crown jewel of strategic influence, Kwajalein, in fact, has to compete for business, particularly now that ICBM tests are few and far between. The atoll, Hirniak argued, did offer some unique advantages over other ranges. Its isolation—and location close to the equator—made it ideal for space launches. But more importantly, it was remote. The Republic of the Marshall Islands covers 750,000 square miles of mostly ocean; the actual land area is roughly the same size as the District of Columbia. That made it ideal for secrecy.* It also offered a "clean" radio frequency environment. As Schad pointed out, "Unlike

---

* Of course, in the Cold War, the Soviets tried to keep tabs on Kwajalein. Longtime residents recalled notices in the *Kwajalein Hourglass* urging USAKA personnel to report sightings of the *Brand-X*, a Russian spy ship that occasionally lurked off the atoll. "All that technology on the island, and they want housewives to watch out for it?" laughed one Kwaj veteran.

other ranges, we don't have to deal with the typical things like TV stations, radio stations, cell phones, garage door openers, those sorts of things. It makes it very easy for us to control that environment out here at the range."

In short, the Army could pretty much do what it wanted with minimal interference. As Schad put it, "From an environmental impact perspective, it's a lot easier for customers to deal with the RMI government on those types of issues—compared to what it is at other ranges."

Across the lagoon from Kwajalein, just off Enubuj Reef, a hulking, three-bladed propeller juts above the waterline, rusting brilliantly in the sun. This is the enormous center screw of the *Prinz Eugen*, a German heavy cruiser that survived World War II only to be abandoned in Kwajalein Atoll. She lies capsized on the reef, the upper deck of the bow touching bottom, 110 feet below. The water was choppy as Anjo Kabua, the son of Iroijlaplap (paramount chief) and former Marshall Islands president Imata Kabua, cut the engine on our boat so we could snap a few pictures; the stern, rudder, and screw were all that was visible above the surface. Anjo, upon hearing of our desire to visit Ebeye Island, had offered us a personal tour.

The *Prinz Eugen* was handed over to the U.S. Navy after Germany's capitulation in World War II, and in 1946 the cruiser was one of the target ships for Operation Crossroads, the first series of postwar atomic tests. Bikini Atoll in the northern Marshall Islands was selected as the site for the first demonstration of atomic firepower after Hiroshima and Nagasaki. In part, Operation Crossroads was a test of the effects of the bomb on naval ships. It was also a major exercise in public relations, demonstrating the awesome new weapon to the rest of the world. The U.S. government invited twenty-two foreign observers (including a pair of Soviet scientists) to watch the test and brought along a boatload of print and radio correspondents.

Before the test, however, something would have to be done with the people of Bikini Atoll. Navy commodore Ben Wyatt, the U.S. military governor of the Marshall Islands, was dispatched to inform islanders that they would have to sacrifice their ancestral home "for the benefit of mankind." The powerless Bikinians acquiesced to the wishes of the

Navy, believing that they eventually would be able to return. They were banished to uninhabited Rongerik Atoll; just before their deportation, their fateful meeting with Wyatt was restaged for the benefit of the newsreel cameras.

The Able shot—the first test of Operation Crossroads, a device dropped from a B-29 bomber—was a bit of a disappointment. The bomber crew missed the target ship, and some observers were less than impressed by the size of the atomic detonation. But the Baker shot (an underwater detonation) was much more dramatic, sending up a giant plume of water crowned by an enormous halo of radioactive spray and steam. Several target ships, including the Japanese battleship *Nagato*, were sent to the bottom by the Baker shot. The *Prinz Eugen* initially survived the blast and was towed to Kwajalein Atoll, the command post for Operation Crossroads. Slowly listing from the shock of the under-water detonation, the German cruiser was towed into the lagoon, where she eventually ran onto the reef and capsized. We took a few more pictures of the atomic relic, and Anjo fired up the engine again.

At the Kwajalein dock, we had watched dozens of Marshallese workers line up to board an old Army landing craft bound for Kwajalein. The transport was one of the many indignities that Mar-shallese complain about: Americans travel around the various islands of Kwajalein Atoll in fast, air-conditioned boats, while the Marshallese workers are transported in slow, open World War II–era landing craft.

Around fourteen hundred Marshallese work on Kwajalein. Most are contract employees of KRS, the base contractor. Another hundred or so work as "domestics"—housekeepers and gardeners for the Americans. The Marshallese workforce on Kwajalein, in turn, support a population of around fourteen thousand people, all crowded onto the small island of Ebeye.

Because journalists are let onto Kwajalein so infrequently, and are forced instead to report from Ebeye, life on Kwajalein is typically painted as something akin to a large group of mad scientists living in a beachfront country club. It is by no means luxurious—a longtime resident described the place as a "suburb of Huntsville." But its neatly manicured lawns make a rather stark contrast to Ebeye, usually referred to as the "slum of the Pacific." USAKA is the second-largest employer in the Marshall Islands (the first being the RMI government), and each employee on Kwajalein typically supports an extended family on Ebeye, where twelve people might share a cramped 650 square feet of living space. Still, with the average Marshallese employee making around ten thousand dollars per year on Kwajalein, Ebeye is the best place in the Marshall Islands to look for a job.

Economic migration is only one part of the picture. In the early 1960s, the military also relocated Marshallese from islands in the central corridor of Kwajalein Atoll to create a target area for the ICBM tests. Even back in 1980, when the population of Ebeye hovered around six thousand, the overcrowding was considered severe, and Americans on Kwajalein issued frantic letters warning of an impending disaster. Poor sanitation led to periodic outbreaks of disease. A polio outbreak occurred in 1963; hepatitis infection rates soared in the 1970s; a typhoid epidemic broke out in 1982; cholera claimed several lives in 2000. By 2007, the population density had reached 66,750 per square mile—more crowded than Manhattan, and worse because Ebeye didn't have high-rise buildings. Water and fuel supplies on Ebeye were unpredictable. Most of the workers waiting for the ferry during our visit were carrying a plastic jug to carry home fresh drinking water.

Relations between the Marshallese and the Americans have been mixed. The Army likes to stress its efforts to promote cultural exchange between the two, as well as the amount of money USAKA operations have injected into the local economy. The Kwajalein women's club puts a happy face on things, organizing bingo tournaments to raise charity funds and staging a "Christmas drop" on Ebeye every year ("Each kid gets a gift bag from Santa," explained the Army's host nation officer). But the perspective of the Marshallese is of an already-tenuous relationship getting more strained.

Noda Lojkar, the Republic of the Marshall Islands liaison to USAKA, recalled growing up "very pro-American" on Ebeye in the 1960s, watching John Wayne movies at the outdoor movie theater. "I think it really changed after 9/11, because of security," Lojkar told us in his small office next to the USAKA headquarters. "Two or three hundred people would come to Kwaj, you know, to just relax and go to the snack bars. We used to have carnivals that they would hold annually on Kwaj, and they would bring people from Ebeye to go to that. But now security's so strict, and some of the security guards at the dock, they get people who don't know the culture, they don't understand the Marshallese. There's a cultural clash and mistreatment of people."

But more than the heavy-handed treatment at the Kwajalein dock, the "host nation landscape," as military officials called it, is clouded by a much more complex issue: land ownership. The Marshall Islands were once part of a Trust Territory administered by the United States, and following independence, the country remained heavily dependent on U.S. economic assistance. The U.S. government pays fifteen million dollars a year to the RMI to lease the eleven islands on Kwajalein Atoll. But there's a catch: The government of the Marshall Islands does not actually hold title to the land; a group of individual landowners does. The Land Use Agreement between the government and the senior landowners of Kwajalein Atoll governs the use of the islands. The current agreement is set to expire in 2016, and the landowners— including a former president and several other influential figures in Marshallese politics—are holding out. The U.S. government, they say, is shortchanging them, and they want to raise the rent. They are threatening an end to the agreement, a move that would theoretically force the Americans out.

It had turned into a chokingly hot midsummer day by the time Anjo Kabua docked our boat at the Ebeye pier, so it was with some relief that we followed him into a waiting GMC Suburban with air-conditioning and tinted windows. The plywood storefronts, concrete-block shanties, and bungalows were ramshackle and crowded. Crowds of children played barefoot in the streets. Ebeye was not an idyllic place for a beach vacation—much of the northern shoreline was given over to an open trash dump—but it was not the fetid slum described by Kwajalein residents.

The striking paradox of Ebeye is that it's a poverty economy with a steady stream of income. "This is where the money is," explained Tom Butler, a native Californian who ran the Ralik Store, a small grocery store on Ebeye. The employment on neighboring Kwajalein guarantees a stable income for the residents who work there. "There's more money in this place than in Majuro, if you really look at it. It's just that steady chunk of change. It's twenty-five million dollars a year in payroll [from Kwajalein employees]." Take the MoneyGram offices near the harbor, he said. People didn't receive remittances from the United States or other islands—the local money went the other way. "No one sends money to Ebeye," Butler said. "I would love to see the numbers of what they send from here."

The Ralik Store stocked a little bit of everything: hardware, packaged food, and bottled water. The bestselling items, Butler told us, were disposable diapers and Hawaiian-style flip-flops. We had stopped to chat in the small warehouse behind the store, where Butler stored pallets of toilet paper and canned goods. Lynyrd Skynyrd played on the boom box, while one of the employees teased a puppy chained up in the open storeroom; the beach just beyond the back steps was littered with empties and cigarette butts. Looking out over the lagoon, Butler lit up a cigarette and took a drag. He first came to the Marshall Islands in 1989, he said, and had mixed feelings about Ebeye. "I love it," he said. "And I hate it."

Butler was married to a Marshallese woman with whom he had a young daughter. He was critical of the RMI government, but even more critical of the U.S. presence on Kwajalein. To fly out of the Marshall Islands, he had to use the airport on Kwajalein. But to even go the few steps from the dock to the airport, he had to wait hours for an official military escort. As an American citizen, he could not visit Kwajalein and, rather ironically, had even fewer rights than the Marshallese, who could, with permission, enter the U.S. base.

Compared with the amount that a single ICBM mission costs, the rent the U.S. government paid for the use of Kwajalein was a pittance, Butler noted. And the Kwajalein Land Use Agreement was shaping up as a major campaign issue in the upcoming election. Butler couldn't vote, but his sympathies were clear. "Fifteen million dollars a year," he said, looking up at the pallets of toilet paper in his storehouse. "I swear to God, the Senate spends more on toilet paper for the Capitol building per year!"

Blame, however, was a two-way street. To alleviate overcrowding on Ebeye, the Kwajalein Atoll Development Authority had built a causeway connecting Gugeegue, Ninji, and other small islets north of Ebeye. A heavy-machine operator from Hawaii had built it, scooping out reef rock to fill in the shoreline between the small islands. The job had been completed in 1992, but the construction had not alleviated the housing situation. The Marshallese owners of the land on the other islands didn't want new development. In some respects, the causeway was a private road for the landowners who lived on Gugeegue, including our escort's father, the former president, and his relatives. For non-land-owners, the majority of the population, it did little to alleviate over-crowding. On our way back down the causeway, we passed the heavy earthmoving equipment on the side of the road, rusting away in the salt spray, a symbol of a project gone nowhere.

After our tour of Ebeye, we stopped near the dock, where we met Marshall Islands senator Jeban Riklon, reclining in a chair underneath an awning. As he picked leisurely at a coconut, Riklon explained his position on the Land Use Agreement. "They know that the Land Use Agreement expires in 2016," he said. "It's very simple to understand. The language is very simple—you don't have to be an attorney to understand. In Marshallese custom, we own the land. It's not like other places in the world. This is something different here. We own the land; it's not the government that owns the land."

The Marshall Islands gained independence with the signing of the Compact of Free Association in 1986. In Section 177 of the compact, the U.S. government accepted its responsibility to compensate Marshallese citizens for damages resulting from the years of atomic testing, and a Nuclear Claims Fund was established to direct payments. By the time we arrived in the Marshall Islands, however, the $150 million originally provided for the fund had been spent; the Nuclear Claims Tribunal, established to decide compensation cases, was set to shut its doors for lack of operating funds. It had paid out only a fraction of the money awarded. And the Nuclear Claims Fund, in the view of the Marshallese, had only been an initial sum for compensation.

The disparity between money paid out by the U.S. government to compensate American "downwinders" and funds given to the Marshallese was striking. As a group of Harvard Law School student advocates noted in 2006, over $1 billion had been awarded as compensation to U.S. citizens exposed to atomic tests, while only $72.9 million in personal injury awards had been given to Marshallese residents who had suffered much higher levels of exposure. However, the U.S.-RMI compact had been renegotiated in 2003, and the new agreement did not extend to nuclear issues. The United States and the Republic of the Marshall Islands had agreed to phase out direct economic aid by 2023, but a trust fund established by the U.S.

government to help the Marshall Islands move toward greater self-sufficiency did not look like it would provide a sustainable income for the country. Kwajalein now was the ultimate bargaining chip in negotiations with the U.S. government.

But what did the old nuclear claims from the 1950s have to do with the current rent dispute over a U.S. base? Tony de Brum, a Kwajalein senator and former finance minister, was an ardent critic of the Land Use Agreement. De Brum was the rising star of Marshall Islands politics, a leader of the political opposition. His allies were anxious to unseat the current government, which they felt had negotiated an agreement not in their interests. The Americans, however, had a more cynical view. While acknowledging his political acumen, they made sure to point out that de Brum was not even from Kwajalein; rather, he had been given land by the former president so that he could run for the Senate. He grew up in Arkansas, Americans whispered on Kwajalein.

De Brum, in fact, was not on Kwajalein when we visited him. He was hosting a party at his wife's home on Majuro, a short flight from Kwajalein. As the plane circled in, we could see dozens of fishing trawlers anchored in the lagoon. The Marshall Islands sold fishing rights to foreign governments; next to funds from the U.S. government, it was probably the biggest source of income. Taiwan, in particular, wielded outsize influence. In return for bankrolling foreign travel for RMI officials, Taiwan expected the Marshall Islands to vote its way in international organizations.

If de Brum was indeed the anointed son of the opposition, they had chosen well. He had a senatorial presence, smooth and affable, and the purring baritone of a born orator. He looked as if he would be at home at a cocktail party in Manhattan, in a hearing on Capitol Hill, or here in the Marshall Islands, sitting in a circle of his peers and enjoying a backyard barbecue. He knew the ins and outs of Washington and had even employed disgraced political lobbyist Jack Abramoff. ("He did good by us," de Brum said.)

Many of the Kwajalein landowners were at the party, including former Marshall Islands president Imata Kabua. Local musicians played Marshallese songs on a Casio keyboard, including a political lament about the compact set to a Dire Straits tune. De Brum was sitting in a circle of men drinking kava, a nonalcoholic brew made from *Piper methysticum*, a plant root native to the western Pacific. The kava, scooped out of a communal bowl, had a muddy, slightly peppery taste. It produced a mild, clear euphoria, working like a topical anesthetic to numb the lips and tongue. Dinner was heaping side dishes of marinated fish, breadfruit chips, rice, and roast pig. The banquet's pièce de résistance was a sea turtle, served up in its shell.

Over breakfast the next morning, de Brum made the case plainly. "Kwajalein is the only bargaining chip we have," he said. "You asked last night, the Kwajalein thing, why is it connected to the nuclear issue? It was the United States that created that linkage for us." The people of the Marshall Islands, de Brum said, made a sacrifice: By allowing the military to validate its nuclear arsenal here, they helped the United States prevail in the Cold War. Today, the Kwajalein missile range still helped the United States preserve that superpower status, but also at a price—the islands were at the target end of missile shots from Vandenberg. "Suppose some day the United States says, 'OK, good-bye guys, we're gone,'" he said. "What are we going to be left with? This is not just a matter of banging a car and paying insurance for any damages you might cause; this is much more permanent than that. Like any other island group, you cannot separate the people from their land. That damage is permanent."

But whether negotiating nuclear claims or the Kwajalein rental agreement, de Brum said, the young government of the Marshall Islands was always on unequal terms with the United States. U.S. negotiators easily lapsed into patterns of colonial administration, dictating terms to the Marshall Islands; the nuclear compensation issue was a part of that, he insisted. "Just because the Marshallese people are not as quote-unquote sophisticated as the American people does not mean that they should be deprived of their day in court."

"Ever been deep-sea fishing?" the man on the bar stool slurred.

"Nope."

"Ever slept with a hooker?"

We were sitting at the Ocean View Club, whose name suggested a menu of fresh oysters and cold white wine, but which, in fact, was an open wood A-frame structure selling beer and assorted schnapps. Only the ocean outside—with its enormous waves crashing on the reef—lived up to the name. Since the club was located next door to our hotel, the Kwajalein Lodge, we had taken to visiting the place to drink an evening beer and watch the ocean. Anne Greene had warned us that the close-knit community would be curious about outsiders, but questions about hookers weren't quite what we expected.

Skip, as our neighbor at the bar introduced himself, was picking at giant hunks of sashimi and dipping them in a shallow Tupperware container filled with soy sauce and wasabi. In Honolulu or in New York, those slabs of raw yellowfin tuna would have cost a fortune; here at the Ocean View Club, the fish was casually laid out on the top of the bar like a bowl of peanuts. Skip had clearly been drinking at the club for some time. Doubling as the food services administration office, the Ocean View is the favorite haunt of contractors from Roi-Namur, a remote site on the north of Kwajalein Atoll where around 180 work-ers—almost all of them men—maintain the radar equipment. Roi is an unaccompanied post—no children allowed—and the more family-oriented residents of Kwajalein often described the Roi employees as "site rats," or reclusive types with limited social skills. On their occasional visits to the "big island" of Kwajalein, Roi Rats can park on a plastic chair at the Ocean View, pop open a two-dollar beer, and watch the waves crash onto the coral reef.

Along with water sports, beer is the main entertainment on Kwajalein Atoll. Eugene Sims, a longtime civilian manager on Kwajalein who first came to the island in 1945, recalls the heroic amount of beer that soldiers and sailors drank in his book, *Kwajalein Remembered* (which he dedicates to "all of those who have known the 'Kwaj condition'"). He describes visiting a brewery during a stateside vacation and learning that the tiny island of Kwajalein is the company's largest export account. "Maybe we did drink a lot of beer on Kwaj and Roi?" he writes. "I had never given it much thought. I began to recall some earlier days on Kwaj when about the only thing to do after work was have a beer, eat chow, go to one of the outdoor theaters, and be back in the sack before 2200 hours for another hot sleepless night."

After the capture of the island in 1944 from the Japanese, Kwajalein was designated as a rear-area rest-and-relaxation facility for troops serving in the Pacific. The Army and the Navy built open-air beer halls—usually simple plywood huts—and issued chits rationing out ten-cent beers. Before refrigeration was widely available, beer drinkers took extravagant steps to chill their brew (Sims, for example, recalls sending cases of beer aloft in aircraft cargo holds or using fire extinguishers to blast down tubs of beer with cold CO_2). With time, infrastructure and air-conditioning had changed the routine, but beer remained a constant. In the Ocean View Club, a lonely flyer taped to the wall advertised twice-weekly Alcoholics Anonymous meetings, but it seemed almost an afterthought. After all, it's hard to be anonymous in a population of just over eighteen hundred. Kwajalein was like a sick twist on the seemingly pleasant notion of "everybody knows your name."

One evening, Anne Greene invited us over to her house for dinner with some of her friends, including a few long-term Kwajalein residents. "So you don't think we're all strange," she joked while extending the invitation. In fact, most of the residents were not that strange; they were just isolated far from home. Over homemade chili, the guests debated the problem of Kwajalein. They were sympathetic to the Marshallese, cynical about USAKA, and critical of many elements of U.S. policy. But they also felt that the Marshallese were not doing enough to improve the country's prospects.

Smoking a cigarette on her front porch and sipping a Diet Coke, Greene expressed many of the frustrations that embody the odd relationship between Americans and Marshallese. The U.S. government, while the source of many of the problems in the Marshall Islands, did not offer a good solution. Health problems—such as rampant diabetes—were beyond a quick fix. A native diet of fish and indigenous fruit had been supplanted by fast food and processed starch. "They subsist off chicken and white rice," she said. "They'll pick the vegetables off their food."

After dinner, Anne's husband, David, a genial engineer whose love of the water had kept the family on the island for so long, talked about the questions he got from Czech journalists. They were surprised to learn that many of the engineers on the island were quite skeptical about missile defense, he recalled, and he was equally surprised by their questions.

For visiting journalists, Kwajalein embodies so many things: economic disparity, nuclear weapons disputes, and controversies over missile defense. But for longtime residents like Anne and David Greene, who had raised two sons and spent nearly three decades on Kwajalein, it was about something else entirely. "Why is it so hard to understand?" David Greene asked. "We enjoy the details of our work. We like the life here. We get a paycheck."

In the Pentagon, colonels may be a dime a dozen, but on Kwajalein, the commander has a supreme status. On our last day there, Greene called us to let us know that Colonel Stevenson Reed, the USAKA commander, had just returned from a trip and would be available to meet with us. Reed, as it turned out, had just visited his higher headquarters in Huntsville, where he had spent the week in budget briefings. The numbers did not look good. He was facing a $50 million budget cut. Flipping through a binder, Reed opened to a page with the current operating budget for fiscal year 2007, about $237 million, already down from the previous year. "This is not an easy time for the Department of Defense," he said. "This is not a time where we have a lot of money. The country doesn't have a lot of money to just give."

Reed met us in an office festooned with decorations and awards from his military career. He had spent most of his time in the Army as an air defense artillery officer, a typical career path for those involved in missile defense, but here he had to juggle different roles: military commander, part-time diplomat, head of the community of Kwajalein. We asked him about one of the issues we'd heard discussed, the idea of a causeway between Ebeye and Kwajalein, which would eliminate the long ferry ride for the workers. "Well, if they fund it, it is [possible]," he replied. "That is not a part of what we'll be funding. I would love to see it, and then I would not have to have boats taking people back and forth." However, he noted the rusted-out equipment we had seen on our trip to Ebeye. "If you look at the previous causeway from Ebeye to Gugeegue, it's not successful."

Good intentions, it seemed, were never enough.

With all the declining Kwajalein budgets and an uncertain mission for the future, what justified the enormous expense of maintaining this outpost in the Pacific? The ICBM mission—though arguably important—could hardly be called essential. Kwajalein, as we had learned, had to compete for work against other ranges. The atolls were covered with radar and sensors—much of it secret—used to track foreign ballistic missiles. But as a couple of island residents had pointed out to us, the U.S. government had looked at, if necessary, moving them. What was really essential about maintaining a U.S. presence in the Marshall Islands? Reed's answer was simple: just in case we need it.

For well over fifty years, Kwajalein and the Marshall Islands had been, above all else, a convenient strategic outpost: for the Japanese waging war in the Pacific, then for the U.S. military in its race to develop new, more powerful nuclear weapons, and then as a giant bull's-eye for ballistic missiles. The tragedy of Kwajalein and the Marshall Islands was that the only thing worse than the American presence would be the absence of the American presence. Kwajalein wasn't absolutely vital to U.S. security; it was just convenient. And at least according to Reed, not much—in that key respect—was going to change.

"You have to have a contingency plan for what you are going to do in the Pacific if Guam actually comes under attack," Reed said. "What's the fallback position to launch from? You have to have contingencies. We don't clearly know what that is, because this is all so new. But I really believe that Kwajalein is going to be a place of strategic interest for our country."

CHAPTER 10

Take Me to Your One-Eyed Baby

Promoting Nuclear Tourism in Kazakhstan

In the late summer of 2006, the government of Kazakhstan was readying a media blitz. President Nursultan Nazarbayev was planning to visit Washington, D.C., in September, and the government had commissioned a series of print and television advertisements to drum up advance publicity. The goal of the campaign was simple: rebranding Kazakhstan. The former Soviet republic's leaders wanted the country to shed its image as a Central Asian backwater in favor of something more appealing—a moderate Muslim-majority state that had sworn off nuclear weapons in favor of economic growth.

In the fifteen years since gaining independence from the Soviet Union, Kazakhstan had emerged as the economic powerhouse of Central Asia. It had plentiful reserves of oil and gas; it had a shiny new capital, Astana; and Almaty, the country's largest city and former capital, was known for its nightlife. Yet in spite of the effort to portray Kazakhstan as a paragon of modernity, the television commercial, which featured a thundering introduction set to the chime of synthesizers, had a curiously retro feel. It began with a stentorian voice-over: "*Stable and prosperous, Kazakhstan has become the economic engine of Eurasia . . .*" The commercial then faded to footage of the avuncular Nazarbayev, strolling alongside Russian president Vladimir Putin: "*It is a case study for the successful economic transition from socialism to capitalism, dismantling its nuclear arsenal in the process . . .*" A montage of optimistic images then followed: Nazarbayev taking the oath of office; construction under way in Astana; Kazakh tenge, the national currency, sifting through a counting machine.

As part of the media blitz, the government of Kazakhstan placed a four-page ad in the *New York Times* promoting Kazakhstan as a multiconfessional democracy, an oasis of economic progress and religious tolerance in the otherwise despotic landscape of Central Asia. It was precisely what the Kazakh government wanted, a riposte to troublesome Western journalists, who insisted on writing about Nazarbayev's crackdown on his domestic opposition. And although observers had declared the country's recent elections as rigged, Kazakhstan had signed on to the Bush administration's "coalition of the willing"—and sent a token military contingent of twenty-seven combat engineers to Iraq. In any case, the Bush administration wasn't bothered by the conduct of Kazakhstan's government. A day after Vice President Dick Cheney had publicly scolded Russia for backsliding on democracy, he made a point of flying to oil-rich Kazakhstan to personally congratulate Nazarbayev on his presidential election victory.

The Kazakh president's preparations for visiting the United States may have dominated the news back home, but he was being upstaged in the U.S. press by some unexpected—and unwanted—publicity for Kazakhstan, a movie called *Borat: Cultural Learnings of America for Make Benefit Glorious Nation of Kazakhstan*. Borat Sagdiyev, the alter ego of British comedian Sacha Baron Cohen, had created a public relations nightmare for Kazakhstan. In the guise of a Kazakh TV journalist, Baron Cohen traveled in character around the United States, speaking fake Kazakh ("Jagshemash!"), conducting hoax interviews ("How much do you tip prostitute?"), and pulling off elaborate publicity stunts.

For Roman Vassilenko, the press attaché for the embassy of Kazakhstan in Washington, Borat was a personal nightmare. Vassilenko was the perfect spokesman for the new Kazakhstan. He was young and idealistic, and—most important for American journalists—he spoke flawless English. But instead of representing the new Kazakhstan, Vassilenko was spending his days battling a fictitious Kazakh journalist. After Borat warmed up a rodeo crowd in Salem, Virginia, with the exhortation "May George W. Bush drink the blood of every single man, woman, and child of Iraq!" Vassilenko had to write an earnest letter to the local newspaper, politely explaining that Borat had nothing to do with Kazakhstan, a tolerant, modernizing democracy.

Kazakhstan was in the middle of marketing itself as a moderate country and energy powerhouse. Baron Cohen claimed he was mocking American prejudice, but he was inadvertently demolishing the real Kazakhstan's image in the process, and Kazakh officials' befuddled response only played into the joke. After Borat hosted the MTV Europe Music Awards in 2005, Yerzhan Ashykbayev, a spokesman for the Foreign Ministry, hinted that Borat was part of an elaborate political conspiracy. In a statement that could have been lifted straight out of a Borat skit, he said, "We do not rule out that Mr. Cohen is serving someone's political order designed to present Kazakhstan and its people in a derogatory way. We reserve the right to any legal action to prevent new pranks of this kind." Borat's response, posted on his Web site: "I fully support my government's decision to sue this Jew."

As Borat rained terror on Kazakhstan's image makers, we were planning our trip to see whether a country's attempt to market itself as a model of nonproliferation could really work. As it happened, our trip to Kazakhstan corresponded to the run-up of publicity for the Borat movie, which likely explained why our e-mail to the public affairs office at the Kazakh embassy in Washington was quickly answered by an enthusiastic phone call. Vassilenko's voice nearly choked with emotion when we told him of our plans to visit the Semipalatinsk Test Site, once a key part of the Soviet Union's vast nuclear weapons complex. Like the caretaker of the lonely Bates Motel, it seemed as if he had been waiting for a journalist to call. "I'm so happy you contacted me," Vassilenko said. "I'm so happy you want to visit Semipalatinsk."

Starting in 1949, the Soviets detonated 456 nuclear devices at the Semipalatinsk Test Site, located on the barren steppe of eastern Kazakhstan. The site was framed on its southwestern frontier by mountain ranges and on the east by the Chagan River. The Soviets built a small administrative city on the banks of the Irtysh River. The secret city, Kurchatov, was located at the edge of the site and housed thousands of workers involved in the clandestine effort. During Soviet times, the territory was off-limits to the outside world. News of nuclear detonations would be reported in terse dispatches by Western wire services.

The intense secretiveness of Kurchatov and its activities spawned rampant speculation among U.S. intelligence officials, including, at one point in the 1970s, reports that the Soviets had built a "death beam," a massive laser with capabilities beyond any comparable U.S. weapons (there was no such laser, though it's sometimes argued that the erroneous report spurred the United States' Strategic Defense Initiative laser efforts).

But in Kazakhstan, even abbreviated information wasn't available. Local villagers living around the Semipalatinsk Test Site were ignorant of nuclear tests in their backyard. And when the government scientists and military personnel packed up and went back to Moscow in 1991, they left the Kazakhs to clean up the radioactive mess. Kazakhstan has been struggling to come to grips with the environmental legacy of Soviet testing ever since.

Much as in Nevada, the legacy of atomic testing in Kazakhstan is still unclear. "Downwinders" in the United States blame atmospheric testing for a host of medical problems. Around Semipalatinsk, local hospitals treat cancer patients and children born with birth defects, but establishing a positive link between those health problems and nuclear testing would have required precisely the sort of studies that weren't carried out during Soviet times. Whether the health problems are the results of testing—or a general legacy of heavy industry, alcohol abuse, and poor diet—is still up for debate.

Either way, nuclear testing has become part of Kazakhstan's national lore, and Vassilenko was particularly happy to have journalists visit a key part of that history. Promoting Kazakhstan's nuclear legacy has become central to the country's diplomatic mission in Washington. The embassy's official Web site, for instance, features a banner on the main page announcing, NUCLEAR NIGHTMARE OF KAZAKHSTAN, in brazen red capitals over a photograph of a mushroom cloud, which alternates via rollover with a ghastly image of a one-eyed "Cyclops" baby floating in a bottle of formaldehyde, a deformed fetus whose defect is attributed— at least by the embassy—to nuclear testing. Kazakhstan has taken nuclear victimhood to a whole new level.

But the legacy of nuclear testing is only one half of the national narrative. After independence, in 1991, Kazakhstan suddenly and unexpectedly found itself in possession of the fourth-largest nuclear arsenal in the world, an inheritance that gave it, at least on paper, the status of superpower. The country had 148 silos for housing SS-18 ICBMs, each missile packed with multiple nuclear warheads. Long-range bombers were parked at Soviet air bases, along with a strategic arsenal of air-launched cruise missiles. According to reported numbers, Kazakhstan in 1991 had 104 ICBMs and forty strategic bombers, which gave the newly independent country an arsenal totaling 1,360 warheads. And it got them all without massive investment in a nuclear weapons complex.

Nazarbayev, then Kazakhstan's Communist Party boss, was a sup-porter of Mikhail Gorbachev's attempts to keep the Soviet Union intact, but he was also mindful of forces that were pulling his republic away from Moscow. He consolidated his local power base, maneuvering to the presidency of the republic in 1990. He stayed on the sidelines when a group of incompetent regime stalwarts attempted a coup against Gorbachev in August 1991, condemning the plotters only after it was clear the putsch would fail. Kazakhstan reluctantly became independent in December 1991. Fifteen new states emerged from the breakup, and four of them—Russia, Ukraine, Belarus, and Kazakhstan—had nuclear weapons on their soil. These new nations appeared on the map just as Yugoslavia was violently spinning apart, and the world was faced with the terrifying prospect of three infant republics, nuclear armed, with uncertain politics and potential ethnic divides. Within a few short years, an accord was reached on dismantling those nuclear arsenals and returning the warheads to Russia.

According to the current founding myth of Kazakhstan's modern statehood, Nazarbayev wisely and selflessly gave up the country's nuclear arsenal. The reality was a bit more complicated. The final collapse of the Soviet Union was precipitated by the Belovezhskaya accords, where the presidents of the Russian Federation, Ukraine, and Belarus ripped up the treaty that held together the Union of Soviet Socialist Republics (USSR). In 1991, after agreeing with the other newly independent countries to give up its nuclear weapons, Kazakhstan suddenly backtracked. "Kazakhstan is a big country and it can't stand unarmed between China and Russia. China has one billion people and it is not clear who will come to power in the future. In Russia the situation is so unstable," a spokesman for Nazarbayev was quoted as saying.

Over the next few years, Kazakhstan—led by Nazarbayev—nego-tiated technical and financial assistance as well as security guarantees in exchange for finally agreeing in 1994 to give up its nuclear stockpile. In a top-secret deal with the United States—dubbed Project Sapphire—Nazarbayev also agreed to allow the United States to whisk away some six hundred kilograms of highly enriched uranium that was stored in the country. By 1995, Kazakhstan, Ukraine, and Belarus were nuclear free and signatories to the Nuclear Non-Proliferation Treaty. Over a decade after disarmament, however, the government of Kazakhstan wanted to remind the international community that it is both a victim of nuclear tests and a model of disarmament. In promoting Semipalatinsk as a nuclear tourism destination, it sought to balance those two roles.

We flew to Semipalatinsk by way of Astana, which looked like Skypad Apartments from *The Jetsons* transplanted to the middle of the steppe. The city was built, quite literally, in the middle of nowhere. In the 1990s, the very arrogance of a planned city rising out of the barren wastes of northern Kazakhstan was mocked by diplomats, who dreaded the prospects of moving from Almaty, a boomtown with a flourishing nightlife, to Astana, a city that every guidebook noted was once named Akmola, or white death. When Nazarbayev designated Astana as the new capital of Kazakhstan in 1997, reporters flew here to write tongue-in-cheek stories about the deluded autocrat and his plans for a post-Soviet Brasília.

But we arrived to find the city to be an almost appealing mix of futurist architecture and Soviet nostalgia. Japanese architect Kisho Kurokawa had designed the airport—a soaring glass structure—to match the modernist ambitions of Astana. Inside, we paused to look at a display case featuring a scale model of the new residential apartment complexes going up in the capital. Kazakh planners, it seemed, favored a revamped version of Stalinist architecture; the buildings still had that ponderous, wedding cake design, but were updated with sleek, smoked-glass facades. Notably absent on the roads were the rusting Eastern Bloc–built cars that congested Russian streets. Most people were driving European and Japanese cars.

Downtown Astana featured a mix of Western-themed restaurants meant to lure visiting foreigners and new shopping areas fueled by a booming oil economy. But the ubiquitous feature of the new capital was the president; his portrait hung in businesses, museums, and even our four-star hotel. There were also posters: Nazarbayev shaking hands with world leaders; Nazarbayev greeting young Kazakh schoolchildren; Nazarbayev embracing religious minorities. There was constant Nazarbayev on television, speaking solemnly yet optimistically to his fellow citizens. Nazarbayev was not on the level of Saparmurat Niyazov, the megalomaniac dictator of Turkmenistan, who renamed the months of the year in his own honor. But Nazarbayev's omnipresence was a reminder that whatever the level of economic development, Kazakhstan's path to democracy was still a bit rocky.

And even economic development has its limits. The difference between the showcase capital and Semipalatinsk began with the flight. We flew in a rickety Antonov turboprop that touched down on an aging runway leading to a squat, utilitarian terminal. A lone fuel truck was parked on the barren airfield. Passengers and crew unceremoniously began hauling their baggage to the pavement. Our final destination, however, was Kazakhstan's National Nuclear Center, located in Kurchatov, about two hours' drive from Semipalatinsk over poorly maintained roads. Vladimir Afonin, an administrator from the atomic center, had agreed to pick us up at the airport. As we looked around for him, we caught sight of a small delegation of people waiting for us at the arrivals gate.

"Hello, you are welcome in Semipalatinsk!" said a rotund Kazakh man in a jacket, tie, and trench coat. The crossed flags of Kazakh-U.S. friendship were pinned to his lapel, and he was holding a sign with our names. In halting English, he introduced himself as Aidar Samayev, an employee of the Semipalatinsk *akimat*, or mayor's office. At Vassilenko's recommendation, we had contacted the local government before our trip. Officials there had promised to arrange some interviews in Semipalatinsk, particularly at the local cancer clinic, after our return from the test site.

Samayev—who, with his curly hair and rotund figure, bore an amusing resemblance to Kim Jong-il—had arrived at the airport with Zhanna, a matronly Kazakh official. A local television news crew was in tow. A microphone was thrust in our faces by a tall female newscaster: "Would you like to comment on the purpose of your visit to Kazakhstan?" Bewildered, we mumbled a few polite phrases about Kazakh-U.S. relations and mutual understanding.

In Soviet days, it was a tradition—or perhaps requirement—for government officials to accompany the rare foreign journalist on a preset itinerary, ensuring that reporters saw only the people and places that officialdom wanted them to see. In many towns, particularly in provincial areas, this tradition has carried on, in part out of misguided hospitality and in part perhaps simply because it is how things were always done. We realized that, like it or not, we were about to fall headlong into that trap. Informed of a visit by foreign journalists, the mayor's office, in fine Soviet tradition, wanted to showcase the town of Semipalatinsk. Brandishing an itinerary, Zhanna informed us of our schedule. Four days booked solid with meetings in Semipalatinsk, with scheduled breaks for lunch and dinner. We took a closer look at the list of meetings. Local poverty, AIDS official, *akimat*. "But the test site," we protested helplessly. "Test site later," Samayev replied. Where was our ride to Kurchatov? Zhanna gave a curt reply: "The people from the institute left already."

We debated for a minute about what to do. The empty terminal offered no place where we could confer discreetly about a course of action. Samayev tailed us through the airport asking questions: "Where did you learn your Russian? How long have you been studying the former Soviet Union?" With him at our elbows, we walked out of the terminal and to the driveway out front. It looked as if we would be staying in Semipalatinsk for a while; our bags were already being loaded into a waiting Volga sedan. As the trunk was about to slam shut, we spotted an amused-looking man standing next to a Toyota Land Cruiser with the hatch open. It was, we figured correctly, Afonin, waiting to take us to Kurchatov. We quickly grabbed our bags from the trunk of the Volga, loaded them into the Land Cruiser, and promised to call Samayev just as soon as we returned.

The car sped off toward Kurchatov, leaving behind a crestfallen Samayev. Zhanna was still holding our itinerary. Our driver, a Kazakh in wraparound shades and a black turtleneck, kept a steady hand on the wheel, all the while cracking sunflower seeds and neatly placing the shells in an empty tin on the door. In the passenger seat, Afonin glanced back with a smile. "I was wondering where you were," he said.

The Soviets tested their first atomic device, RDS-1, at the Semipalatinsk Test Site on August 29, 1949. The device—dubbed Joe-1 by U.S. atomic scientists—was essentially a copy of the Fat Man implosion device that was tested at Trinity and exploded over Nagasaki. Soviet bomb designers had acquired technical details of the design through an espionage ring that penetrated the heart of the Manhattan Project. The spy work saved the designers considerable trial and error, but the Soviet bomb program also drew on the leadership of physicist Igor Kurchatov, who showed the same theoretical genius and relentless drive as Robert Oppenheimer.

The mood of the scientists and technicians preparing for the test, code-named First Lightning, must have been somber. The Soviet atomic bomb project was overseen by Lavrenti Beria, Stalin's murderous, frog-eyed chief of the NKVD, the secret-police force that preceded the KGB. The punishment for failure would have been severe. Like the Trinity site, the land selected for the Soviet atomic bomb test was remote and inaccessible: an expanse of arid grassland about sixty miles northwest of Semipalatinsk. A few people—nomadic Kazakhs—lived in the zone. They were unceremoniously evicted.

Over the next four decades following that first test, the Semipalatinsk Test Site served as the main Soviet nuclear testing center, the Cold War mirror to the Nevada Test Site. (The Soviets also touched off over one hundred nuclear devices on Novaya Zemlya, an archipelago in the Arctic Ocean, similar to U.S. tests in the far-away Marshall Islands.) The Semipalatinsk site—referred to in Russian as the *polygon*—eventually covered a territory of 18,500 square kilometers, roughly the size of Belgium or Israel. As our truck bounced over the rutted roads leading toward the site, we could see why the place was ideal for testing. It was located in a natural depression with very few water sources, perfect for observation. There were few signs of life, save for the arresting sight of herds of wild horses. (Vassilenko might have resented Borat's jokes about Kazakhs drinking fermented horse urine, but horse meat is still a prized delicacy in Kazakhstan.)

At the height of the Cold War, nearly fifty thousand people lived in the town of Kurchatov, the administrative center at the edge of the *polygon*. Part of the USSR's network of secret cities, Kurchatov was known only by its postal codes, Moscow-400 or Semipalatinsk-16. The place was cordoned off from the outside world by a barbed-wire fence, and military guards controlled access to the city, funneling traffic through a main checkpoint. But residents enjoyed a high standard of living, at least by Soviet measures. There were no shortages of butter or kielbasa.

We drove past the old Soviet checkpoint, passing row after row of collapsing facades of three- and four-story apartment buildings and military barracks. If Mercury, Nevada, looked like a ghost town, the abandoned main boulevard in Kurchatov looked like it had been hit by heavy shell fire. The small city had once been a pleasant oasis in the middle of the dry steppe, but the hulking granite statue of Kurchatov now cast an ominous shadow over the town's empty main square. The bearded figure gazed away from his Kazakh successors, who now occupied the buildings and institutes once used by Soviet weapons scientists. After shutting down the test site, Nazarbayev issued another decree in 1992 declaring the city of Kurchatov a scientific center dedicated to the peaceful use of the atom.

Kurchatov was no longer a classified city. The last underground test had been conducted at the site on October 19, 1989. And in a decree signed on August 29, 1991, the anniversary of the first Soviet atomic test, Nazarbayev had ordered the closing of the Semipalatinsk Test Site. Without testing, Kurchatov lost its purpose. Eventually, more than three quarters of the city's residents—mostly ethnic Russians with no ties to the newly independent Kazakhstan—packed up and left. The Russians, as locals now like to say, took everything but the glass in the windows.

Closing the test site was one matter, but wishing a world-class research institute into existence was quite another. Without nuclear weapons, Kurchatov was drained of scientific talent. And today, Kazakhstan's National Nuclear Center is a lab still in search of a purpose. In his modest office overlooking the town square, Zhenis Zhotabayev, the head of the center, explained his basic mission: conducting a radiological survey of the Semipalatinsk *polygon* and other sites in the country where the Soviets had conducted nuclear testing. The Soviets had collected extensive data at the test site, but after the collapse of the USSR, the Russians had packed it up and taken it back to Moscow.

In building the National Nuclear Center, Kazakh scientists like Zhotabayev were essentially starting from scratch. Zhotabayev grew up in provincial eastern Kazakhstan in the 1950s, the son of a local Communist Party official. During our interview, he recalled sitting in his classroom as a child and hearing an earth-rattling sound. "We were taking a test and finished early," he told us. "Suddenly there was this powerful—I wouldn't say explosion. It was more like a powerful crack! Like a thunderclap, but much, much stronger. And the glass rattled. We felt the earth shake." Zhotabayev paused for a moment. "We didn't know about the testing."

With his wavy, shoulder-length white hair, Zhotabayev looked a bit like the Kazakh version of American physicist Richard Feynman. He described the operations to clean up and monitor the test site as an arduous endeavor. The Kazakhs received some international help ("not as much as we'd like, of course"), but in order to survey every part of the sprawling site, they still needed to take hundreds of thousands of samples. They had only succeeded in mapping out about 20 percent of the total territory. Zhotabayev said they had received help in dismantling some test infrastructure, but when it came to data that could help map out the extent of the radioactive contamination, the Kazakhs had gotten nothing. "Russia hasn't given us anything," he laughed. "To be completely frank, we are starting here from zero."

But cleaning up the site—and conducting an extensive radiological survey—was not exactly world-class science. It was more like nuclear custodial work. Zhotabayev wanted to tell us about the research work of the National Nuclear Center, which now encompasses four institutes, including the Institute of Nuclear Physics outside Almaty and the Institute of Atomic Energy in Kurchatov. Despite Kazakhstan's unhappy experience with nuclear weaponry, the government has declared developing nuclear power a priority, and Zhotabayev was positively brimming with enthusiasm about that project. "You know that the president and the prime minister have in recent speeches said that it's time to pursue the development of nuclear energy, and we've already been moving in that direction," Zhotabayev said optimistically.

Rising from his cluttered desk, he showed us some reactor models. The Japanese, he said, had shown interest in cooperation, and he had the crossed flags of Kazakhstan and Japan on his desktop to prove it. It was hard not to sympathize with Zhotabayev, but reviving the fortunes of Kurchatov seemed a remote prospect at best. By the mid-1990s, things had really bottomed out. Dilapidated apartments were being sold for as little as two hundred dollars, and no one thought the town had a future.

Yet trying to revive the city of Kurchatov is still the goal. After our meeting with Zhotabayev, we took a walk across the square in front of the former Communist Party headquarters, where we met with

Anuarbek Mukhtarkhanov, the *akim*, or mayor, of Kurchatov. He, too, had ambitious plans. Sitting in his office—underneath a portrait of a benevolent President Nazarbayev—the mayor spoke effusively of hopes for a "technopark" that would lure investment to this remote corner of the steppe. "The government of Kazakhstan has turned its attention to this," he told us. "The park of nuclear technology has started its work." And last August, he added for emphasis, they had founded a state-owned joint stock company.

We expressed doubt that anyone could be persuaded to invest in a venture in which the Kazakh government held 100 percent of the shares, but the *akim* continued his pitch: Kurchatov would have an "engineering center" and a "business incubator," and by 2011 the center would be funded purely "on the republic level." There was a plan for growth, he emphasized. "By 2009, we are planning to have a centralized hot water supply." (Hot water was notably infrequent.) As further proof of their efforts, Mukhtarkhanov said, the city had grown by about six hundred people in recent years. By 2015, he said, the *naukograd*, or science city, of Kurchatov would have a population of fifteen or sixteen thousand.

Kurchatov was two hours from a regional airport, it had spotty hot water on a good day, and the city center looked like it had been visited by Genghis Khan. What would attract people to the city, we asked? The *akim* rubbed his fingers together in the universal symbol for money. "Of all the towns in the region of eastern Kazakhstan, we have the highest average salary—forty thousand tenge per month." That amounted to a little over three hundred dollars.

Yelena Starenkova, the vice mayor, had a different story. When we sat down with her alone in her office, she confided to us the real problem. Semipalatinsk, the largest city in the region, was soaking up most of the aid money. The awkward showdown we had faced at the Semipalatinsk airport suddenly became clear; it wasn't just an over-abundance of municipal hospitality, it was also very much a question of which city would be highlighted in the "nuclear tragedy" story: Kurchatov or Semipalatinsk? The two cities were in a battle for the nuclear legacy, and there was money at stake.

Everyone, Starenkova complained, had heard about Semipalatinsk, but no one had ever heard of Kurchatov. "Our city is in the shadow of Semipalatinsk," she said. "Everything [nuclear] is associated with

Semipalatinsk in the mind of donor countries. The Methodist church helped us a bit. The old *akim* tried to set up a sister cities program, but it didn't work out. And whenever the media show up, they just want to shoot the derelict apartment buildings for local color."

Indeed, Kurchatov was not yet dead, but it looked like a marauding army had recently passed through. On an early-evening stroll, we passed rows of run-down housing and the empty shell of the Univermag, once the city's main department store. There was the occasional sign of life. A few children played in a weed-choked lot, while teenagers in tracksuits lounged on the hood of a Volga sedan. But the only construction was at Beria's old cottage. The last Soviet general in charge of the Semipalatinsk complex donated the secret policeman's former residence to the Russian Orthodox Church. An enthusiastic young priest was overseeing a small crew of army conscripts who were plastering the interior. The city, named after the Russian scientist who had led the Soviet Union to nuclear glory, was a shell of its former self.

It was an atomic ghost town.

Back when nuclear blasts shook the barren steppe of eastern Kazakhstan, Soviet scientists and their families in the city of Kurchatov took precautions. Schoolchildren went inside, residents shut their windows, and officials passed out iodine tablets to protect workers from radiation. Valentin Kuklev, a civilian employee involved in nuclear testing, told us of another precautionary step taken by rank-and-file technicians: They drank. "I'll tell you what kind of antiradiation measures we took," he recalled when we met with him back in Moscow. "The main one was alcohol, pure distilled spirit. Before every test, we drank grain alcohol."

Kuklev, who had worked for the Goskomgidromet, the unpronounceable Soviet state meteorological service, said he and his colleagues were given radiation suits and gas masks, but they tossed the burdensome equipment aside. The nuclear tests were often conducted at ten A.M. Moscow time (midday in eastern Kazakhstan), so as a prophylaxis, Kuklev and his co-workers would start drinking the night before.

Nuclear tests at the site ended in 1989, and our hosts at the National Nuclear Center gave us the same reassurance we had heard at the Nevada Test Site: Most of the Semipalatinsk *polygon* was at background radiation levels, though there were still pockets of elevated contamination.

The day after our arrival in Kurchatov, we were led on a tour of the test site. Our guide, Yuriy Strilchuk, showed up wearing what appeared to be a homemade uniform, consisting of old fatigues, fashionable aviator sunglasses, and a camouflage hat. He was carrying a handheld dosimeter, something we hadn't seen on our trip to the Nevada Test Site the previous year. As our official minder, Strilchuk was there to make sure that we didn't get more than our allotted dose. The precautions were somewhat comical, considering that—as the Lonely Planet *Central Asia* guidebook pointed out—tourists wishing to visit the test site could also simply hop a cab from the neighboring city of Semipalatinsk, thus bypassing any formalities.

Strilchuk had the occasional chore of escorting reporters out to the test site. And that meant reassuring visitors about the effects of radiation. *Radiophobia*, as Russians like to call fear of radiation, affects everyone differently. Strilchuk recalled with amusement how some German journalists had arrived at the test site equipped with ventilators, and how a pair of Polish TV producers had been afraid to get out of their car. But others were fearless to the point of absurdity. One Scandinavian camera operator had lain down in the radioactive dirt to get a better shot of ground zero.

We drove along the heavily potholed road in a blue Niva, a Russian-built off-road vehicle, passing an abandoned collective farm, where a few wild horses and cattle roamed the grass. An air defense artillery unit had once been stationed here, protecting the site against potential attackers. But now the security around the place was nonexistent. We stopped at the unmanned perimeter gate, where Strilchuk took a first dosimeter read, about twelve to fourteen microroentgens per hour—essentially background levels, he told us.

Years of nuclear detonations at Semipalatinsk had scarred the landscape. In addition to aboveground tests, the Soviets detonated nuclear devices inside a series of horizontal tunnels carved out of Site D, or the Degelen Mountain Complex, as well as inside vertical test holes drilled at the Balapan Testing Field. They also conducted a series of "peaceful" atomic tests similar to the Sedan test at the Nevada Test Site. An underground nuclear explosion conducted in 1965 left an "atomic lake" at the Balapan site, formed in the massive crater left by the test.

Craters weren't the only thing left behind. The Soviets had also left a live nuclear device inside Tunnel 108-K, carved out of Degelen Mountain. The device—emplaced in June 1991—was a "special" design with an uncertain shelf life; a brochure produced by the National Nuclear Center noted euphemistically that the device inside 108-K was left under "off-design" conditions such as the flooding of the tunnel. In 1995, it took a complex engineering operation and a thirty-kilogram charge of high explosives to destroy the device and seal it in place.

Strilchuk stopped the car, and we got out at the outer perimeter of the first nuclear test. A smashed beer bottle and a discarded boot lay next to testing infrastructure. For the first test, the Soviets divided the site into fourteen pie-shaped sectors to study the blast effects on different kinds of structures and equipment. In one sector, they parked military vehicles and equipment; in another, they constructed civilian buildings and a typical village street. There were factory buildings, fortifications, and a railroad bridge. And much as American scientists did in Nevada, their Soviet counterparts also included a biological testing area, where they studied the effects of blast and heat on live animals, including dogs, pigs, sheep, and horses. Even a few camels were corralled within the blast radius. At the outermost perimeter, where we had stopped, all that was left were bits of peeling concrete and random rebar.

Soviet weapons scientists also designed a series of diagnostic towers, built in concentric circles around the shot tower. There were three types—A, B, and V, coded after the first three letters of the Cyrillic alphabet. Soldiers nicknamed the structures Annushka (Annie), Bukashka (Little Bug), and Verochka (Little Vera). We parked at a type B (Bukashka) about three thousand meters from ground zero. Diagnosticians had set up film equipment here to record the event; they shot footage indirectly through mirrors and glass, presumably so the intense flash from the fireball would not damage the photographic equipment. The glass was no longer intact; anything of value inside the three-story concrete tower—metal, mirrors, diagnostic cable—had been hauled away by local scavengers long ago or removed when the Soviet scientists left.

There was more evidence of rampant scavenging at the site. Next to the tower, a shallow trench had been excavated. At one time, over five hundred kilometers of communications cable connected the entire infrastructure around the test site. Local metal hunters eager to unearth valuable aluminum scrap had stripped almost all of it away. Kurchatov officials were understandably concerned that the irradiated metal from the site had made its way to the global scrap market, but there was little they could do. The former test site, though officially off-limits, is not protected by gates or security. We asked Strilchuk about the penalties for trespassing on the test site. "Oh, if we run into them, they get a warning," he replied.

Outside the Bukashka tower, Strilchuk got a reading of nine micro-roentgens per hour ("That's background level," he said). We drove on. About three hundred meters from ground zero, the Soviets had built a railroad bridge. The reinforced bridge piers were toppled like some ancient column; the concrete fragments of the bridge were strewn in the grass. Strilchuk—who had an excellent command of the history of the first test—stopped to explain a piece of lore. The Americans had dubbed that test Joe-1 after Joseph Stalin, but the Soviets had coded it RDS-1, which in many history books stands for *reaktivny dvigatel Stalina*, or Stalin's rocket engine. But the real provenance of the name, Strilchuk said, remained a mystery, perhaps even to the Russian physicists. In one joint meeting between the Kazakhs and the Russians in the 1990s, scientists from both sides attempted to get to the bottom of the mystery, but only came up with more variations: *Rossiya delaet sama* ("made in Russia") or *Rossiya daet sdachu* ("Russia strikes back"). No one really knew for sure, Strilchuk said.

We continued on foot toward the center of the site. Strilchuk's dosimeter confirmed that the levels were at background—less than ten microroentgens per hour—for the better part of our trip. But as we moved closer to the hypocenter the number on the readout slowly crept up. Around 220 meters from ground zero, the dosimeter gave a reading of sixty-six microroentgens. A few steps farther and the display jumped to six hundred microroentgens, a level Strilchuk compared to getting a chest X-ray. When we finally reached ground zero, Strilchuk paused for another dosimeter read. The counter on the LCD screen had spiked to over two thousand microroentgens per hour. Strilchuk warned us not to linger there for longer than ten or fifteen minutes.

It was here that the Soviets detonated their first nuclear device in 1949, just four years after the Trinity test in New Mexico. Unlike the Trinity site, which was never reused in atomic testing and was even-tually adorned with a historic marker, the site of the RDS-1 experiment was reused and the original Soviet ground zero had been bulldozed over a few times. Visitors to the site were sometimes disappointed, Strilchuk said: "They say this can't be the real site; they want to know where the crater is."

Walking around ground zero, we saw pieces of molten rock, named *kharitonchiki* after one of the leading Russian nuclear weapons scientists, Yuly Khariton. The porous black pebbles weren't quite as pretty as the greenish Trinitite found at White Sands Missile Range, but they were equally intriguing. We were politely rebuked when we picked up a piece. According to Strilchuk, they were still dangerous to handle. "Just because I pick it up doesn't mean you should," he said.

Was a *kharitonchik* any more radioactive than a piece of Trinitite? How much was myth and how much was reality almost didn't matter. The secrecy surrounding nuclear testing created a climate of distrust. After a ten-minute stay, Strilchuk ushered us back to the Niva. A ten- or fifteen-minute stay at the center, plus the trip to the site, gives about the same dose of radiation as on a transatlantic flight, he explained. But you should have worn boots, he scolded, pointing to our Converse sneakers. "You had better wash those when you get back to town."

The day after our tour, we returned by car to Semipalatinsk. Driving back toward the city limits, we were reminded that this was still the ex-USSR. We passed a tank-driving range, where a Kazakh motorized infantry unit practiced driving its Soviet armored personnel carriers. A sign on the roof of a large apartment building, no doubt a holdover from Soviet days, carried a stern public service announcement: PEDES-TRIANS BE DISCIPLINED ON THE ROAD.

Back in the city, we met up again with Samayev, our fast friend from the airport. Samayev worked in the international section of the mayor's office of Semipalatinsk, a city of around four hundred thousand. He met us at the hotel smiling and with a fresh itinerary in hand, anxious to show off the city. His mission, as we quickly came to understand it, was to ensure that we never left the city—or at least not until we had absorbed every fact and figure he had memorized about his beloved hometown.

As we drove with Samayev, he explained that Semipalatinsk is the old Russian name for a city czarist officers once called the "devil's sandbox." The Kazakhs now call it Semey, which Samayev helpfully translated as "soul place." It was an industrial city with not much else to lure visitors. Almaty had mountains and discos; Astana had shiny new architecture. Semipalatinsk was downwind from the Soviet Union's main atomic test site.

But it wasn't a hard sell for Samayev, who wanted to share his vision of Semipalatinsk, a city that had so much to offer to the outside world ("museum of miniature dolls," "Dostoyevsky house," "famous mosque"). For the next few days, he was like a third hand, forever present, reluctant even to part in the evening. Our first stop on the nuclear tour was the memorial to the victims of atomic testing. Called *Stronger Than Death*, the gargantuan public sculpture featured a granite woman kneeling protectively over her child. Hovering overhead was the silhouette of a mushroom cloud. The sculpture reflected the Soviet taste for the literal in public art. But what effect did five decades of nuclear testing really have on the local population? At the Semipalatinsk Institute of Radiation Medicine and Ecology, answers were frustratingly elusive.

During the Soviet era, the main task of the institute was not to provide treatment for fallout victims but to dispatch top-secret reports to the Institute of Biophysics in Moscow. Now it serves the public. With some research assistance from the Japanese, the institute has created a database of over a quarter of a million people affected by testing. Researchers focus on understanding the effects of radiation; documents rescued from Soviet times, once marked top secret, now feed into their studies. They have concluded, not surprisingly, that the region has an elevated cancer rate.

Boris Gusev, director emeritus of the institute, takes a measured approach to their work. "Not all pathologies can be attributed to the aftereffects of radiation," he said. "Unfortunately, our region also has heavy industry. More than half of illnesses can't just be attributed to radiation; it's the overall ecological situation. We don't try to encourage hysteria, and we take a realistic and objective approach to the whole problem."

Samayev, who was sitting in on our interview, shifted in his chair. It was a nuanced point that didn't fit the narrative of Semipalatinsk as a victim of nuclear testing. On our way to the next appointment, however, he brightened up, and the monologue continued. There was Samayev on Afghanistan ("They didn't appreciate what the Soviets did for them"), Samayev on Islam ("Muslims can eat pork; when the Quran was written, we didn't know about modern sanitation"), and our personal favorite, Samayev on the Soviet era ("not altogether a bad thing").

In between interviews, Samayev gave us sections of his Web site to edit, hoping to maximize the presence of useful, English-speaking foreigners. His Web site, he hoped, would eventually draw tourists to the many fine museums and monuments of Soul Place—as well as to the nuclear test site. "A short visit will not pose any danger to human health, rather the pervasive atmosphere will give you an emotive impression of the tragedy," read his proposed text.

Our next visit was to the mayor's office. We met with the mayor's chief of staff, Yerlan Maikenov, a man in a charcoal-colored suit with a matching mustache. Once again, the local press had been invited, this time to cover Maikenov's meeting with the foreign journalists. We were ushered into a cavernous office and seated at a long table, where Maikenov was thumbing through some information about us that had been faxed from the embassy in Washington. Sitting under the presidential portrait, Maikenov began by reading us a prepared speech about the trauma and effects of nuclear testing ("We have seventy sites around the city where preventative measures are taken for the population; we have invested ten million dollars into a cancer center. There is compensation for those who lived in the areas most affected by testing, including those residing in the zones of maximum risk . . .").

When we asked him for his thoughts on nuclear weapons, we got his first unscripted response. "Well, I'm a peaceful person. I don't even like to hold a knife," he said. "But of course if you must defend yourself . . ." He paused for a moment before remembering the party line: "I must bow before our president, who made the wise decision to turn away from nuclear weapons."

On our way back to the hotel, Samayev continued on the delights of Soul Place ("beautiful botanical garden," "children's zoo," "nice rivers"). We passed on his offer of evening entertainment ("I can offer a night excursion, town square, music disco"). Back at the Hotel Semey, we found that toilet paper was scarce, but prostitutes were readily available in the hallway. The Soviet-era hotel had seen better times (though Samayev had complimented the neorealist mosaic floor in the lobby, lamenting that no one made such designs anymore). We considered telling Samayev we might skip the next day's attractions and go directly to the airport. But we remembered one important thing: We hadn't yet seen the one-eyed baby.

After arriving the next morning at the Semipalatinsk State Medical University, we were ushered past a reliquary of Lenin statues and into a small two-story building housing a medical museum. Its walls were lined with jars of deformed fetuses, a horror show featuring encephalitic heads, misshapen bodies, and missing limbs. And there, floating in formaldehyde, was the one-eyed baby from the embassy Web site. "It's the only Cyclops baby in any museum," the caretaker proudly informed us. The line between victimhood and exploitation is a delicate one. Staring at the display, we suddenly felt like rubberneckers at a catastrophic car accident.

On our trip to the airport, we got a final lecture from Samayev—on the local churches ("beautiful"), on Dostoyevsky ("spent wonderful time in Semipalatinsk"), on the future of Kazakhstan ("hope not all good things from Soviet era are lost"). We felt trapped in a Borat skit.

At the airport, our host was not ready to let us go. He followed us through security and twice waved off a guard who insisted he leave. Whatever his faults, Samayev was an embodiment of local hospitality and national pride. In guiding us around Semipalatinsk, he showed us a country that was proud of its independence, if still a bit confused over its national identity. We worked hurriedly to finish editing his text on local culture, which touched on the neglected beauty of Soviet-era architecture and public art. We concentrated on the final passage:

> While you stay in Semipalatinsk, the city with blended old and new, with ancient history, the city bathed in green, you will spend an unforgettable time and I am sure that you will try to make your own contribution to the economic development of the land which suffered from nuclear testing.

We handed the paper back to Samayev, and airport security escorted him out.

*   *   *

A few months after our return from Kazakhstan, we attended the official dinner for President Nazarbayev in Washington. He arrived in the capital with a large entourage in tow, beginning his visit with the unveiling of a new statue at the embassy of Kazakhstan. The gold-hued statue featured an ornate nomadic archer poised stiffly atop a winged cat.

The curse of Borat, however, had followed Kazakhstan all the way to Washington, where Sacha Baron Cohen, in full character, held a press conference outside the embassy, assuring reporters that Nazarbayev's visit to Washington was to promote his film. The actor attracted a bigger crowd than the Kazakh president; the *Washington Post* reckoned there were about fifty journalists on hand to record Borat's press conference.

"My name Borat Sagdiyev," he said. "I would like-a make a comment on the recent advertisements on television and in media about my nation of Kazakhstan saying that women are treated equally and that all religions are tolerated." As his sidekick brandished the *New York Times* ad, Baron Cohen continued: "These are disgusting fabrications! These claims are part of a propaganda campaign against our country by evil nitwits Uzbekistan, who, as we all know, are a very nosy people with a bone in the middle of their brain."

But the dinner held that night at the Capital Hilton on Sixteenth and K streets in northwest Washington was designed to send a very different message: Kazakhstan was at the forefront of nonproliferation. The reception hall leading to the banquet room was decorated with pictures and tributes to the country's disarmament, and the Kazakh delegation mingled with VIPs like former national security adviser Brent Scowcroft and former senator Sam Nunn, who had spearheaded much of the U.S. counterproliferation work in the former Soviet Union. At one of the head tables sat Linton Brooks, the head of the NNSA.

We were seated on the fringes of the ballroom at a table with a former foreign service officer now working for Beltway contractor Washington Group International, along with a few other former midlevel bureaucrats and people vaguely associated with the oil industry. We sat and listened as Nazarbayev was welcomed by CNN founder Ted Turner, who had become the largest private sponsor of nonproliferation work, cofounding the Nuclear Threat Initiative. Turner got up to introduce "President Narabee-off."

After a long round of applause, Nazarbayev rose to the podium. Security guards with earpieces scanned the room. Nazarbayev began his speech, in Russian. The main topic was nuclear disarmament, but part of the speech seemed to be a critique—albeit a very polite one—of the politics of his hosts, the U.S. government. "A paradoxical situation is taking place in the world which in essence runs contrary to principles of international law: Some are allowed to have nuclear weapons and even modernize them, while others are forbidden from having them or even developing them," he said. "This is not right, unfair, and not evenhanded."

But about twenty minutes into his presentation, Nazarbayev made an interesting digression: "When I made the decision to eliminate nuclear weapons, Kazakhstan *was offered* by a certain party a very large amount of money so it would be the first Muslim-majority country in the world to declare itself a nuclear-armed power." Nazarbayev didn't name the country, and following his appearance, the embassy of Kazakhstan released an official English translation of the speech that curiously omitted the key passage about the unnamed country's attempt to bribe Kazakhstan into becoming a nuclear state. It was an intriguing aside, but no one at the Kazakh embassy would offer any comment.

Nazarbayev's take on nuclear disarmament was simple and attractive. Kazakhstan wisely and selflessly gave up its nukes, and won international guarantees of sovereignty and security in return. The reality was a bit more complex. Kazakhstan never really had operational control of nuclear weapons on its territory; it did not have the infrastructure to maintain a nuclear arsenal; and it had some financial incentives to surrender the warheads. Still, the results were real. The five countries of Central Asia—Kazakhstan, Kyrgyzstan, Uzbekistan, Tajikistan, and Turkmenistan—signed a treaty on September 8, 2006, creating a nuclear weapons–free zone in their region. Semipalatinsk was the site of the signing.

A few weeks after Nazarbayev's departure, Roman Vassilenko gave us his thoughts on the visit over lunch at a sushi restaurant near Washington's Dupont Circle. After dealing with the president's visit and coping with Borat, he was happy for the break (at his press conference, Baron Cohen had called out Vassilenko by name, labeling him an "Uzbek impostor"). Vassilenko was disappointed that U.S.

media was still not emphasizing the critical role he believed Kazakhstan had played in preventing nuclear proliferation, but he was upbeat about his country's future.

In fact, he was due to return to Kazakhstan, where he would take a more senior government post. The Kazakh government's advertising campaign, he conceded, had been "a bit heavy-handed." But the Borat movie was opening in theaters, and he felt the government needed to act fast. He offered the embassy of Kazakhstan's official statement on the movie: "The only actual facts about Kazakhstan in the movie are the country's geographic location and its flag." As we parted ways, he conceded the one good thing about the Borat movie.

"At least now people know where Kazakhstan is," he said.

CHAPTER 11

Barbarians at the Gate
In Search of Russia's Secret Nuclear Cities

Our first inquiry into visiting Russia's closed nuclear cities should have given us a clear indicator of how the rest of the trip would go. It began with Viktor Mikhailov.

"How old are you, anyway?" he asked, exhaling cigarette smoke through Soviet dentistry. "You've already forgotten your basic high school physics. You can't possibly be qualified to write on this subject."

We had arranged a meeting with Mikhailov, the former chief of Russia's atomic energy ministry, hoping that he might advise us on how to get access to Russia's nuclear cities. But things were not going well. Mikhailov—once a top nuclear weapons designer and winner of the Lenin Prize, the Soviet equivalent of a Nobel laureate—was working his way through a pack of Marlboro reds, irritated that his visitors had not read his autobiography, *Ya-yastreb* (or, as he icily translated the title, "I . . . am . . . hawk").

"Ask Sergei Kiriyenko and you'll get the answer: yes or no," he said, referring to the current head of Rosatom, Russia's federal nuclear agency. "Of course," he added with a slightly malevolent smile, "the security services will have a say in this as well."

Russian nuclear cities are in many ways mirror images of their U.S. counterparts. The United States had Robert Oppenheimer and Edward Teller, and the Soviet Union naturally had its own pantheon of scientists—such as Igor Kurchatov and Yuly Khariton—who fathered the Soviet atomic bomb. The year 2006 would mark the sixtieth anniversary of the founding of the All-Russian Scientific Research Institute of Experimental Physics in Sarov, a.k.a. Arzamas-16, the Russian equivalent of Los Alamos. We put in formal requests to visit the Russian laboratories, hoping the authorities would welcome the opportunity to showcase the accomplishments of the country's weapons designers.

There had been a brief interlude in the 1990s, when a select few Western journalists had been allowed into Russia's nuclear cities, but by 2006, when we traveled to Russia, the atmosphere was substantially different. Under the presidency of ex-KGB colonel Vladimir Putin, the Kremlin had reinvigorated its culture of official secrecy. The president's reinforcement of "vertical power" in Russia was affecting all parts of society. Putin was moving to consolidate the Kremlin's authority, which meant reining in oligarchs who had amassed money and influence under President Boris Yeltsin. It was becoming impossible for journalists to approach even the lowest municipal official without a sheaf of letters on company stationery, preferably plastered with impressive-looking stamps. The usual response to our entreaties was demands for more paperwork. This power play extended to the nuclear cities, which were becoming even more closed in recent years. And as one arms control expert warned us, Russia's atomic bureaucrats strongly objected to what they called "nuclear tourism."

Difficult as things may have been for journalists in Russia, it was becoming equally difficult for U.S. officials who worked in counter-proliferation programs. In an effort to stop the threat of "loose nukes," the U.S. government had underwritten a host of endeavors in the former Soviet Union under the mantle of the Cooperative Threat Reduction Program to help eliminate existing WMD stockpiles, upgrade security at nuclear facilities, and dissuade weapons scientists from moonlighting for rogue nations. Spearheaded by senators Sam Nunn and Richard Lugar, the Cooperative Threat Reduction Programs bankrolled efforts to secure nuclear materials across the former Soviet Union. Russian facilities received over half a billion dollars a year. The country's nuclear complex had been on the receiving end of around $1.6 billion since 1993 for facility security alone. Yet access to nuclear sites for U.S. officials, particularly under Putin, proved fickle. In August 2005, a high-level U.S.

delegation visiting Russian nuclear facilities was briefly detained in the Siberian city of Perm. The delegation was led by Lugar.

Money was flowing to the former Soviet Union, because as Nunn put it, "the gravest danger in the world today is that a nuclear weapon will be used by a state or a terrorist group." And the most likely origin of that weapon was the Russian arsenal. We wanted to travel to Russia to see if the billions being spent on preventing nuclear terrorism—arguably a more pertinent threat than the Russian arsenal itself—were really making the world any safer.

We had thus turned to Mikhailov for help. He had spent much of his career at Arzamas-16, the country's oldest and largest nuclear center, eventually rising through the ranks to become the minister of atomic energy. He had also helped oversee U.S.-Russian cooperation, including groundbreaking joint U.S.-Soviet underground nuclear tests in 1988 at the Nevada Test Site and the Semipalatinsk Test Site in Kazakhstan. We met with Mikhailov in Moscow at the Institute of Strategic Stability, a think tank affiliated with Rosatom. When he entered the room—wearing his gray flannel suit and lapel pin—he did little to blunt the impression of an imperious Soviet functionary. The staff in the waiting room rose in obsequious unison to shake his hand. We had been forewarned that Mikhailov, a strong advocate of Russia's nuclear deterrent, could be a bit abrasive.

By way of introduction, we explained our project, our visits to the U.S. national laboratories, and our desire to conduct similar interviews with weapons scientists in Russia. Mikhailov swiftly cut in. "What would you have to talk about with them?" he interjected, stubbing a butt in an ashtray. "Just banal things. 'How do you live?' 'What's your house like?' 'Do you have a family?' All these banal questions."

The days of U.S.-Soviet cooperation, apparently, stirred little nostalgia for Mikhailov. He suggested that the American weapons scientists lacked broad theoretical knowledge outside of their narrow field, disparaging in particular the scientific abilities of Siegfried Hecker, director emeritus of the Los Alamos National Laboratory. When we mentioned Mikhailov's pioneering work on joint U.S.-Soviet tests, he scoffed, saying, "I found the Americans weren't even such great scientists."

Mikhailov may not have had fond feelings for Americans, but neither was he a favorite of the Russian government. He had been forced to

resign from his ministry post in 1998, during one of the government
shake-ups that occurred with increasing frequency under erratic, binge-
drinking president Boris Yeltsin. Reports at the time noted that Mikhailov was opposed to downsizing Russia's nuclear weapons complex.
Since his ouster, the old academician had become one of the most
prominent public advocates for maintaining a robust nuclear deterrent.
Russia's nuclear arsenal, he had written, "is a guarantee of free choice
of a way forward not only for our people but for all nations who cannot
accept the American 'freedom and democracy.'"

We understood now why Mikhailov had titled his autobiography *I
Am a Hawk*. It would have been easy to dismiss him as an unrepentant
cold warrior with a sense of injured pride. His prickly apparatchik
routine certainly reinforced the impression, but that would have been
too simplistic. Mikhailov, when he was in government, had been an
advocate for making the nuclear cities more open. But his view today
reflected wider concerns about the future of Russia's nuclear deterrent.
That spring, in fact, an article in *Foreign Affairs*—titled "The Rise of
U.S. Nuclear Primacy"—had sparked a major uproar in the Russian
press. The authors, Keir Lieber and Daryl Press, had argued that
Russia's nuclear capability had seriously deteriorated since the end
of the Cold War. The cornerstone of nuclear deterrence—mutual
assured destruction—was at an end, they suggested. "Today, for the
first time in almost 50 years, the United States stands on the verge of
attaining nuclear primacy," they wrote. "It will probably soon be
possible for the United States to destroy the long-range nuclear arsenals
of Russia or China with a first strike."

The piece fueled even more unease over America's intentions.
NATO's eastward expansion—the alliance now included the Baltic
states and former Warsaw Pact members—had stoked Russian fears of
encirclement. And the Bush administration's push for a ballistic missile
shield, advertised as a defense against rogue regimes like Iran or North
Korea, had also provoked suspicion. Russian military leaders insisted
missile defense was actually designed to neuter Russia's nuclear might,
a belief that was only reinforced when the United States announced
plans to house interceptors in Poland and a tracking radar in the Czech
Republic.

Hence Russia's desire for a strong deterrent. Mikhailov, in fact,
noted with pride that there was "no shortage" of young Russians who

wanted to work in the nuclear complex. They had better pay, good benefits, and guaranteed housing. "If you want to go to a closed city, write to Kiriyenko," he suggested again. "Of course, the situation has become much more complicated. The security services are really tightening the screws. I myself have complained about this."

Mikhailov stamped out his final cigarette. Our meeting was at an end.

During the Cold War, the Soviets built a network of closed cities called the Zakrytye Administrativno-Territorial'nye Obrazovaniya (literally, closed administrative-territorial entities) to house secret weapons projects. The ZATO were off-limits to ordinary citizens. Often built with the labor of conscripts or prisoners, the secret cities were surrounded by barbed wire and guarded by soldiers; residents could not enter or exit without a pass. It was the Soviet *propiska*—a system of residence permits that restricted travel within the Soviet Union—on steroids. Like Los Alamos in the days of the Manhattan Project, Soviet secret cities were often in isolated locales. Classified research needed to be conducted in utmost seclusion. And like Los Alamos—once identified as P.O. Box 1663, Santa Fe, New Mexico—Soviet secret cities were often known only by postal codes.

Residents of these cities enjoyed a high standard of living, at least for the USSR. The authorities understood that scientists, technicians, and their families needed above-average housing, schools, and libraries to compensate for their isolated lives behind the wire. In an economy of shortages, central planners ensured that the shelves in the local grocery stores were always well stocked, a measure that kept Russia's nuclear arsenal secure. Jim Toevs, the head of nonproliferation programs at Los Alamos, described the system as the "five Gs": guns, gates, guards, groceries, and gulag. As Toevs put it, "Why would you put all this at risk to try to steal some material that you couldn't get out of the country?"

The secret cities included two premier atomic weapons design centers: Sarov (known by the postal code Arzamas-16) and Snezhinsk (designated Chelyabinsk-70). In many ways, the cities of Sarov and Snezhinsk were the mirror images of Los Alamos and Lawrence Livermore. Some weapons scientists even jokingly referred to Sarov as "Los Arzamas." Industrial towns such as Ozersk—formerly known as Chelyabinsk-65 or Chelyabinsk-40—were also part of the nuclear archipelago. Ozersk housed the Mayak Production Association, an industrial facility that produced plutonium pits, the triggers for modern thermonuclear weapons.

Russia still maintains a massive arsenal (over fifty-eight hundred operational nuclear warheads, according to a 2006 estimate prepared by the Natural Resources Defense Council); it boasts top-flight nuclear research institutes, a network that in scale and geographic reach rivals the U.S. weapons complex. But by the mid-1990s, there was general agreement that the Russian nuclear weapons labs were at the breaking point. Once known for their high standard of living, the closed cities seemed more like provincial backwaters. In October 1996, a despondent Vladimir Nechai, the director of Sarov's Institute for Experimental Physics, where famed Soviet dissident Andrey Sakharov once worked, shot himself. Russia, in the meantime, was close to hitting rock bottom. After a financial collapse in August 1998, the country resembled a sort of Slavic Nigeria, a lawless, resource-rich kleptocracy. Salaries went unpaid for months; bureaucrats and bandits struggled for control of state assets; and a new war in Chechnya was under way. The place seemed on the brink of collapse.

If Russia in the 1990s was not a direct strategic threat to the United States, its crumbling infrastructure presented a new security concern: the possibility that terrorists or so-called rogue states would obtain nuclear weapons, material, or know-how from the former Soviet Union. Securing Russia's arsenal became a major worry for the U.S. government. Department of Energy scientists, as well as Pentagon officials, began making trips to Russia to jump-start cooperative programs meant to secure key sites. Some scientists returned from visits to Russia with horror stories about poorly secured stockpiles of fissile material.

Larry Satkowiak, the director of nuclear nonproliferation programs at Oak Ridge National Laboratory, described to us his visit to the Research Institute of Atomic Reactors in Dimitrovgrad with a team of experts from the Department of Energy. "I was the first American to go into this building," he said. "And this building had literally hundreds of kilograms of highly enriched uranium and weapons-grade plutonium—it was a warehouse—stacked on a loading dock." The material was stored behind wooden doors with some rudimentary alarms. Anyone with a crowbar could get in.

Much of Russia's nuclear security had broken down after 1991, reaching critical levels by the late 1990s. The great unknown, however, was whether in the midst of that upheaval any significant quantities of nuclear material—or worse, a complete weapon—had actually ended up in the hands of the highest bidder. Many of the fears of nuclear watchers were further confirmed in January 2007, when authorities in the former Soviet republic of Georgia announced they had arrested a Russian nuclear smuggler. The man, Oleg Khintsagov, was caught in a sting operation while allegedly trying to sell a quantity of highly enriched uranium, material suitable for making a bomb. During questioning, Khintsagov confessed he had acquired the material in Novosibirsk, one of Russia's major scientific cities. But the most alarming—and most controversial—claim of nuclear theft was made in 1997, when General Alexander Lebed, who had been Yeltsin's national security adviser, reported that over one hundred "suitcase nukes," or nuclear demolition weapons similar to the U.S. military's SADM, had essentially gone missing.

Lebed's claim, later discredited, was seized upon by Curt Weldon, a Republican congressman from Pennsylvania and longtime Russia watcher. Weldon, a senior member of the House Armed Services Committee, had during his many terms in Congress emerged as something of a foreign policy gadfly, making, by his own account, some forty-five trips to Russia alone. He had also, in recent years, jetted to other nuclear hot spots, like North Korea and Libya. Some of his antics—like promoting the theory that a military intelligence program had identified several members of the 9/11 terror cell prior to the 2001 attacks—rankled Democrats and Republicans alike. But Russia, and Russia's nuclear arsenal, was his top international priority, and in 2003 he made a groundbreaking trip to Zheleznogorsk, formerly Krasnoyarsk-26, a plutonium-producing plant in Siberia.

We met with Weldon in his congressional office a few months before our trip to Russia, where he showed us the mock-up of a suitcase nuke, which he said a former CIA official had built for him. He then spent two hours blasting U.S. policy toward Russia. "Whether it was proliferation, corruption, or efforts to develop a strong leadership in the Duma, our leadership in Washington was a dismal failure," he argued.

According to Weldon, the root cause of poor U.S.-Russian relations—and of the United States' inability to foster genuine nuclear cooperation—lay in its turning a blind eye to corruption under Boris Yeltsin. The U.S.-funded Cooperative Threat Reduction Program was also rife with corruption, he charged, noting that Russia's former minister of atomic energy had been indicted in the United States for siphoning off money meant for nuclear projects.

Weldon had his own solution. A few years earlier, he had been approached by Alexander Kotenkov, Putin's representative to the Duma, the Russian parliament. Kotenkov's proposal was to work through a nongovernmental organization that would serve as an intermediary between the Russian and U.S. governments for cooperative programs, particularly ones involving nuclear weapons. Only it wasn't exactly nongovernmental. The entity, called the International Exchange Group, was openly governed by Putin's allies. The board of governors included Kotenkov, members of the Duma, and military officials. And rather than funneling money directly to the labs, or to private businesses working with the labs, the money would all be run through this government-controlled NGO.

To prove how serious they were, Kotenkov's cohorts got Weldon into Zheleznogorsk, where no American had previously been. Weldon recalled it as "a beautiful city in the middle of Siberia," but also "a terrorist's dream." He was taken into a mountain, where the Soviets had built plutonium reactors far away from the prying eyes of American satellites. "We took a photographer," he said. "There were no limitations." He described the mountain, still filled with thousands of small containers of weapons-grade material, but with very little external security. It was also a place that had been, up to that point, beyond the reach of any American delegations, he said. "There we are in the mountain with no one from the State Department, no one from Defense Department, Energy Department, or CIA."

Weldon came back from Russia and offered to help set up this new approach—working with Putin's inner circle—to getting access to new WMD sites. Yet the scheme never got off the ground. Weldon blamed "lawyers and bureaucrats" in the Pentagon and the State Department. He gave us copies of the agreement that would have allowed the United States access to biological weapons sites, as well as of a ninety-seven-million-dollar contract that the Pentagon, through the Missile Defense

Agency, had initially awarded to the International Exchange Group "for the purpose of facilitating certain MDA projects for missile defense cooperation in Russia." But no checks were ever cut to the Russian group, Weldon said.

It was easy to see why government lawyers would balk at the plan: It sounded a bit like institutionalized corruption. Money would be paid to an NGO openly controlled by Putin's people. That NGO, in turn, would guarantee government participation in a variety of cooperative projects ranging from missile defense to nonproliferation. It would also guarantee the presidency's direct control over the labs and their international projects. In the case of WMD sites, it would function as a pay-for-access plan. Weldon, for his part, didn't seem to have a problem with this. "I don't want to do anything illegal, but I want to get access to weapons-of-mass-destruction sites," he said.

But Weldon did have one good point. Access to Russian sites was important. More than just nuclear tourism, it cut to the very heart of cooperation and, more importantly, homeland security. "The terrorists' dream is to get into Russia, where all the biological, chemical, and nuclear materials are," he said. "We don't have a way to counter that. All that gobbledygook about homeland security doesn't mean anything, because that's where the weapons of mass destruction are; that's where they were built. If we don't have the confidence of the Russians to get into those sites, then we're not going to be able to win this battle."

"Oh no, you can't possibly do that," said Sergei Novikov with an indulgent smile. "It's prohibited by the laws of the Russian Federation."

Novikov, the top press official for Rosatom, was considering our request to visit a closed nuclear city. With his boyish looks, well-cut suit, and suave manners, Novikov stood in sharp contrast with Mikhailov, the truculent cold warrior. Novikov, however, was no more helpful. He recalled that a member of the Kremlin press pool—a wire service reporter, he said, and a U.S. citizen—was prohibited from entering the city of Sarov, even during an official visit by President Putin. "So you see," he continued with evident satisfaction, "it's quite impossible."

We were sitting in an upscale coffee shop across the street from Rosatom headquarters. After half a decade of high oil prices, Moscow was a boomtown, with scads of BMW dealerships and sushi joints.

Nearly a decade after the 1998 crash, there was no shortage of places to find a good espresso in Moscow. Meeting in the coffee shop, Novikov explained, would spare him the trouble of getting foreigners cleared to enter the building.

It was obvious that getting a permit to visit a closed city—even for a seemingly innocuous request to visit one of their museums—would be impossible. Foreigners visited as part of official delegations, which were the subject of endless rounds of government-to-government talks. For Russian citizens, getting in was a bit easier, but the process was shrouded in secrecy. A Russian arms control researcher, for instance, told us about his visit to Sarov a few years earlier. He had phoned a contact at the energy ministry to inquire about arranging a visit. The curt reply: "We'll call you back."

What ensued was a scene from *Harry Potter* crossed with *Dr. Zhivago*. The ministry phoned back three hours later and instructed the researcher to go to Moscow's Kazan train station, report to a certain ticket booth, and give his name. A cashier issued him a ticket for another city—a destination other than Sarov. He boarded an overnight train, and in the middle of the night, his carriage was decoupled from the rest of the train and diverted to another track. When the train arrived at the main gate, uniformed guards boarded and entered his compartment. After riffling through a series of alphabetized cards, they handed him his pass.

But that was in 2001. Five years on, the power of the FSB—the successor to the KGB—was much stronger, and now getting into the closed cities was much harder. Members of the FSB were actually embedded in Rosatom. While the Russian government liked to emphasize nonproliferation cooperation with the United States, particularly when it came to solving problems *outside* of Russia, it was not keen to publicize the fact that the United States was spending half a billion dollars a year on threat reduction programs inside Russia. Not only did it suggest that Russia's facilities were less than optimally secured, but it seemed to indicate that foreigners—*Americans*, no less— were poking around inside the country's most sensitive nuclear sites. Rosatom, however, was willing to offer us an alternative: a visit to a Russian nuclear power plant.

In anticipation of the twentieth anniversary of the 1986 Chernobyl disaster, Rosatom wanted to highlight the security and safety upgrades to Russian nuclear power plants. The explosion and reactor fire at Chernobyl—and the failed attempt by Soviet authorities to cover up the incident—had accelerated the collapse of the USSR. It had also put the brakes on the nuclear power industry in the former Soviet Union. Now Russia was launching a drive to build forty new reactors over the next two decades. The effort—which complemented the Global Nuclear Energy Partnership, the Bush administration's renewed push for nuclear energy—promised to have far-reaching consequences.

Building more nuclear power plants was part of the Russian government's plan to free up more oil and gas for export. The global appetite for hydrocarbons was good for Russian business, and by 2006 the state coffers were swollen with petrodollars. But promoting nuclear power required a serious public relations effort, both at home and abroad. In part, it meant opening up Russia's secretive nuclear power industry to the press and selling wary consumers on the idea of nuclear safety. Since the doors to the secret cities were proving hard to open, we decided to accept Novikov's offer.

Several weeks later, a formal invitation came through for a press excursion to the Smolensk Nuclear Power Plant. We were instructed to assemble around midnight outside the Rosatom headquarters, where we were ushered on board an aging Soviet passenger bus with brown curtains. In addition to a few Russian reporters and a pair of bewildered Swiss journalists, an entire busload of Bulgarians was joining us for the trip. Russia's nuclear-power-station construction company, Atom-stroyexport, was bidding against a Czech consortium to build two nuclear power reactors in Bulgaria, and Bulgarian energy journalists were being aggressively courted by the Russians.

While the Smolensk facility was only 220 miles from Moscow, it was a seven-hour bus ride to get there. Russia might be flush with cash, but much of the Soviet infrastructure was still crumbling. Minders from Rosatom thoughtfully loaded the bus with a crate of beer, a case of vodka, and some boxed lunches for the trip. The road was in abysmal shape, and the clinking of bottles kept the passengers awake for most of the night. The bus finally pulled into its destination around seven A.M. Desnogorsk—the company town built around the Smolensk power plant—boasted a Soviet-era "palace of culture," but showed little evidence of the encroachment of Russian capitalism. A local tour guide armed with a microphone lectured the sleep-deprived visitors as the vehicle lurched around town. "Over thirty thousand people live in our atomic city," she recited. "Construction here began in 1971. We have four schools and nine kindergartens. You may see on your right the palace of culture. The youth center is over there. It all belongs to one enterprise: the Smolensk power plant."

The Smolensk plant employed RBMK reactors. In other words, its three one-gigawatt, graphite-moderated power blocks were the same basic design as Chernobyl's Reactor 4, which exploded in 1986. Inside, an enormous Lenin mosaic adorned the front entrance, a reminder of the plant's Soviet heritage. We disembarked from the bus and went through security turnstiles. In the men's changing room, a matron with blazing cranberry hair barked at the visitors to strip down to their underpants and change into white smocks.

On the tour, plant management showed off the new technology and automated security controls that had been installed since 1986. The facility now boasted a faster emergency shutdown system, enhanced fireproofing and safety systems, and a redesign meant to limit and localize damage in the event of a catastrophic event. The plant had also switched to a safer type of fuel. More important, the Russians had changed the way personnel worked in the facility. Aleksandr Potapov, the deputy head of NIKIET, an energy research and development institute in Moscow, had described to us how the Chernobyl disaster promoted a "culture of safety" at Russian nuclear power plants. "There was this overconfidence before Chernobyl," he said. "The reasoning went, we could put a man in space, we could harness the atom, and we didn't think this kind of disaster was possible."

In the corridor to the control room, the nuclear plant's nerve center, we passed another massive Soviet-era sign: THE ATOM WORKS FOR PEACE. Despite the upgrades, Chernobyl still hung over Russia's nuclear industry like an ugly, radioactive cloud. The Bulgarian energy journalists didn't seem impressed. As the bus lurched back toward Moscow, we passed through the Russian countryside—a landscape of decaying farm equipment, cheap brick houses, and tiny subsistence plots. The Bulgarians pointed to the street signs ("Engels Street!") as we passed through provincial towns. One of them gestured to a modest two-story cottage: "*Mestny oligarkh,*" he said in Russian with lavish irony. "Local oligarch."

The Bulgarians may have been enjoying a laugh at the expense of their giant eastern neighbor, but the joke was really on them. As Europe was quickly learning, Russia's vast energy resources were a much more effective guarantor of power than its aging nuclear arsenal. In early 2006, during the coldest winter in a quarter century, Russia turned off natural gas deliveries to Ukraine over a payment dispute. The move seemed calculated to punish Ukraine, which had drifted from Russia's orbit following the pro-democratic Orange Revolution in 2004.

Panic ensued in European capitals. Cutting off Ukraine threatened deliveries of gas further downstream. A year later, Belarus—a quasi-totalitarian state run by a former collective farm director—was in the crosshairs. When Russia cut off oil supplies to Belarus in another payment dispute, European supplies were once again threatened. Russia, quite literally, had Europe over a barrel. By 2006, high global energy prices had helped restore Russia's swagger. Russia was the largest producer of gas in the world, and it was rapidly catching up with Saudi Arabia as a top oil exporter. Monolithic energy companies like Gazprom and Rosneft were tightly interlinked with the Kremlin, and energy was a much more practical foreign policy tool than a nuclear arsenal. Nuclear weapons hawks like Mikhailov seemed inconsequential in the brash, oil-rich new Russia.

Back in Moscow, we went to see Evgeny Velikhov, president of the Kurchatov Institute, Russia's premier nuclear energy research facility. Founded in 1943, the institute was named in honor of Igor Kurchatov. We met Velikhov in the "international little house," a cottage for receiving foreign visitors located just outside the gates of the facility. While the Kurchatov Institute is no longer involved in nuclear weapons research, much of the institute is still secured behind gates and requires high-level approvals to visit. We waited in the hallway, where a Russian television reporter was also getting ready to interview Velikhov.

A well-known scientist among Western politicians, Velikhov had been instrumental in international efforts to develop ITER, an experimental thermonuclear reactor. In contrast to the scowling Mikhailov, Velikhov was positively bubbly about his work at the institute. Switching back and forth enthusiastically between English and Russian, he held forth about his career at the lab and how he rose from junior scientist to director there. Velikhov's passion—in contrast to Mikhailov's—was not for nuclear weapons, but for promoting nuclear power.

"If it weren't for Chernobyl, one hundred percent of our electricity would be produced by nuclear power, and we would have the chance to export all of our natural gas," he told us. "Now we are moving in this direction again."

With the Kurchatov Institute's international "brand," Velikhov was also an effective evangelizer for nuclear energy. The institute, for instance, was leading an effort to create affordable new reactor designs for growing electricity consumers like India. The institute was also studying the concept of the "floating nuclear power plant"—essentially a nuke on a barge that would be operated by Russian specialists and would plug into the local electricity grid. Velikhov outlined the main advantages of this approach. Less-developed countries did not have power grids capable of absorbing a one-gigawatt power station, he said, and Russia had decades of experience operating naval reactors, both on submarines and on nuclear-powered icebreakers. And more important, if a country agreed to buy a floating nuclear plant, it had no need for home-grown nuclear specialists. "Just like you have with big passenger aircraft—Boeing or Airbus—you sign an agreement for full support," he said. "You are just leasing the plane."

Following our interview, Velikhov invited us to visit behind the gate of the institute so we could see a crucial piece of Russian nuclear history. We could see the F-1 reactor, the longest-running operational reactor in the world, Velikhov suggested. The institute also preserved the legendary "forester's cabin," home of Kurchatov—the Soviet equal of Oppenheimer. The cabin today is a museum dedicated to Kurchatov. For nuclear tourists, it was like an invitation to Los Alamos National Laboratory, the chance for a rare glimpse of an atomic landmark. But the Kurchatov Institute was still a part of the nuclear complex, and the FSB had the final say over who could go behind the gate—even for a visit to Kurchatov's library. We would have to submit another formal letter requesting permission to visit.

A few days passed, and we received a call from Raisa Vasilyevna Kuznetsova, the director of the Kurchatov museum. "Meet me on Kurchatov Square in one hour," she said. "I'll be waiting by the monument."

Ready to begin our tour, we headed north toward the Oktyabrskoye Pole metro station. It was hard to miss the monument. The disembodied head of Kurchatov dominated the square like a misplaced relic from Easter Island. A graffiti artist had tagged his lip with a silver marker. A woman in a matching brown leather coat and hat was waiting by the granite pedestal, holding a red leather attaché case. It was Kuznetsova, upright as a howitzer shell. "We won't be opening the museum to you, I'm afraid," she began, somewhat brusquely. "But I brought you some books."

She handed us a thick book titled *Kurchatov in Life*, a collection of the scientist's papers and correspondence, and a brochure for the museum. When we noted that Velikhov, the head of the institute, had invited us on a tour, she snapped back, "Velikhov is not the one who decides these things." Kuznetsova then gently upbraided us for not submitting the right correspondence. "You probably didn't manage to send the letter in time," she said. In any case, she continued, repairs were under way at the museum. A group of "junior rocket scientists" recently paid a visit, and they managed to break the staircase. Instead of a tour, she suggested we review her book. After all, she had spent nearly thirty years collecting documents from Kurchatov's personal archive.

As she escorted us back to the metro station, Kuznetsova described her obsession with the bearded scientist and how she came to work at the museum. "It came to me in a dream," she said. As the midday Moscow traffic streamed by us, Kuznetsova described her dream of Kurchatov, a convoluted tale that began on a giant ocean liner. Falling overboard, she nearly drowned, but was saved by distant voices guiding her to a desert island. The dream ended in a forest clearing, where Kuznetsova spotted a little house—and Kurchatov. "He says, 'I'll show you something interesting, come with me!'" Kuznetsova recalled. "I was so happy, and I said, 'Of course, of course!' And we go into the old house. And Kurchatov asked, 'Would you like to live here? It's your house now. I want this to be my museum.'"

As we listened to the museum's caretaker recite her odd love affair with Kurchatov, it reminded us of the heroic status the nuclear weapons scientists enjoyed in Russia. Kurchatov, father of the Soviet Union's nuclear weapons program, was honored with statues, a prestigious institute, and even a city in Kazakhstan. There were no labs or cities named for Oppenheimer. While still revered as the father of the atomic bomb, he lost his security clearances and was pushed out of national security work. But maybe that fall from grace—justified or not—was healthier than deification.

We reached our metro destination, and Kuznetsova bade us good-bye. "Maybe next time," she said cheerfully.

In 1991, in the immediate aftermath of an attempted coup in the Soviet Union, the U.S. Congress passed a set of initiatives designed to help safeguard nuclear weapons in the countries of what would shortly be the former USSR. Those programs, under the broad mandate of "threat reduction," had grown by 2007 to more than one billion dollars a year. The largest chunk of money went to the International Science and Technology Center, which provided immediate financial support to scientists to prevent them from selling their knowledge to rogue nations. The second-largest amount was for the Initiatives for Proliferation Prevention, designed to foster business cooperation with Western firms.

A central hub for such conversion projects is Chelyabinsk Oblast, a region in the foothills of the Ural Mountains where several of Russia's closed cities are clustered. Snezhinsk—previously Chelyabinsk-70—is home to the All-Russian Scientific Research Institute of Technical Physics, a laboratory that designs and fabricates nuclear weapons, while Ozersk—the old Chelyabinsk-65 or Chelyabinsk-40—houses the Mayak Production Association, the industrial facility that produced plutonium pits. Both cities are now back on the map but remain off-limits to outsiders.

We set up our interviews at Dalnyaya Dacha, a sanatorium—the rough equivalent of a summer resort—in the foothills of the Urals, just outside the town of Kyshtym. We flew in a gleaming new apple green Boeing operated by Siberian Airlines to Chelyabinsk, a sprawling industrial town. It was a two-hour drive from there to Dalnyaya Dacha, winding through a ghostly landscape of birch and pine. It was almost idyllic. WE WISH YOU HEALTH, read the inscription on the ominous, wrought-iron gate of the sanatorium. But behind the gate, the aging residential buildings shed chipped stucco, and not far off in the distance, an industrial plant belched out dark gray smoke. We began to feel a little ill.

There didn't seem much about the isolated sanatorium that would draw visitors, but out on the crumbling front steps of our hotel, we found a small crew of middle-aged men, wearing pressed slacks and golf shirts, the unmistakable casual-Friday uniform of the American middle manager. "I don't think we can work out all the problems in the thirty months we have," said one khaki-clad man. Another nodded in silent agreement, and all three paused to glance at us as we passed. They hardly seemed surprised to run into fellow Americans here. The remote lodging, only a short drive from the closed cities of Snezhinsk and Ozersk, was a way station for foreigners working on the swords-to-plowshares schemes that seek to downsize Russia's massive nuclear weapons complex.

We settled into a sparsely furnished room that sported a radio that received just one channel, the Russian state broadcasting network. Outside, a weathered sign pointed to seemingly nonexistent amenities, such as a sauna and a movie room. For all its lack of conveniences, though, Dalnyaya Dacha was ideally located for working on nuclear conversion projects. How had these efforts progressed? We spent a few days interviewing Russians from Snezhinsk and Ozersk who had been involved in conversion programs sponsored by the United States and the United Kingdom.

The participants we spoke to were relentlessly upbeat. We sat in a conference room as enthusiastic, and relatively young, scientists were ushered in to present PowerPoint slides. Aleksei Shagin, a beneficiary of Western assistance, showed us a brochure for his company, which had received aid from the Closed Nuclear Cities Partnership, a U.K.-funded enterprise. The photo showed a blue-eyed, blond-haired girl playing on pint-size furniture. Shagin used to work at Mayak, the plutonium production facility; now his private firm, Bur-Invest, manufactured children's furniture. A young pair of former weapons scientists we spoke with ran a consulting business that advised companies on their energy efficiency. They were well versed in terms such as "guerrilla marketing," but in most cases their business, like the children's furniture manufacturer, was dependent on government customers.

Starting a business in a closed city also carried an extra dimension of uncertainty. The security services can refuse entry to the city without any explanation, a risk for both American and Russian investors. Robert Felton, an American medical doctor turned entrepreneur, made business contacts in Russia through a U.S. program that helped Russian weapons scientists forge partnerships with Western commercial enterprises. His company, Numotech, won a ten-million-dollar loan from the Overseas Private Investment Corporation to launch a commercial venture with Spektr-Conversion, a partner company in Snezhinsk. Spektr-Conversion's highly trained engineers and scientists would use their expertise to produce medical equipment such as affordable prosthetics. That sounded like a worthy humanitarian task—as well as an excellent business venture. But in the paranoid atmosphere of Putin's Russia, Felton, too, found that working in a closed city could be a real nightmare. "I've had a lot of problems going to Russia," Felton said from his office in California. "The FSB put me in a corner and interrogated me for hours, thinking I was a spy. I was almost arrested once. I was detained in Russia—didn't get on a plane because of this project. Strange and bizarre things like that happened."

Felton had approached the enterprise with caution; the U.S. Department of Energy had invested in a similar initiative in another closed city, Sarov, with little success, he said. Numotech and its Russian partners found a good site, and they spent over two years (and hundreds of thousands of dollars) lining up all the approvals. Then Putin decided to shake up the regional administration. The old mayor of Snezhinsk landed in jail, and Felton was forced to start from scratch. "We had all the approvals in order, and now we had to start all over," he said.

Anatoly Ivanov, the director-general of Spektr-Conversion and Felton's partner, met with us at Dalnyaya Dacha. He didn't come with slides or pictures, and we talked on a bench outside the main building as mosquitoes the size of hummingbirds swarmed around our legs. Ivanov was upbeat, but much more realistic than some of the other scientists we had met. The partners had received final approvals, and the venture was going forward. "We think we can set a good example—if you start a joint venture, it'll show them how you can do it," Ivanov said. "And step-by-step, the closed cities will open."

The Spektr-Conversion project, however, had met with indifference—and little economic assistance—from Russian officials, Ivanov said. "From the Russian side, you look at it and think, golly gee, the Americans are more interested in seeing this succeed than the Russians!" he said. "But of course, the Americans' motives are different. They don't want Russian nuclear weapons scientists to go off to work in Iran or Iraq or wherever."

Were these programs worth all the hassle? For less money than the United States had spent on cooperative threat reduction, it could simply pay all the underemployed Russian weapons scientists to retire, Elizabeth Turpen, a senior associate at the Henry L. Stimson Center in Washington, had told us. Why, then, keep up the charade? The simple answer, she explained, was that U.S. taxpayers—and Congress—would never tolerate the notion of charity. Much of the initial funding that flowed to Russia's "WMD scientists" was in crisis mode, she said, when there was an immediate concern about a breakdown at the Russian labs. The technologies offered by private businesses were often solutions in search of a problem. Opportunities to promote meaningful cooperation, such as on nuclear energy or infectious diseases, were not seriously pursued. "We kept people in place with busy work," she said, and now the programs were being nickeled-and-dimed.

In Washington, groups like the private Nuclear Threat Initiative have tried bringing attention to the danger of nuclear smuggling, producing *Last Best Chance*, a docudrama starring Fred Thompson. Yet perhaps even more than nuclear materials, it is knowledge that poses a proliferation threat. Weapons and materials can be controlled, but people are more difficult. Turpen noted that the U.S. government, in funding Russian scientists, had no way to know if they were moonlighting on work that could contribute to proliferation. And one American scientist, a former arms control adviser, told us that one concern was that nuclear weapons designers from the closed cities could be teaching classes to foreigners right outside the gates. In other words, places like Dalnyaya Dacha could be hosting evening seminars on plutonium production. Turpen offered one note of optimism: "Russian scientists aren't out to create doomsday," she said, "unless they're destitute."

In late summer of 2000, U.S. Energy Secretary Bill Richardson traveled to the closed Russian city of Sarov to unveil an ambitious new project. It was a "technopark"—a free zone that would operate adjacent to the closed city. Such an idea, it was hoped, would help overcome some of the problems faced by other cooperative endeavors in closed cities. The nuclear weapons scientists would continue to live in the safe confines of a closed city, and yet they would work in a relatively free area where they could cooperate with outside businesses. "The new Sarov Technopark at Avangard is a successful example of how Russian nuclear weapons scientists and plants of the Cold War era can join private industry in the twenty-first century," said Richardson at the groundbreaking ceremony.

It seemed like a good idea at the time. September 11 was still just another day of the year, WMD was not part of the popular lexicon, and Russia's new president, Vladimir Putin, seemed a promising partner for the United States. Richardson said the U.S. government planned to spend at least $4.5 million the following year on similar projects. Sarov would remain closed to ensure security for sensitive nuclear materials, but an open territory just outside the fence would house the technopark. The United States helped pay for it, Russia promoted it, and six years later, we were curious to see how the experiment was going.

After being denied permission to go inside the city itself, we sought an invite to the Sarov Technopark, a part of the city that was not bounded by the perimeter fence. The idea, as with other technoparks, was to create a zone conducive to private enterprise. While the area was described in public relations materials as an "open access" zone, it took many faxes, formal letters, and phone calls before we finally won permission. Open access, we were learning, does not necessarily mean accessible.

Sarov is over four hundred kilometers from Moscow. We traveled overnight by train to Nizhniy Novgorod, known as Gorki in Soviet times, the residence-in-exile of Andrey Sakharov, the famed Soviet dissident and father of the Soviet Union's hydrogen bomb. Sakharov lived there in a first-floor flat on Gagarin Street in the 1980s with his wife, Elena Bonner, and their "housekeeper," a KGB employee who would let security agents in the window to rummage through the apartment.

In Nizhniy Novgorod, we hired a Volga taxi that reeked of gasoline for the two-hour drive to Diveyevo, the village closest to Sarov. Once in the village, we were instructed to use a local pay phone to ring the technopark staff, who would provide further instructions. We weren't quite sure what would happen at that point, though something involving blindfolds seemed plausible. Just a few kilometers away from our destination, we called the technopark just to let them know we were running on schedule. A few minutes later, as we reached the outskirts of Diveyevo, we received a frantic phone call from our assistant in Moscow. The meeting had been canceled. "But we just spoke to them!" we protested.

We immediately rang the technopark, where a brusque secretary picked up the phone. Every single staff member at the technopark had been summoned at the last minute to Moscow, she explained, a lie so blatant that we were caught off guard. No one, except her, was present in the building, she said; we could hear voices in the background. "Was anyone reachable by mobile?" we asked. "No, they all have their phones turned off" was the brusque reply. "Could we just stop by to see the place?" "I'm not authorized," the secretary said. Was there at least some literature available? Again, the answer was no. We were just outside the gates of Sarov. Of course, we still didn't even know where the technopark was located.*

We stopped in Diveyevo, the site of a historic women's convent, nauseated and exhausted after our two-hour ride. The nuclear city of Arzamas-16 was built on the grounds of the Sarov monastery. The Soviets had shuttered both the convent and the monastery in the 1920s. St. Serafim of Sarov, a Russian monk and mystic occasionally compared to St. Francis of Assisi, was an Orthodox spiritual leader in the early nineteenth century. The monastery's old grounds are still off-limits, but the Diveyevo convent was returned to the Russian Orthodox Church in 1991. Nadezhda, a local guide, took us on a tour. There wasn't a hint of bitterness in her voice, even as she described how the historic Preobrazhensky Cathedral was used as an indoor target range by the secret police. The buildings were now all under renovation, the chapels had been restored, and devout young couples strolled the grounds. In the convent, we forgot our frustration over the failed visit to the "open" technopark.

The culture of suspicion around Russia's closed cities cuts both ways. It has, Western experts maintain, helped control the spread of WMD. But it has also left Russian scientists living there in a state of perpetual dependence on outside assistance. So long as the cities are closed, there

---

* In later Web research, we found several different businesses claiming to be located in the technopark. All shared the same street address and e-mail.

can never really be open business. Elizabeth Turpen, who had studied the problems of the closed cities as a congressional staffer, acknowledged this contradiction. She recalled the anarchic days of the 1990s, when destitute Russian scientists were said to be job hunting in places like Iran, Iraq, and North Korea. Keeping Russia's closed cities fenced off was the "least worst" option, she decided. "In 1999, I came to the conclusion the fences are our friend, because things were so bad," she said.

Yet, can a closed city be compatible in the long term with an economy able to sustain scientists in anything other than nuclear weapons? The United States' Lawrence Livermore lab is close to Silicon Valley. Scientists can leave Los Alamos at will and seek work anywhere in the country. There is, on neither side of the debate, any long-term plan for Russia's scientists and the cities they live in. While Russia and the United States have cooperated on a number of initiatives to prevent the spread of nuclear technology, not even the most Pollyannaish diplomat would describe the relationship as warm and friendly. Cooperation with Sarov has been halting at best. The city is still closed, and the technopark was hardly a magnet for free enterprise. Perhaps the only place we saw in the region that had successfully opened to the outside world was the Russian Orthodox convent in Diveyevo, and it was thriving.

In Nizhniy Novgorod, we had almost a full day to pass before our overnight train back to Moscow, so we asked our taxi driver to drop us off at the home of Andrey Sakharov. The small apartment—now a museum—had no visitors, and we wandered the rooms in silence. One exhibit featured a display of correspondence from Americans, including scientists who lobbied on Sakharov's behalf. Almost all personal mail intended for him was intercepted and never received, the exhibit explained.

We were surprised to find one note, written by a Soviet émigré to Sakharov, calling a pair of U.S. scientists "sons-of-a-bitch" because they weren't willing to link U.S.-Soviet scientific cooperation to human rights issues. The KGB allowed the letter to be delivered to Sakharov presumably because it would undermine his morale. But the note underscored a larger point. U.S. cooperation with the Soviet Union, and now Russia, has always been fraught with contradictions. The United States wants Russia to open up, but it also wants nuclear security. As the closed cities open up, they pose risks of proliferation. But private businesses in closed cities (or secretive technoparks) can never survive in the long run. What foreign partner would tolerate traveling all the way to Sarov, only to be turned away at the door?

There are no easy solutions. The United States has regarded corruption as a small price to pay in the name of nonproliferation. For the first time, standing in Sakharov's museum, we perhaps even understood Mikhailov's disdain for the West. Representative Weldon's approach would get access to the closed sites, but it skirted at the edges of legality. His projects, in the end, went nowhere. "The U.S. government evaluated Rep. Weldon's proposal and determined that it would be more appropriate to keep the U.S./Russia missile defense dialogue in government-to-government channels, rather than paying non-government entities to engage in these important discussions," a spokesman for the Missile Defense Agency told us. "Consequently, no U.S. funds have been spent on the proposal."

In fact, just a few months after our return from Russia, Weldon's unconventional approach to dealing with Eastern Europe landed him in hot water at home. That October, the press revealed that Weldon was under investigation by the Federal Bureau of Investigation for allegedly helping steer contracts to Russian and Serbian businesses in exchange for consulting fees for his daughter. Weldon denied the charges—but under a cloud of suspicion, he was voted out of office in November 2006.

On our return to Moscow, we described our aborted road trip to one of the directors of the Closed Nuclear Cities Partnership. He chuckled and said it was good we had visited the monastery. He suddenly remembered that one of the technopark managers was in the office that day. "Elena from Sarov," he said, offering to introduce us. A few minutes later, he returned with Elena Diyakova, who shot us an icy look.

"Oh yes, I heard you came all that way," she said unapologetically and handed us a brochure. It was a flimsy pamphlet for the technopark, written in stilted English and quoting Putin as saying, "Such Technoparks is of great social and economic importance."

According to the brochure, construction started on Building Two in 2005, five years after then–secretary of energy Bill Richardson visited.

It still wasn't open for business.

CHAPTER 12

Got Nukes?

Nuclear Junketeering in Iran

Our flight to Tehran was leaving in a few short hours, and we still didn't have our visas. We had been trying for months to get into the Islamic Republic of Iran, and as the minutes passed, we could see our chance to visit the Esfahān Uranium Conversion Facility slipping away.

Iran has no formal diplomatic relations with the United States, but it maintains an Interests Section in Washington through the embassy of Pakistan; it also keeps a small staff tucked discreetly away in a sky-scraper on Third Avenue in New York City as part of its permanent mission to the United Nations. Months earlier, we had written a letter to Javad Zarif, ambassador and permanent representative of Iran to the United Nations, reminding him of his president's promise to open Iran's nuclear facilities to scientists, journalists, and students. And on the advice of a journalist who had recently visited the country, we also spoke with the head of the Iranian mission's press section, Mohammad Mohammadi, who received us over tea and cookies in a small waiting room and listened patiently to our request.

We had few illusions about a visit to Iran. If experts from the International Atomic Energy Agency (IAEA) couldn't divine the secrets of Iran's nuclear ambitions, it was unlikely that two journalists would somehow uncover a hidden weapons program (or, even less likely, somehow prove that such weapons were not the goal). We had a good sense, however, that nuclear tourism in Iran could provide us with insights into why Iran, which insisted on developing an indigenous capability to enrich uranium, was setting itself on a collision course with the United States.

To Mohammadi, however, we simply explained that we wanted to learn about Iran's declared nuclear energy program. Mohammadi told us that his superiors at the foreign ministry in Tehran had recently put all visa applications for U.S. journalists on hold. And he was particularly unhappy with Ted Koppel, who had traveled to Iran, promising to film a balanced documentary for the Discovery Channel. The documentary that resulted, *The Most Dangerous Nation*, had made the government even more suspicious of Western journalists. "I will do my best," he said with a weary sigh. "I am not promising anything, but I will ask for the visa."

Months passed with no word. Another journalist, recently returned from Iran, suggested hiring a "fixer," a private company in Tehran that arranged interviews and provided translation services for foreign journalists in Iran. They, too, promised to help, but months passed with no word. Then, early one morning in February 2007, we got an unexpected call from the fixer: The Islamic Republic of Iran's Atomic Energy Organization would be organizing a tour of the Uranium Conversion Facility in Esfahān. Could we be in Tehran by Saturday? Our visas would be taken care of.

Four days later, we were still waiting. If we didn't catch our flight, we wouldn't make our six A.M. rendezvous on Saturday at the Atomic Energy Organization's club in Tehran. We were almost out of time, and in Washington and New York, consular officials told us they didn't have paperwork authorizing our visas. We took a chance and drove to the Washington-based Interests Section to plead in person with the head consular official. He wanted to know what our book was about.

It was about nuclear tourism, we confessed. We were professional journalists, we explained, and we were writing about our travels through the nuclear world. As he listened to our reply, we felt our hearts sink. How far-fetched was the notion that Americans—declared nuclear tourists—would be allowed to see a controversial nuclear facility in the midst of a diplomatic confrontation with the United States?

The consular official listened politely, and smiled. As he flipped through our passports, he chatted casually in colloquial English. He had studied political science at the University of Kentucky, he told us offhandedly. Finally, he sighed and explained that he knew about the trip to Esfahān—our names were indeed on an official list that had been sent to the Interests Section—but without visa approval from the Foreign Ministry, his hands were tied. "I'll try to call the night shift of the Foreign Ministry," he said finally.

He disappeared again with our passports, and we returned to the waiting area, watching other visitors—mostly Iranians—wait for paperwork. One young woman—likely American—tucked stray wisps of blond hair under a head scarf, required for all women in Iran and in the country's diplomatic missions abroad. We had, by that point, spent several hours in the waiting room; with a quick mental calculation, we figured that if we didn't get our visas within half an hour, there was no chance we would make our flight.

Our trip to Iran arose out of a strange promise made in October 2006, when the Islamic Republic News Agency published a brief—but intriguing—news item. Iran's president, in a bid to demonstrate Iran's transparency, was offering to open up its nuclear facilities to foreign tourists. "Upon permission granted by President Mahmoud Ahmadinejad, the organization is currently working on ways by which foreign tourists can view Iran's nuclear facilities," an Iranian tourism official told reporters. He added that the president "issued the authorization to prove that Iran's nuclear activities are peaceful."

For many months after that announcement, we waited anxiously for our opportunity to become the world's first nuclear tourists to Iran, but our visa applications went nowhere. Now, quite unexpectedly, the Iranian government was inviting an assortment of journalists and diplomats to visit the Esfahān Nuclear Technology Center, a fortified industrial complex on the outskirts of the historic Persian city of Esfahān. Significantly, the center housed both the Uranium Conversion Facility, a 120,000-square-meter industrial plant that produced uranium hexafluoride, a key step in the enrichment process, and a nuclear fuel manufacturing plant.

The timing, it seemed, was auspicious, since nuclear weapons were back in the news. In October 2006, North Korea had conducted an underground test of a nuclear device, sparking fears of a new arms race in Asia. At that point the United States was in the fourth year of Operation Iraqi Freedom, a war that began as a hunt for weapons of mass destruction. And the Bush administration was ratcheting up the pressure on Iran—a member of the "Axis of Evil"—over its nuclear program. Nuclear proliferation was the topic of the month for policy wonks and television anchors, and Iran had emerged as ground zero of the nuclear debate.

Iran was a signatory to the Nuclear Non-Proliferation Treaty, the international compact that created an exclusive club of five established nuclear-weapons states: the United States, Russia, the United Kingdom, France, and China. Iranian policy makers had declared ambitious plans to construct nuclear power plants with a total capacity of over twenty thousand megawatts, saying Iran had a right under the NPT to develop its own nuclear fuel cycle. Iran denied seeking the bomb. But if the Iranians were pursuing peaceful nuclear power, they were doing it through rather surreptitious means. During a visit by IAEA director general Mohamed ElBaradei in February 2003, the Iranians confirmed the existence of a pilot fuel enrichment plant at an underground facility in Natanz, as well as of a large-scale enrichment plant under construction at the same location. The Arāk heavy water reactor, which could potentially produce bomb-grade material, was also in the works. In a report issued in June 2003, the director general summed up a general failure by Iran to report its nuclear activities to the IAEA—including the import of natural uranium, the processing of uranium, and the storage of nuclear waste.

"Although the quantities of nuclear material involved have not been large, and the material would need further processing before being suitable for use as the fissile material component of a nuclear explosive device, the number of failures by Iran to report the material, facilities and activities in question in a timely manner as it is obliged to do pursuant to its Safeguards Agreement is a matter of concern," his report dryly stated. In less bureaucratic language, Iran was still years away from a bomb, but it was acting as if it had something to hide.

For potential nuclear tourists from the United States, travel to Iran was complicated by the lack of bilateral diplomatic contacts. Formal relations between Iran and the United States never resumed following the 1979 Islamic Revolution and the subsequent hostage crisis, when Iranian militants held U.S. diplomats captive for 444 days. The State Department staffs an Interests Section in Havana; it holds talks with North Korean officials. But it has no presence in Iran, although its interests are represented through the Swiss Embassy. At cocktail parties abroad, U.S. diplomats are advised to refrain from even informally recognizing Iranian diplomats, in a grown-up version of school yard ostracism. Nicholas Burns, the undersecretary of state for political affairs, summed it up neatly in February 2007: "It is the world's most unusual diplomatic relationship."

Relations sank to a new low after President Bush lumped Iran in the Axis of Evil with Iraq and North Korea in his 2002 State of the Union address. Just a few months earlier, Iranian and U.S. diplomats had met around a conference table in Bonn, Germany, to hammer out a new future for Afghanistan after the fall of the Taliban. With a few choice words, the president torpedoed any official Iranian goodwill toward the United States after the terrorist attacks of September 11, 2001. A subsequent high-level overture from Tehran—sent through a Swiss intermediary in the late spring of 2003, shortly after the fall of Saddam Hussein in Iraq—was reportedly ignored by the White House.

If lost opportunities were not enough, Iran had a new president, Mahmoud Ahmadinejad, the former mayor of Tehran. Dressed as a populist in a cheap Chinese Windbreaker, Ahmadinejad somewhat unexpectedly won office on promises to deliver a better standard of living to ordinary Iranians. While domestic success proved elusive— the price of fresh produce, for instance, stubbornly continued to rise— Ahmadinejad scored easy points in his confrontation with the West and the United States. In a speech at the "World Without Zionism" conference in Tehran in 2005, he suggested that Israel should be wiped off the map. His remarks about the Holocaust (questioning whether it happened) and religion (he believed in hastening the return of the Hidden Imam, the Shia vision of apocalypse) were not reassuring either. The former mayor of Tehran and the ex-governor of Texas seemed to be on a collision course. And our chances of getting a visa appeared slim.

Fifteen minutes after the Iranian consul disappeared with our passports, he returned shaking his head. "I'm very sorry," he said gravely.

Before we could protest, he broke into a broad smile. "Just kidding, here are your passports," he said, handing the two small blue books back to us.

Our passports were stamped with ten-day visas.

"Don't do anything without permission," he warned. "And in Esfahān, don't leave your group."

Our visas, however minor a point, were an important lesson: Iran does not have a monolithic political system. While its government is frequently described in the Western press as authoritarian, in many ways it lacks the strict hierarchy of a true authoritarian regime that one comes to expect in places like, for example, Belarus or Cuba. During our stay in Iran, we would have constant reminders that there were multiple political factions vying for control, and our trip to Esfahān demonstrated just how confused the lines of authority were.

We arrived in Tehran just as the government was kicking off a ten-day celebration in honor of the anniversary of the Islamic Revolution, the return of the Ayatollah Khomeini from exile, and the collapse of the shah's regime. Rumor had it Ahmadinejad would make a major announcement about Iran's nuclear program at the culmination of the festivities. We landed in Tehran in the middle of the night—only to be delayed in customs for almost two hours as security officials tried to find someone on duty to fingerprint us. The Iranian government had responded to U.S. security regulations requiring that international visitors be fingerprinted by demanding the same of American visitors; we were apparently the only two Americans on the plane, and the fingerprinting equipment wasn't set up. Another delay ensued when it was decided that only a female officer could take a woman's fingerprints.

Still bleary-eyed from a daylong layover at the Frankfurt airport, and exhausted by the uncertainties of the visa process, we arrived at the hotel with time only for a quick shower. We were packed into a minibus with a group of television journalists worrying aloud about how they would set up a news feed to make the evening broadcast. We headed out first to the "nuclear club" of Iran's Atomic Energy Organization, a brief visit that gave us the first taste of how disorganized, or at least rushed, the preparations for the delegation had been. What had initially been presented to us as a select group of reporters turned out to be several busloads of journalists and diplomats from Iran and abroad, though notably few Americans were in the crowd. As we arrived at the gate, confusion ensued as guards first demanded that all of the journalists be confirmed against a master list and provided with badges allowing them into the facility. After an hour of arguing—and the realization that only a small number of the journalists present were actually on the list—the guards finally relented and began to let everyone through without even checking their identifications.

We entered a building that resembled a modern exhibition hall—a colorful model of an atom was perched atop the interior entrance—and were led into a spacious banquet room upstairs. Preparations for something had clearly been made, though for what was not exactly clear. Places for the journalists—now numbering around a hundred—had been set up, along with a large breakfast buffet. We had been told that the morning would start with a press conference (though we hadn't been told who would conduct it). After an hour, we began to realize that nothing of the sort would take place. Whatever had originally been planned had fallen through the cracks of coordination. We were eventually herded back onto buses to begin the long ride south.

Esfahān is 420 kilometers from the capital, just over five hours' drive, if you don't factor in Tehran traffic. But in Tehran, as we learned, traffic is always a factor. On the midmorning ride out of town, our bus convoy found itself wedged among the procession of vintage Peugeots, Citroëns, and Paykans.* Tehran's population has grown to over twelve million (out of Iran's total population of some sixty-five million), and traffic congestion has reached epic proportions. The delay gave us time to contemplate the elaborate, larger-than-life murals that dotted Tehran's facades. Painted in vivid colors, many depicted martyrs of the 1980–1988 Iran-Iraq war—referred to in Iran as the "Imposed War"—which consumed hundreds of thousands of Iranian lives. Some were quite striking, showing vivid scenes of battle overlaid with Persian script and portraits of dead heroes. Other murals were devoted to the Palestinian intifada or, on a more banal note, exhorted residents to pick up trash. While certain elements of Iran may point to hope for political pluralism, ever-present political art is one of the most common—and perhaps more unsettling—visual features of authoritarian governments.

---

* The ubiquitous Paykan, a poky sedan modeled after the 1960s Hillman Hunter, has approached the status of national joke in Iran, something akin to East Germany's Trabant.

The tour bus lumbered south along the modern, multilane highway through the desert south of Qom, past the serrated ridges of the Kuh-e Karkas ("mountain of vultures") that sliced out from the desert floor. Here, among the jagged red mesas, still dusted with snow, it was hard not to think of the lonely familiarity of the southwestern United States.

In the early afternoon, we exited the highway on the outskirts of Esfahān. Amid a drab sprawl of concrete housing blocks cluttered with electric transmission lines, a highway exit sign in Farsi and English read: KHORASGAN MUNICIPALITY WISHES YOU A HAPPY COMFORTABLE JOUR-NEY. This was the road to the Esfahān Uranium Conversion Facility. A few kilometers down the two-lane road, our coach approached a checkpoint. The security struck us as amazingly light. A simple perimeter fence skirted the facility; there were no sensors or barriers like we had seen in places like Y–12 in Tennessee. A few antiaircraft guns were emplaced outside the perimeter, pointing lazily at the sky. The Iranians, quite clearly, were preparing for an attack from the air, although the primitive double-barreled guns appeared a quixotic defense in the age of satellite-guided bombs and cruise missiles.

Our escorts from the Uranium Conversion Facility gave us a short briefing. There would be no photography of the outer complex, they warned us, saying that getting the layout of the place might help Iran's adversaries (although it was unclear what, exactly, we could photograph that would be any more valuable than a high-resolution satellite photo available on the Internet). We were then instructed to leave all of our equipment on the bus and were escorted into a small cafeteria, where we were seated with plant employees enjoying plentiful helpings of rice pilaf, lamb kebabs, and lentil soup. After lunch, already several hours behind schedule, the press conference was set to begin. Reporters from the Iranian press and the international media crowded into a conference hall, where a tabletop model of the facility was set in a glass case. Someone had built a display of industrial equipment with small signs in mystifying English. A plastic hard hat was marked with a sign that read, "ball valve," a metal pipe with the description "2 in-schedual 40," a standard—but misspelled—pipe sizing. The doorway leading to the press conference was decorated with a panoramic photo of the facility captioned "Nuclear Energy Is Our Obvious Right."

The Esfahān Uranium Conversion Facility is a key part of the Iranian nuclear complex. Declared to the IAEA in 2000, the facility was designed to produce uranium hexafluoride (UF_6), uranium oxide, and uranium metal. It could provide feedstock for the uranium enrichment facility at Natanz or fuel for the heavy water reactor under construction at Arāk. In 2004, an agreement reached between three European Union states and Iran led to the temporary suspension of nuclear activities at Esfahān. As part of the deal, the Europeans offered Iran a light water research reactor, which would not produce plutonium that could be readily diverted to military use. But the deal broke down after the election of Ahmadinejad. In what foreshadowed an escalating battle of wills, the Iranian authorities informed the IAEA in August 2005 that they would break the seals and resume their work at Esfahān. By the time of our visit in February 2007, the Iranians had produced 250 tons of UF_6 at Esfahān.

The press conference began with an eye-glazing, information-deprived thirty-minute presentation on the scientific activities of Esfahān's Nuclear Technology Center. The heavy reverb from the microphone, flashing PowerPoint slides, and amateur translation made the presentation feel like a bad acid trip. Finally, after a concluding slide marked "Tanks for your time and attention!," Ali Asghar Soltanieh, an owlish physicist with a closely trimmed salt-and-pepper beard, took questions from the press. But the question-and-answer session was a bit of a circus. Soltanieh, who served as Iran's permanent representative to the IAEA, mostly evaded hard questions. There was Soltanieh on Iran's recent acquisition of antiaircraft missiles ("I think it is not relevant to the context"); on safety at the facility ("You shouldn't be worried, as long as you are not inhaling or swallowing nuclear material"); and on the installation of new centrifuges at the facility in Natanz ("There is no obstacle to cooperating with inspectors").

He was momentarily flummoxed, however, by a question from a BBC reporter based in Tehran. "If you want to show us how transparent you are, why don't you take us to Natanz?" she asked. "Well, I . . . I passed the request to the authorities," he stammered. "In principle, I think there are no obstacles . . ." The reporter persisted, explaining that she had had no luck in getting permission to visit Natanz, which by that point had become much more critical to international concerns about Iran's nuclear ambitions. The Iranian authorities insisted that they had opened up the Uranium Conversion Facility to the press and visiting diplomats to prove to the international community that there was no diversion of material to nuclear weapons programs. But the press visit was in many ways theatrical; journalists and diplomats were not qualified to judge whether Iran was delivering on its promises.

Despite the obvious fact that the Iranian government was not allowing anyone inside Natanz, Soltanieh fell back on platitudes. "We are willing to open our doors to everybody!" he said. "I remind you that our president informed the [UN] General Assembly—and unfortunately the Western media did not highlight this important suggestion by our president—he invited the whole world to come to Natanz, not only the media. The whole world!" Soltanieh finally moved on to the next questioner. "Well, anyway, your request will be passed to them."

Soltanieh led the tour through the Uranium Conversion Facility at a brisk pace, explaining in precise English how the facility worked. Members of the press were issued the uniform of nuclear tourists: billowing surgical caps, white smocks, and disposable plastic booties. The diplomats were given sky blue smocks to distinguish them from the journalists. It looked like a battalion of Smurfs was invading the place.

The diplomats were the first to be escorted into the main hall. An impatient crowd of journalists lined up in the corridor, sweating into their bunny suits and waiting their turn. A Japanese journalist rehearsed his stand-up. A female correspondent struggled to keep her *hijab*—the obligatory Islamic head scarf—tucked in neatly underneath her surgical cap. Christiane Amanpour, CNN's chief international correspondent, was also waiting in the corridor. A local photographer snapped a photo of her as she stood in the queue, wearing a black scarf and penny loafers. For the Iranian press, Amanpour's visit to Esfahān was news in itself. Born in London to an Iranian father, the television news star lived for a time in Tehran before the Islamic Revolution. She was a returning Persian celebrity, albeit not necessarily a welcome one, given her critical reporting on the regime in Tehran.

We paused in one room while photographers snapped pictures of what is likely the most recognizable part of the uranium enrichment process: yellowcake, milled uranium oxide. The fine powder, the same luminous shade as Big Bird, was stored inside hulking industrial vats with small windows. The uranium concentrate could be further processed and converted into fuel for a nuclear reactor. It could also be mixed with fluorine gas to be converted into UF_6, a gaseous compound that could be fed into centrifuges for further enrichment through isotope separation. The enrichment process—separating minute amounts of fissionable uranium-235 from uranium-238—was the key issue. If enriched to a lower level, 3 or 4 percent, the uranium would be suitable for a reactor. Enriched to 90 percent, it would be weapons grade. "As you notice, the whole system is a closed system," Soltanieh said, speaking through his white surgical mask. "It means input is calculated by IAEA. Every gram of yellow chalk inside . . . is measured, and outside it could be measured. Therefore, they can have accountancy very easily."

As the tour progressed, the pack of reporters and photographers converged in a narrow, fluorescent-lit corridor. Like paparazzi fighting for a glimpse of a celebutante's fresh corpse, they were jockeying for a photo opportunity. And like a celebrity sighting, the target was quite mundane: the place where the IAEA had installed surveillance cameras to monitor Iran's nuclear ambitions. As the crowd surged toward the door, two camera operators shouldering bulky Sony Betacams began a shoving match. Things escalated.

"Stop pushing," hissed a cameraman to his rival.

This was the highlight of the tour. "We agreed to put two additional cameras in, so that you are sure that these capsules are not moved during this process when the inspectors are not here," Soltanieh explained. "And two hundred and fifty tons of UF_6 have been produced here, and everything is under the IAEA."

The tour was meant as a gesture of transparency. On December 23, 2006, just six weeks earlier, the UN Security Council had slapped sanctions on Iran in retaliation for its refusal to halt its nuclear enrichment efforts. Security Council Resolution 1737 made it clear that the Islamic Republic of Iran must suspend its sensitive nuclear activities—including its enrichment-related work at Esfahān—or face serious consequences. The resolution had been spurred by the IAEA, which had singled out Iran for a pattern of secrecy regarding its nuclear ambitions. While the international community had closed ranks, the government of Iran still insisted its enrichment program was part of a peaceful drive to develop nuclear power.

The journalists would broadcast the message of openness. And the diplomats from nonaligned nations—Cuba, Malaysia, Egypt, Bolivia, Slovenia, and Sudan—would add a veneer of respectability to the occasion. In our quest to learn about nuclear proliferation, we had traveled all the way to the deserts of central Iran, sat through a shambolic press conference, and nearly got caught in a stampede to look at surveillance cameras. And all of that, we realized, might well be a facade.

But an interesting question arose during the press conference: How serious would the environmental consequences be if the facilities in Esfahān were attacked? The subject was not far from the minds of Iran's nuclear officials. After all, there was already chatter in the press about the "Osirak option," possible military strikes against Iran's nuclear infrastructure. In 1981, Israel successfully destroyed the French-designed Osirak nuclear reactor, under construction in the Iraqi desert, through an elaborately planned air attack. The Uranium Conversion Facility at Esfahān, presumably, was high on the U.S. targeting list. Soltanieh had a ready answer: Any attack against a nuclear installation, during either operation or construction, would be an environmental disaster. "There is a serious concern . . . about the ecological consequences of an attack if there is nuclear material," he said. "That is, of course, a fact. That is why through you—in the media—we expect that these concerns would be expressed to the whole world."

And that is also why we would be treated to a lengthy excursion around the historic city of Esfahān on the day following our tour of the Uranium Conversion Facility. The excursion was not solely for cultural edification; officials clearly hoped that the media would take home the message that an air strike would potentially destroy the city's cultural wealth. It was hard to miss the subtext: If you try to bomb the Uranium Conversion Facility, you might end up striking a UNESCO World Heritage Site. A British television producer on the tour was not too happy. Outside the ornate, forty-columned Chehel Sotoon palace, she quietly fumed: "We've got *work* to do."

The main stop on our tour was the Naqsh-e Jahan Maidan, the royal square built by Shah Abbas the Great in the early seventeenth century. Bounded by a two-story arcade, the Maidan features some of the great achievements of Islamic architecture—the Sheikh Lotfollah Mosque, the Royal Mosque, and other landmarks—lavished with luminous blue tile work and intricate calligraphy. But the full magic of the place was not apparent until we climbed the stairs of the Ali Qapu Palace for a view of the skyline. The weather was overcast, but we could see the minarets shrouded in mist and silhouetted against the granite mountains.

After our morning outing, Saeid Baktash, the director of the Esfahān Cultural Preservation and Tourism Office, welcomed the journalists for a short presentation on the cultural and archaeological heritage of the city. While we sipped pulpy orange soda, he reeled off the facts and figures ("UNESCO World Heritage Site . . . 1,210 registered historical landmarks . . . eight thousand years of civilization") and the tourism statistics ("three million visitors last year"). He concluded with a plea for more visitors. True, Esfahān was a backpacker's dream. But the Maidan was completely empty of tourists, except for a small tour group of giggling Iranian schoolgirls and a young Iranian man with a faux-hawk. The souvenir vendors inside the deserted covered bazaar looked like they had been roused from a long nap. One of our guides quietly dismissed Baktash's boosterish talk: "The tourists are all from Iran!"

Esfahān had the potential to be one of the world's greatest tourist destinations. Its architecture, history, and hospitality were a seductive mix. But Esfahān was becoming better known for its nuclear connection.

On the long trip back to Tehran, on a particularly sparse stretch of highway, we passed another road sign marking an exit to a small mountain town. It was the exit for Natanz, home to Iran's disputed uranium enrichment facility. Nearby, an air defense artillery battery was visible from the highway, double-barreled guns pointed skyward.

Iran's history with nuclear research was not always that of a pariah state. Quite the opposite: Iran in the 1970s was the poster child for nuclear energy, at least in the eyes of some. "Guess Who's Building Nuclear Power Plants?" read a 1970s advertising caption. Featuring a stately picture of the shah in full-dress uniform, the ad was paid for by American power companies trying to reach a domestic audience. Iran's nuclear efforts dated back to the shah's regime and the Eisenhower-era Atoms for Peace program. In the 1960s, the United States supplied a five-megawatt thermal research reactor in Tehran, which went critical in 1967. The shah subsequently stepped up the country's nuclear research efforts. During the 1970s, as oil revenue flooded state coffers, Iran concluded contracts with three supplier countries—the United States, Germany, and France—for the construction of nuclear power plants and the delivery of nuclear fuel. It also bought a billion-dollar stake in a European consortium's uranium enrichment facility in France.

In 1976, the *New York Times* reported, "Iran is expected to complete about 20 nuclear power plants with total capacity of 23,000 megawatts between now and '94, at a cost unofficially estimated at more than $20 billion." The 1979 revolution put those plans on hold, as countries suspended their nuclear cooperation with Iran. The ensuing Iran-Iraq war effectively stalled any further progress over the next decade. Iran remained heavily dependent on oil and gas revenue, even as population growth further drove demand for energy. During the disastrous Iran-Iraq war, the authorities discouraged birth control, leading to a surge in the birth rate. By the 1990s, Iran's younger generation—over two thirds of the population was estimated to be under thirty—was shaping up as a major force in politics, putting pressure on the Islamic regime and helping elect the reformist government of President Mohammad Khatami.

The revival of nuclear programs began in the early 1990s, when Iran started negotiations with Russia over the completion of a nuclear power plant in Bushehr, on the Persian Gulf. The Bushehr project was begun by Germany's Siemens in the 1970s, but work stopped after the Islamic Revolution. Russia concluded a contract with Iran in 1995 to complete the Bushehr reactors; despite opposition from the United States (which dissuaded Ukraine from taking part in the project), construction work proceeded, albeit slowly and fitfully. The old Siemens design was a mismatch with Russian technology, and by mid-2007 the Bushehr plant was still not online.

A bigger proliferation concern, though, was evidence that Iran was seeking technology that might help it master the enrichment process. On August 14, 2002, Alireza Jafarzadeh, the U.S. spokesman for the National Council of Resistance of Iran, an exile group, publicized evidence of Iran's clandestine nuclear facilities at a press conference in the Willard InterContinental Washington, a D.C. hotel two blocks from the White House. The news reports that followed, as well as U.S. intelligence, helped spur the IAEA into action. Over the next few years, Jafarzadeh would make public many details of Iran's nuclear program, naming high officials involved in nuclear research and development, providing satellite images of clandestine facilities, and furnishing documents that pointed to the Islamic Revolutionary Guard Corps' interest in nuclear weapons technology.*

The IAEA followed with a series of visits to Iran, beginning with Mohamed ElBaradei's February 2003 trip, during which the Iranian government confirmed the existence of the Natanz enrichment facility. While ElBaradei did not directly accuse Iran of violating the Nuclear Non-Proliferation Treaty, he strongly hinted that the country was engaged in clandestine activity. Faced with sanctions, and persuaded by the intervention of three European states, Iran agreed in October 2003 to suspend all enrichment and reprocessing activities for an "interim period." At the end of that year, Iranian officials signed an additional protocol that would allow IAEA experts to make "snap inspections" of its nuclear facilities.

Ironically, three decades after encouraging Iran's nuclear energy ambitions, the United States disavowed the arguments once used on the shah's behalf. In 2005, Secretary of State Condoleezza Rice put it succinctly: "Our view is that Iran needs no civil nuclear power." Within a year, however, the Bush administration conceded that Iran was entitled to nuclear energy, and Rice shifted course in a May 31,

---

* The role of Jafarzadeh was one of the most unusual parts of the story. The NCRI had been designated a terrorist group by the U.S. State Department for its links to the Mujahedin-e Khalq (MEK), a militant Iranian group that had allied with Saddam Hussein's regime during the Iran-Iraq war. The MEK had a curious ideology—a mélange of Marxism, Islamic fundamentalism, and feminist rhetoric—and a *New York Times* reporter who visited Camp Ashraf, the MEK's base in Iraq, described a bizarre, almost cultlike devotion to the MEK leader, Maryam Rajavi (Massoud Rajavi, the MEK's founder and Maryam's husband, disappeared shortly before the fall of Saddam Hussein's regime). Exactly one year after Jafarzadeh revealed the existence of Iran's hidden nuclear network, his small office inside the National Press Club was shut down by the Treasury Department for being a front for the MEK. When we met him in April 2007, Jafarzadeh had rebounded. He occupied a plush office in downtown Washington, where he ran a consulting firm, Strategic Policy Consulting, and worked as a paid terrorism analyst for Fox News.

2006, speech. "The Iranian people believe they have a right to civil nuclear energy," she said. "We acknowledge that right."

On our return to Tehran, we went to meet with a top member of the Majlis, Iran's legislative assembly, which had been a driving force behind Iran's bid to develop nuclear technology. We arrived twenty minutes late for our appointment. Tehran's complicated traffic rules meant we had to park outside the Baharestan district and hire a taxi; by the time we made it through security, our interview subject was no longer waiting in his office. A scrawny legislative aide escorted us to a committee room, where a hearing appeared to be in progress. Legislators and staff were conducting their business in the corridors, sharing gossip on cell phones. It looked like a congressional office building in Washington, except no one was wearing a tie.

We were eventually ushered into an ornate, mirrored waiting room with massive chandeliers shaped like tulip bulbs inside the old Majlis building, a neoclassical structure across from the modern new one, and finally into a formal interview chamber. With his closely trimmed salt-and-pepper beard and chubby cheeks, Aladdin Boroujerdi looked a bit like a Persian Robin Williams. But as the head of the national security and foreign policy committee in the Majlis, he was known as one of the main hard-liners in the Iranian legislature. After exchanging a few pleasantries through a linebacker-size translator, he held out his palms to begin the formal interview: "*Bismillah ar-rahman ar-rahim* [In the name of God, the compassionate, the merciful]. . ."

Boroujerdi's argument for nuclear power rested on a basic principle. "Our future generations are going to be deprived of fossil fuel facilities in our country today," he said. "We are not thinking only of ourselves." A looming fuel crisis, in fact, must have been weighing on Boroujerdi's mind. The following month, the government voted to introduce gasoline rationing, a measure designed to eliminate subsidies that cost the government billions of dollars a year. The new measure would hit ordinary Iranians particularly hard. While oil-rich, Iran lacked refining capacity and relied on imported petroleum. Nuclear energy would help solve the energy crunch. But Iran's pursuit of atomic power underscored the dilemma of nuclear know-how being inherently "dual use." Master the basics of uranium enrichment, and you have the technology for creating weapons material. Official U.S. policy was to deny Iran a nuclear weapons *capability*.

Determining whether Iran's nuclear energy program overlapped with a weapons program was the crux of the issue.

On the subject of nuclear weapons, Boroujerdi echoed the sentiments of others we had spoken with in Iran. "Sixty years have passed from the Second World War," he said. "And in view of all of the technological advances that have so far been made by human beings, I don't believe that a nuclear bomb and moving to this direction would be of any use . . . Therefore there is no place in our defense doctrine for nuclear weapons, ever."

Iran's commitment to the Nuclear Non-Proliferation Treaty preceded the 1979 revolution. The country ratified the treaty in 1970, and it had been in force ever since. But some legislators had hinted the country might withdraw from the treaty in response to outside pressure. The international community would then have no oversight at all of Iran's activities. Boroujerdi said he was opposed to withdrawal—unless Iran was pushed. "We have the Non-Proliferation Treaty for three decades now," he said. "That means we have been committed not to make the atomic bomb. We have accepted the limitations that have been imposed upon us."

But, Boroujerdi added, Iran also expected to take advantage of the "opportunities the Non-Proliferation Treaty could provide." He was highlighting, of course, that the treaty does not create a distinction between enriching uranium for nuclear fuel and enriching it to levels suitable for making a bomb. The Nuclear Non-Proliferation Treaty, opened for signature in 1968, was designed to limit membership in the nuclear weapons club to five recognized nuclear powers while restricting the spread of nuclear weapons technology. The scope of the treaty is sweeping, but also vague. Under Article VI, for instance, the members of the nuclear club commit to the lofty goal of "general and complete" disarmament—at some unspecified date in the future.

The interpretation of Article IV is also ambiguous: "Nothing in this Treaty shall be interpreted as affecting the inalienable right of all the Parties to the Treaty to develop research, production and use of nuclear energy for peaceful purposes." The Iranian government felt it was perfectly entitled to develop its own domestic enrichment capability, including the hundreds of new centrifuges being installed in Natanz. For Iranian officials, continued suspension of reprocessing came at a high price. Iran's scientific base would erode, losing its nuclear know-how. As Boroujerdi told us, that was unacceptable. "All the activities of these facilities could not remain in a state of limbo," he said. "That means all of our scientists, all our facilities, they would lose everything, the base."

Spurred by this concern, the Majlis intervened, calling on the government to continue nuclear energy research and the process of enrichment; the Esfahān Uranium Conversion Facility was promptly reactivated. On August 8, 2005, two days after Ahmadinejad's inauguration, Iranian scientists began feeding uranium ore concentrate into the process line at the Esfahān facility. On January 10, 2006, Iranian officials broke the IAEA seals at Natanz. The U.S. government ramped up its military posture, sending aircraft carriers to the Persian Gulf. The United States and Iran appeared to be set on a course for military confrontation.

Operating a centrifuge, it is sometimes said, is as much art as science. A centrifuge works like a supersonic washing machine—separating the enriched uranium atoms (U-235) from the minutely heavier U-238 atoms by spinning the element in a vacuum at ninety thousand revolutions per minute. The parts must be precisely balanced or the entire contraption will fly apart. The difficulty of setting up and running centrifuges, in fact, proved to be one of the main reasons Libya gave up its nuclear weapons program. "You know, they were essentially sent a 'do-it-yourself kit' with very little instructions," Larry Satkowiak, director of nuclear nonproliferation programs at Oak Ridge National Laboratory, told us.

Libya had acquired the plans for building centrifuges—along with blueprints for making a nuclear warhead—from the black market network of A. Q. Khan, the father of Pakistan's atomic bomb program. The country had long been suspected of seeking to acquire the bomb, but after the interdiction of a freighter bound for Libya with centrifuge components, Libyan leader Colonel Moammar Gadhafi agreed to give up his weapons program. International experts descended on Libya to learn more about the country's progress toward joining the nuclear club. In January 2004, experts in centrifuge technology from Oak Ridge traveled to Libya to find out, as Satkowiak put it, "the ultimate capability of the facility had it become fully operational."

The Oak Ridge scientists were to look at the infrastructure that was going to be used to run the centrifuges. They found a new building, with all of the piping ready for the installation of the centrifuges. The Libyan program, Satkowiak recounted, was a mixed bag. "The thing was, they had been working for about eighteen months to two years and were unable to get one to work," he said. It was like an intricate model plane with a thousand different pieces. The Libyans found they could assemble the parts and put them together, but they just didn't get it to work quite right. Over time, Satkowiak predicted, they would have figured it out.

In giving up its centrifuges, though, Libya was giving up very little. Its scientific base was limited, and its technology was acquired from abroad. The Iranians, on the other hand, as Boroujerdi had noted, had gone through a painstaking process of reverse engineering: dismantling centrifuges piece by piece and reconstructing them. That was one reason why the director general of the IAEA remained worried— given Iran's past clandestine activities—that there might be undeclared enrichment activities in Iran. The IAEA also wanted to find out the origin of highly enriched uranium samples it had found in Iran's centrifuge components. ElBaradei called for "further investigation" of the country's nuclear supply network.

Much of the criticism of Iran's nuclear activities is based on what the international community has regarded as concealment and obfuscation. Rahman Ghahremanpour seemed amused by this accusation when we met him in his office at Tehran's Center for Strategic Research, a think tank affiliated with Iran's ex-president Hashemi Rafsanjani. Ghahremanpour, a boyish-looking political analyst, spoke impeccable English and had a habit of breaking into almost teenage giggles when talking about something he found particularly amusing.

We discussed our trip to Esfahān with him, and the fact that we weren't allowed to visit Natanz. "The core issue is Natanz, and suspending enriching in Natanz," he conceded. But he defended the government's hesitancy to let foreigners into the facility there. "One of our main concerns is about leaking some secret information from Natanz," he said with a playful smile. "As you know, one of the debates within this issue is leaking intelligence data or information. Even in safeguard agreements they had said that IAEA had accepted that the secret information of one country should be protected. Why? Because of the commercial issues."

France, he noted, had unique plasma methods for enriching uranium, while Japan had its own ion exchange process. "When we see the centrifuge facilities, we cannot understand anything because of the technical issues, but the engineers, the nuclear engineers, can understand the method and some technological secrets," he said. "And this is why we did not agree to demonstrate the fuel cycle in Natanz. Because before this, unfortunately, some inspectors leaked our specific and secretive data to others."

By others, he meant, for example, the Institute for Science and International Security (ISIS), a U.S. nongovernmental group founded by David Albright, a former UN weapons inspector. ISIS had been providing the public with detailed reports and commentary on Iran's centrifuge work, as well as other aspects of the country's nuclear program. One of the things that ISIS had reported on, in fact, were problems with Iran's fuel enrichment process, including metal contamination. When we noted that, Ghahremanpour erupted again into giggles.

"I have not seen any credible information!" he said. "But I remember in September, *Time* magazine and in particular ISIS argued that there are some technical problems in Natanz in connecting cascades to each other." But today, he pointed out, ISIS had reported that Iran had successfully connected these cascades. "Iran could overcome this technical issue," he said. "But regarding the contamination of UF_6, as you know, we have bought some of it from China and some from South Africa. I have not heard that this contamination is a main obstacle to produce UF_6. And we asked this from experts of [the Uranium Conversion Facility] in Esfahān, and they said that there is no considerable contamination."

When Iran suspended uranium enrichment in 2003, it had proposed a "warm" suspension—not for Esfahān, where the activities were monitored by the IAEA, but for Natanz. That proposal meant they would stop injecting UF_6 into centrifuges. The issue for Iran, Ghahremanpour argued, was whether it could suspend some elements of enrichment without compromising the scientific base. And then there was the issue of what suspension would mean for Iran's painstakingly built enrichment equipment. In fact, when Iran restarted enrichment after suspension, some of the centrifuges were destroyed, he told us.

"We have 'cold' and 'warm' suspension," Ghahremanpour said. "We can agree about warm suspension. What does warm suspension mean? It means you stop injecting UF_6 into the centrifuge. But in cold suspension you should turn off all the centrifuges. Even in the United States of America, the centrifuges are not turned off fully in your enrichment plants, because when you turn off the centrifuge, turning them on may destroy some centrifuges. And technically it is very difficult to resume the lost process."

But the fundamental issue, he said, was gaining the knowledge of enrichment. That specific nuclear know-how was extremely valuable. "You cannot learn it by reading from textbooks or from the Internet," he said, giggling hysterically.

Ghahremanpour and Boroujerdi had both expressed the same point: Iran was focused on maintaining its scientific and technical nuclear base. It wasn't enough to import know-how and nuclear material from abroad, as was being done with the Russians at the Bushehr power plant. Iran wanted its own cadre of nuclear scientists.

Iran argued that its universities were—like universities anywhere—interested in establishing a base in science. The West, however, viewed Iran's universities as a base for forays into weapons research. The Atomic Energy Organization of Iran, which had organized our trip to Esfahān, was the legitimate face of Iran's nuclear complex. But the National Council of Resistance of Iran claimed the regime also had a parallel nuclear effort, using university laboratories as a cover for concealing weapons research.

Nothing illustrated that tension better than our meeting in Tehran with nuclear engineer and physicist Fereidoon Abbasi Davani. We met Abbasi in his office on the campus of Shahid Beheshti University, a state-run university in north Tehran named after a martyred ayatollah. Abbasi, as the saying goes, wore many hats. He was the vice president of student and cultural affairs at the university; he was also the secretary of the Nuclear Society of Iran.

The Nuclear Society of Iran, founded before the 1979 revolution, was a sort of club for students and professors interested in nuclear issues. It remained largely dormant during the Iran-Iraq war, but in the early 1990s, as official interest in nuclear technology revived, the organization came back to life. The society's main goal was to help educate a new generation of Iranian students and scientists who found their access to cutting-edge nuclear research restricted abroad. "Limitations were imposed on Iranian students outside Iran in order to deprive them of access to study and work in the nuclear field and related engineering fields," Abbasi said, gesturing to a tray of Persian sweets and fresh fruit laid out for his visitors. "We decided to start the effort to bring the know-how here."

After the end of the Cold War, universities and institutes in the former Soviet Union, desperate for hard currency, opened up their doors to paying students. Iranian students, Abbasi said, took the opportunity to get an education in Russian and former Soviet facilities, which boasted some of the best theoretical training and practical expertise. But as in Western countries, Iranian students in the former USSR found certain doors were closed to them as well. "Those places . . . kept Iranian students in the marginal issues," Abbasi complained. He was cagey about which institutes housed the Iranian students. "I won't name what those institutes are, but I can say in general the institutes like Kurchatov or the Physics Institute of Moscow," he said. "Iranian students have gone there, but you know, very explicitly, just because some American investment has been done there, they have prevented Iranian students' access . . . Especially when it comes to nuclear reactors."

Much like Boroujerdi, Abbasi saw a conspiracy led by the United States to thwart Iran's ambitions. Even countries like China and India, he said, were doing the bidding of the U.S. government. "Iranian students are admitted," he said. "They get the admission, but in the final stage, when they want to get a visa to enter the country, the governments actually stop the Iranian students from going there."

The Nuclear Society of Iran had forged ahead, sponsoring workshops on various aspects of nuclear technology and mentoring younger scientists. While Iranian scientists lacked top-of-the-line research tools (sanctions also meant a shortage of good measurement equipment, sophisticated software, and research data), Abbasi noted with pride that sanctions had not stopped their research. "I can say these restrictions were fruitless. We were slowed down, but we could get the knowledge and know-how that we needed in other ways. We had to go through nonconventional ways to get the information we needed, either by relying on our young people for getting them or from our friends outside of Iran."

Abbasi concluded with a half-hour lecture on Iran's historic grievances, from the overthrow of Iranian prime minister Moham-mad Mosaddeq in a CIA-backed coup in 1953 to Saddam Hussein's war of aggression. His speech was at moments conspiratorial (the Taliban, he said, destroyed the Buddhas of Bamiyan at the behest of U.S. and Pakistani intelligence in order to give Islam a bad name) and at others touching (he recalled his experiences during the eight-year Iran-Iraq war, when he saw Hussein's army employ chemical weapons against Iranian troops). The nuclear issue, he continued, was just a "good excuse" for bullying Iran. "If the nuclear issue is not the base issue, there would be other things," he said.

"Tell George Bush to stop threatening people!" he concluded with a laugh.

As we got up to leave, Abbasi was reluctant to offer us a business card ("I don't have any," he said).

On March 24, 2007, we found out more about our host. In a resolution tightening sanctions against Iran, the UN Security Council published a list of individuals suspected of involvement in Iran's proliferation activities. Fereidoon Abbasi Davani, described as a senior Ministry of Defense and Armed Forces Logistics scientist with links to the Institute of Applied Physics, was on the top of that list.

If you close your eyes in the lobby of Tehran's Azadi Grand Hotel, you can imagine, for a moment, what it must have looked like in the late 1970s. From the upper floors, there is an arresting view of Tehran's mountains, making the hotel a favorite for regular travelers. The cavernous lobby would have been filled with prosperous oilmen and expatriates, mingling with stylishly dressed Iranian professionals. The raised bar, featuring a grand piano and low-slung tables, would have been packed with young men and women dressed in the latest wide-collar fashions, sipping wine or brandy. Sitting in the lobby, one is overcome by a feeling of déjà vu, which of course makes sense, because the Azadi, prior to the revolution, was a gleaming Hyatt, with a modern open atrium design that could be found in Tokyo or New York.

And then you open your eyes and remember that it is 2007; there isn't even beer. The Azadi, like other Western-owned hotels, was nationalized and renamed after the revolution. Though well maintained, it clearly had not been remodeled in the ensuing years and was beginning to show its age. The rugs were a bit threadbare, the furniture chipped and dented, and the warm earth-toned colors of the 1970s had faded to a homely brown. The newsstand sold vintage English-language paperbacks, the racier covers blacked out with magic marker. Yet the outlines of the Hyatt were still there, and the piped-in music was a bittersweet reminder that you could make it all the way to Tehran, but there was no escaping the soporific saxophone of Kenny G.

To estimate the cost to Iran of nuclear posturing is to understand what being a pariah state entails, both economically and culturally. As we waited on our last day in Iran for a taxi to the airport, we sat in the fading glory of the former Hyatt hotel, sipping juice and coffee. Across from us was an elegantly dressed family of Iranians: a prosperous-looking man, his made-up wife, and their daughter, a sullen Tehrani girl wearing outrageously tight jeans and a low-slung *hijab*. A South Asian man in a cheap business suit was putting the finishing touches on a management presentation. The entire Belarusan soccer team loitered in the lobby, looking bored in their brightly colored tracksuits. There were few if any of the visitors from first world countries that we would expect to find in one of the nicer hotels of the capital city.

We watched as the Iranian family sat and drank their tea—waiting for no one and doing nothing. Perhaps they, like us, were reflecting on what the hotel might have once been, and what Tehran could someday be again—a flourishing cosmopolitan city with business rooted in the country's natural resources. Iran's isolation predated the nuclear crisis, but international sanctions and the looming threat of air strikes had made the city even more of an international ghost town, a way station for visitors from other shunned countries.

While there is room for negotiation, it is hard to resolve how the United States and Iran would come to a lasting understanding. The Iranian government has staked the country's pride on the nuclear issue, and the airwaves are filled with propaganda meant to underscore that point. Our trip to Esfahān could be taken as a sign of openness, but it could just as easily be interpreted as cynical propaganda. The Iranian government knew the press would broadcast pictures of the tour of Esfahān, even as the real controversy centered on the centrifuges in Natanz. In the United States, the Bush administration has taken an equally unequivocal approach to the issue. In October of 2007, Bush, answering a question about Iran, said, "If you're interested in avoiding World War III, it seems like you ought to be interested in preventing them from having the knowledge necessary to make a nuclear weapon."

What links Iran and the United States, as Rahman Ghahremanpour of the Center for Strategic Research observed, is hard-line leadership. Ghahremanpour saw Ahmadinejad and Bush as two sides of the same coin: Ahmadinejad believes in the Hidden Imam, while Bush sees it as a religious duty to destroy Iran's government. "They believe they are destined to give victory to humankind," he told us with a slight giggle. "They believe in a type of millennialism or what we call apocalyptism."

Like most people we met with in Iran, Ghahremanpour said he was not afraid of U.S. air strikes. He noted that bombing Iran would only justify Tehran's withdrawal from the Nuclear Non-Proliferation Treaty. Worse, he argued, air strikes could have "disastrous consequences for the region" as well as for the United States. "Even before 1979, we have influence in Kashmir, in Iraq, in Lebanon, in Jordan, as you know, in Pakistan, and others," he warned. "In this sense, or at the societal level, there will be a harsh reaction by ordinary people against air strikes on Iran."

If Iran's government is not deterred by the threat of attack, it is also, disturbingly, unperturbed by the consequences it has already brought on its population. Instead of moving the country toward energy self-sufficiency, Iran's nuclear program has brought crippling economic sanctions and led it to the edge of military confrontation, isolating the country from the international economy and the scientific community. All Iran has achieved, in sum, is to protect its nuclear base as an end in itself, making it a populist tool for a government that has little else to show in the way of social or economic progress. Although in that respect, it has been successful. Iran's nuclear complex is spread out geographically and enjoys popular support.

"You cannot be assured about the destruction of all Iranian nuclear technology," Ghahremanpour warned us. "The nuclear technology activities are distributed within Iran. If you want to destroy the nuclear technology totally, you should attack all the cities: in Bandar 'Abbās, in Bushehr, in Kermān, in Esfahān, in Natanz and in Tehran, in Karaj, in Mashhad."

And in that respect, he concluded, "destroying Iranian nuclear activity is impossible."

Epilogue

Next Year in North Korea

We seek the total elimination one day of nuclear weapons from the face of the Earth.
                    —Ronald Reagan, second Inaugural
                        Address, January 21, 1985

In December 2006, we attended a meeting in a windowless room inside the James E. Forrestal Building, the Department of Energy's drab headquarters in southwest Washington. It was the seventeenth in a series of public "scoping" meetings on the future of the U.S. nuclear weapons complex. Tables were set out with official information sheets outlining the department's Complex 2030 plan; blue chairs were lined up neatly under the fluorescent lights. Over the previous year, the Department of Energy had held similar meetings in cities around the country, from Livermore, California, to North Augusta, South Carolina. The stated goal was to allow the general public the opportunity to comment on the proposed plans to modernize the nuclear weapons complex.

Most of the attendees were antinuclear. In Oak Ridge, Tennessee, thirty-one of thirty-two participants made statements opposing the modernization plans at the Y-12 plant. Over a hundred people turned out for a meeting in Santa Fe, New Mexico. The Washington meeting was no exception. Peace activists and church representatives stepped up to the podium to condemn the evils of nuclear weaponry.

Ted Wyka, the NNSA official overseeing the meeting, seemed to have been handpicked for his self-control. Wearing a conservative suit, starched white shirt, and understated gold tie, he sat patiently, his head cocked attentively toward each speaker. With hands folded, fingers interlocked, and hair neatly gelled, he listened intently as speaker after speaker launched into denunciations of nuclear weapons.

Sister Marie Lucey, a diminutive nun with salt-and-pepper hair, delivered a brief lecture on stockpile reliability. "We are convinced that plutonium and most nuclear weapons will remain reliable for at least a century, that the number of surplus plutonium pits is actually increasing, and that four thousand more heads in the U.S. current stockpile all provide evidence that there is no need to produce additional pits," she said.

It was interesting to hear a nun discuss plutonium pit production. But Lucey's point was supported by recent scientific studies. Lucey was followed by David Culp, a Quaker lobbyist. He turned to address the Department of Energy officials in the room. "Some of the smartest people in this town work in this building," he said. "And it is a great frustration to me to see you come back again on another failed proposal." In the back of the room, several Department of Energy and NNSA bureaucrats sat in a single row, listening with arms folded. One chewed on the stem of his spectacles. Culp continued with his statement: "You have come to Congress before asking for new nuclear weapons complexes. You lost every one of those fights. You're trying to get testing resumed. You have lost that fight. You have tried to get funding for the development of new nuclear weapons. You have lost that fight."

The Complex 2030 scoping meeting had drawn a healthy assortment of activists, but members of the general public were not lining up outside the Forrestal Building to attend. Besides a dedicated group of activists, few in Washington seemed aware of the meeting or bothered to attend.

The meeting reached something of a climax near the end, when Stephen Young took the stand. For a long, awkward moment, Young stood in front of the microphone, frozen. He bowed his head and, barely suppressing a sob, began speaking. "I work with a group called the Union of Concerned Scientists," he said, his hands trembling. "But I'm speaking today as a human being, a person."

He paused. The tears began to flow. "I am sorry I am crying," he said. "I am."

Wyka's look of attentive concern stayed rigidly in place. But the most painful part of the spectacle was the realization—even on the part of many participants—of its futility as a forum for discussing nuclear strategy. Before the hearing, we had chatted briefly with Wyka about whether debate over the nuclear arsenal was useful. "Absolutely," he replied. "But it's not something that we're going to debate and make something out of." The hearings, he noted, were to provide the public with the opportunity to comment on the nuclear complex, not the nuclear arsenal itself. Such decisions, he emphasized, were for another venue. "Our job is to put that structure in place— the nuclear weapons complex—to handle any types and composition of weapons defined and directed by the president and appropriated by Congress," he said.

There never really *had* been an opportunity to discuss the nuclear arsenal. The Reliable Replacement Warhead did not emerge after a presidential speech; rather, it slipped almost unnoticed into a spending bill. Over the next few years, it became something of a political hot potato in Congress. And after the scoping meetings, the controversy persisted over the future of the nuclear weapons complex.

Where was the debate over nuclear strategy? We had spent two years traveling the world to understand how nations view nuclear weapons. We came away less convinced than ever that there was any strategy to speak of. During our journey across the U.S. nuclear complex, it occasionally felt like we were visiting an Oldsmobile factory: outmoded facilities with a cynical workforce and little in the way of a vision for the future. In the United States, we found a complex adrift, grasping for meaning and purpose. In the absence of political leadership, the nuclear facilities had become a political punching bag—a disservice to those who worked in them.

In our travels abroad, we found a similar problem: a lack of clear purpose. In the Marshall Islands, where the United States had yet to fully acknowledge the legacy of nuclear testing, a sort of inertia had taken hold. The continuing use of Kwajalein sustained a quasi-colonial relationship that kept the islands in a state of dependency. Kazakhstan could not decide whether its nuclear legacy should be as a destination for Armageddon tourists or as a magnet for peaceful nuclear science. In Russia, the United States and its allies threw money at nonproliferation programs without any clear way to gauge their success. Iran's nuclear program—whether peaceful or not—was doing little besides guaranteeing the country's continued political and economic isolation.

In one sense, this strategic ambivalence was undoubtedly the product of a positive evolution. The chances of an all-out thermonuclear war are now remote, or at least decidedly less likely than during the Cold War. But a lack of clear nuclear weapons strategy can be devastating. The United States tacitly condoned Pakistan's and India's nuclear weapons programs; it went to war over an Iraqi WMD program that didn't exist; and, in 2007, it edged closer to military confrontation with Iran, convinced of a shadowy nuclear program. Successive administrations have failed to articulate either an architecture for the present or a plan for the future. There is no leadership with respect to the world's most powerful weapon, a frightening prospect given the state of current affairs. As nuclear weapons expert Joseph Cirincione noted, Iraq is the "world's first nonproliferation war, a battle fought primarily over the perceived need to prevent the acquisition or transfer of nuclear, biological, and chemical weapons."

But if the advocates of the nuclear complex have lost their sense of purpose, then so, too, have its adversaries. Even forceful disarmament advocates like Helen Caldicott readily conceded that point. In January 2007, we attended a press conference in Washington hosted by the *Bulletin of the Atomic Scientists*, the venerable publication best known for its Doomsday Clock, an illustration that since 1947 has symbolized how close the human race is to nuclear extinction.

The occasion of the conference was the decision to set the clock at five minutes to midnight, advancing it two minutes closer to doomsday. The change signaled that the world was in as perilous a state as it had been at the height of the Cold War. Yet in a surprise move, the *Bulletin* added global warming and other environmental threats. "Nuclear weapons still pose the most catastrophic and immediate threat to humanity, but climate change and emerging technologies in the life sciences also have the potential to end civilization as we know it," said Sir Martin Rees, president of the Royal Society and a professor of cosmology and astrophysics, in his explanation of this new amalgamation of deadly threats. Whether the *Bulletin*'s broader focus on environmental threats would bolster public awareness—or dilute its focus on nuclear weapons—was unclear to us.

The lack of vision is also evident in Washington, where the discord has reached the highest levels of the nuclear weapons complex. On January 4, 2007, Linton Brooks, the affable NNSA chief we interviewed at the beginning of our travels, was abruptly fired. For Brooks, the firing offense may not have been the security breaches at Los Alamos but failing to inform his boss, Energy Secretary Samuel Bodman, about computer hacking that had compromised the personal information of Energy Department contractors. Brooks learned in September 2005 that the computers had been hacked, but he didn't inform senior Energy Department officials until months later. Brooks's explanation for the delay was the political equivalent of fumbling with his laces. "It appears that each side of that organization assumed that the other side had made the appropriate notification to the deputy secretary," Brooks told members of a congressional oversight committee.

The nuclear debate, in the meantime, continues to float along like a ghost ship lost at sea. Nearly two years after our visit to Livermore, the lab that Edward Teller built on the foundations of nuclear optimism was selected over Los Alamos to design the Reliable Replacement Warhead. But just a month later, in April 2007, an influential report on the RRW by the American Association for the Advancement of Science questioned whether the administration had laid out any coherent nuclear policy, a seeming prerequisite for developing a new warhead and modernizing the complex. "There has been no presidential or cabinet-level statement from the administration that clearly lays out the role of nuclear weapons in the post–Cold War, post-9/11 world, that makes the case for and defines future stockpile needs, *and that argues the case for the RRW*," the report states (emphasis in original).

Later that year, Tom D'Agostino, who took over for Brooks, sat in on a roundtable in Washington with defense journalists. D'Agostino, like Brooks, was a well-liked bureaucrat trying to cope with a weapons complex that defied solution. When asked what he thought a nuclear weapon of the future might be for, D'Agostino's reply was "I don't know"—a somewhat surprising answer, but also one that seemed to sum up the state of the nuclear arsenal.

In July, shortly after the roundtable, the administration released what could be regarded as the equivalent of a puff piece on nuclear weapons policy: a three-page statement titled "National Security and Nuclear Weapons: Maintaining Deterrence in the 21st Century." The paper was a mishmash of nuclear policy platitudes with few details. It offered little other than an argument for the RRW. Perhaps what was most striking about the policy statement was that it outlined no possible scenario for the use of such a weapon. It did little to convince anyone.

A congressionally mandated study on the RRW released in the fall of 2007 cast doubt on whether the warhead could be developed without underground testing. As 2007 came to a close, Congress refused to fund further work on the RRW, leaving plans for the new warhead in limbo. NNSA officials, however, indicated there was still money for an "RRW-type of program." In other words, RRW was far from dead.

At the same time, the Bush administration announced plans to reduce the number of deployed warheads and shrink the footprint of the nuclear complex in line with what was now being called Complex Transformation (rather than Complex 2030). Still missing was any discussion about the purpose of the nuclear arsenal.

In the spring of 2007, as we were wrapping up the last of our nuclear travels, we received a call from Lieutenant Colonel D. Brent Morris, an instructor we knew at the Air Force Academy in Colorado Springs. Morris, a nuclear engineer, was desperately trying to drum up interest among his cadets in pursuing careers in the nuclear field. He was concerned—not unlike many of the people we had met—that the nuclear weapons business was no longer attracting the best and the brightest. To pique the interest of his students, he had organized a "nuclear rediscovery" field trip—a journey that followed some of our nuclear itinerary. He asked if we would like to come along, so we flew out to Albuquerque for a final trip.

On the drive from Albuquerque to Trinity, we shared a ride with one of Morris's colleagues, who had worked for the Defense Threat Reduction Agency. He had spent the better part of the past year working on Divine Strake, the agency's controversial plan to test high-yield explosives at the Nevada Test Site, a test that, as DTRA director James Tegnelia told a group of reporters, would be "the first time in Nevada that you'll see a mushroom cloud over Las Vegas since we stopped testing nuclear weapons."

The test—already controversial—became a lightning rod for criticism. Our driving companion was still grumbling about Tegnelia's offhand "mushroom cloud" remark. It had, he said, needlessly engulfed the program in controversy, giving ammunition to opponents of the test and ultimately leading to the project's cancellation. It was a waste of twenty-five million dollars in taxpayer money, and a year of his work. "We were robbed of an opportunity," he said bitterly.

When we pointed out that the ominous name of the test might have fed into the public's misgivings, he looked perplexed. It was just a name, he said, noting that the *D* in Divine came from a standard formula used for code-naming demonstration tests. Phenomenology tests, he added, were named Humble. "Like Humble Ginkgos," he said.

As we approached Trinity, we saw that not much had changed in the two years since we had last visited, but we did note a new sign posted at the road leading to ground zero. REMOVAL OF TRINITITE IS THEFT OF GOVERNMENT PROPERTY AND CAN RESULT IN FINES AND JAIL TIME, it warned. The students immediately fanned out on a Trinitite hunt.

We wandered around ground zero, mostly observing the students. It was, if nothing else, amusing to watch the possible future guardians of America's nuclear arsenal as they picked up and handled pieces of Trinitite. "Is nice—verrrry nice!" one declared, mimicking Borat as he inspected another piece of stone. We stopped to look again at the obelisk, where Morris was snapping photos, and chatted with him about the trip. In addition to Trinity, we had accompanied the students to Sandia National Laboratories for briefings (which nearly put the students to sleep) and on a tour of a Triga nuclear reactor, which the students seemed to enjoy more. They also went on a tour of the Manzano Base, where nuclear warheads were once kept in storage (lacking security clearances, we were not allowed to join them). Would any of that convince the students to go into nuclear weapons? "It's a dying breed," Morris said. His hope, he added, was that at least one of the cadets would pursue that route, and the tour would help them understand the nuclear complex they would inherit.

After two years of travels, we now understood why his battle was an uphill one. Without a clear nuclear strategy, the nuclear career track was not likely to be attractive. We began and ended our journey as strong proponents of national security. We came away with a respect for the patriotism and dedication of those who toil in the nuclear weapons complex—both in the United States and abroad. But we also felt it was an enterprise that had lost its way.

Worse, knowledge about nuclear weapons is fragmented. Those who advocate the RRW, for instance, aren't necessarily knowledgeable about the military missions it would be used in, and those with knowledge of military missions often don't know the physics behind the argument for the RRW. Those working on counterterrorism technologies don't really know the worldwide scope of the threat, and those who do study and know the threat don't have any influence over the war plans designed to deter it. There's no single person—or agency—who can put it all together. "Thinking about the unthinkable" was once the task of theorists like Herman Kahn, who pored over the different scenarios of World War III. However controversial his views may have been, considering nuclear war was a serious business. Today, that discussion has largely been abdicated by our top intellects.

Most experts now seem to agree that the gravest future threat is nuclear terrorism, and yet only a small portion of our massive nuclear weapons infrastructure and scientific talent is actively involved in tackling this problem. Even then, there is no unity of effort. Whether our own nuclear weapons could prove a deterrent to such a threat is questionable at best; one could even argue that the main purpose of a terrorist attack using a nuclear weapon would be to provoke a catastrophic nuclear retaliation.

We failed on our travels to find anyone within the complex who could articulate what the current role of the nuclear arsenal is, or should be. Quite the opposite, we learned that conventional weapons are quickly taking on the role that nuclear weapons once played; that Russia is no longer the primary nuclear contingency; and that terrorism, even nuclear terrorism, cannot be easily deterred by our current stockpile of weapons. The nuclear genie, as the cliché goes, can't be put back in the bottle (nor are we convinced it should be), but that doesn't mean we need thousands of warheads on full alert. More than anything, what emerged from our travels was a conviction that it may be time again for the United States to explore practical options for eliminating the nuclear arsenal.

As we sat with the Air Force cadets in the Owl Bar and Cafe, we felt the empty Cold War nostalgia of the place. It was unlikely that more than one or two students, at best, would go into the nuclear field. Visiting historic nuclear weapons sites was interesting, but it was in some ways the atomic age equivalent of visiting the World's Largest Rubber Band Ball or the Museum of Pez Memorabilia.

We asked the students what about their own nuclear tour was most memorable. We expected them to select the top-secret nuclear storage facility at Manzano, or perhaps Trinity. But they all agreed their favorite sight was the deep indigo glow from the Cherenkov radiation released at the bottom of the Annular Core Research Reactor at Sandia. It was a reminder for us that it isn't a deep allure of power that attracts people to the world of atomic weaponry, but the opportunity to work on interesting and worthwhile science. To attract the best and the brightest in the future, the nuclear complex will need better reasons for them to join than weapons maintenance. If dismantling an atomic bomb can be as satisfying as building one—a lesson we learned at Y-12—then surely nuclear counterterrorism is as worthwhile a job as sitting in a silo and waiting to turn the keys.

The issue extends to the entire nuclear enterprise. To imagine that we will continue to sink billions of dollars into weapons whose purpose is so unclear is troubling. And it is clear that the lack of urgency in the nuclear enterprise could make us less—not more—safe. In the late summer of 2007, a B-52 mistakenly loaded with six nuclear-armed cruise missiles flew across the United States, an error attributed to a breakdown in security procedures that would have been unthinkable during the Cold War.

But more troubling, perhaps, is that the rest of the world may lose sight of the alternatives to nuclear proliferation. Without clear, unambiguous leadership from the United States, and without a concerted international effort, more—not fewer—countries will pursue nuclear weapons, and the number of potential nuclear destinations will increase. We were reminded of this fact as we completed the manuscript for this book, when we learned of a new destination for nuclear tourism: China. The Los Angeles Times published a story describing a trip to Factory 221 in Xihai, where China sealed its status as a nuclear power. China clearly recognized the appeal of atomic tourism; it was building a ten-million-dollar Nuclear City museum.

What other countries will join the nuclear club and, by virtue of membership, become an elite tourist destination along the expanding nuclear trail? North Korea, though it has (again) renounced its nuclear ambitions, could reemerge as a threat. Iran's nuclear ambitions remain a focal point of diplomatic tensions.* Syria is now alleged to have a nuclear program. From Asia to the Middle East, more countries have dropped hints that they, too, might seek the nuclear option.

The last president to state a goal of eliminating nuclear weapons was Ronald Reagan. He was inspired, in good part, by a technological fantasy of effective missile defense that twenty years later still proves elusive, even on a limited scale. Yet the notion of freeing the world from nuclear weaponry—while anathema to sitting politicians—is hardly a view restricted to aging peaceniks. In January 2007, George Shultz, William Perry, Henry Kissinger, and Sam Nunn—all serious practitioners of foreign policy—published a *Wall Street Journal* opinion piece advocating this same vision. "Reassertion of the vision of a world free of nuclear weapons and practical measures toward achieving that goal would be, and would be perceived as, a bold initiative consistent with America's moral heritage," they wrote. Maybe the goal of zero nuclear weapons will never be reached, but it's a far better goal than none at all.

We emerged from our travels convinced that the United States has a nuclear arsenal that serves many purposes, but no particular end. From the missile fields of Nebraska and Wyoming to the test range in Kwajalein, much of the infrastructure supporting nuclear weapons continues to exist merely because no one has come up with a compelling reason to shut it down. In the end, we had to return to the question we posed at the beginning: Why take a nuclear vacation?

The things closest to you are the easiest to ignore, and travel is the best way to break free of complacency. Nuclear tourism reminded us of a threat to which we've become inured, living in Washington, amid the constant chatter about terrorism and national security. It took a trip around the world for us to question the rationale behind the nuclear arsenal.

Perhaps that is the power of travel. It confronts the visitor with something that has become quite normal to those who live around it. At

---

* In late 2007, a new U.S. National Intelligence Estimate concluded that Iran had ceased work on its nuclear weapons program in 2003.

the opulent Greenbrier, Bob Conte, the hotel's historian, recounted how hundreds of staffers worked for years atop—and at times inside— a nuclear bunker. Despite the rumors, they never much contemplated the possibility of nuclear holocaust. Why not? "One of the things they relied on is that most of us are pretty narrowly focused on our lives," he said. "We're worried about our jobs and our kids and what's right under our feet. You walk by things and they don't quite register. So you think, it's of no major importance. You don't worry about it. Yet the whole thing was planned around nuclear war."

Notes

Prologue: How to Be an Armageddon Tourist

2   *"This 1,000 mile trip up Interstate I–25 from the Mexican border . . . the epic story of America's obsession with the bomb"*: Leslie Woodhead, "Welcome to Los Alamos," *Financial Times*, September 1–2, 2007.

2   *"Many visitors, even those who are anti-nuclear," . . . who has studied the nuclear complex*: Hugh Gusterson, "Nuclear Tourism," *Journal for Cultural Research*, Vol. 8, No. 1, January 2004, pp. 23–31.

5   *In 1966, the United States had . . . 32,193 weapons in its stockpile*: "Fifty Facts about Nuclear Weapons," Brookings Institution fact sheet. Accessed at http://www.brookings.edu/projects/archive/nucweapons/50.aspx.

5   *By 2006, the exact number . . . to be around 6,000 and dropping*: Amy F. Woolf, "U.S. Strategic Nuclear Forces: Background, Developments, and Issues," Congressional Research Service report, September 5, 2007.

5   *In 2006, the United States spent . . . was $6.34 billion*: Greg Mello, "Weapons Activities Spending 1980–2006," Los Alamos Study Group report.

8   *The United Kingdom and France . . . are surprisingly secretive about their nuclear facilities*: Cassell Bryan-Low and Carrick Mollenkamp, "Atomic Alliance: U.K. Village Is Home to Secretive Agency," *Wall Street Journal*, December 28, 2006.

1. Priscilla, Queen of the Desert: A Visit to the Nevada Test Site

15   *After all, an NNSA advisory panel in 2002 had concluded . . . only a very rough estimate*: "Science and Technology in the Stockpile Stewardship Program," Advisory Committee of the National Nuclear Security Administration report, October 19, 2002.

15 *In either case . . . The NNSA disbanded that advisory panel in 2003:*
    Julian Borger, "U.S. Scraps Nuclear Weapons Watchdog," *Guardian,*
    July 31, 2003.

21 New York Times *journalist William J. Broad described . . . in case*
    someone tried to make off with a nuclear weapon: William J. Broad,
    "Bomb Tests: Technology Advances Against Backdrop of Wide De-
    bate," *New York Times,* April 15, 1986.

22 *Another, Misty Rain, depicted a bikini-clad woman holding an um-*
    brella: Rick Atkinson, " 'Underground Events' Test Mettle of U.S.
    Atomic Arsenal," *Washington Post,* May 29, 1984.

23 *Tests in 1957 exposed some twelve hundred pigs . . . appropriately*
    called the Pork Sheraton: Nevada Test Site Guide, Department of
    Energy, 2001, p. 13.

24 *Diagnostic cables snaking out from the canister . . . would be recorded:*
    Gusterson, *Nuclear Rites* (Berkeley and Los Angeles: University of
    California Press, 1996), pp. 136–37.

26 Footnote: *The aftershock of Sedan was felt again in 2005, . . . "Sudan"*
    nuclear test: BBC World News: "Typing Error Causes Nuclear Scare,"
    March 11, 2005, accessed at www.news.bbc.co.uk/2/hi/africa/
    4338835.stm.

2. When Knowledge Is an Endangered Thing: Travels Through New Mexico's Nuclear Landscape

35 *Oppenheimer—who once wrote a friend . . . of the mesa:* Richard
    Rhodes, *The Making of the Atomic Bomb* (New York: Touchstone,
    1986), p. 451.

35 *"Nobody can think straight . . . Everybody who goes there will go*
    crazy": Ibid.

36 *And that view of a dysfunctional laboratory . . . for being "cowboys" and*
    "butt-heads": Keay Davidson, "Los Alamos Crackdown Imperils U.S.,
    lab physicist warns," *San Francisco Chronicle,* September 18, 2004.

36 *Nanos ordered a complete shutdown . . . save me the trouble":* Original
    document posted on Defensetech.org, www.defensetech.org/archives/
    001020.html.

47 *When it was revealed in 2003 . . . no more than a blip on the radar*
    screen of newspapers: Dan Eggen and Susan Schmidt, "Ex-FBI Agent
    Resigns Post at Nuclear Weapons Lab," *Washington Post,* April 11,
    2003.

3. Wicked Things: Exploring the Future of Nuclear Weapons at Sandia and Livermore

48 *"If that meant staying inside . . . It was suicide, and we all knew it"*: Frank Greve, "Nuclear-Armed Troops Had a 'Green Light' to Suicide," *Houston Chronicle*, August 7, 1994.

51 *As author Richard L. Miller notes . . . a whole series of pelvic X-rays"*: Richard L. Miller, *Under the Cloud* (New York: Free Press, 1986), p. 8.

57 *Writers like William J. Broad . . . fields dotted with cows"*: William J. Broad, *Star Warriors* (New York: Simon and Schuster, 1985), p. 22.

59 *In 2001, the General Accounting Office . . . management for the facility's troubles*: GAO report, June 1, 2001.

59 *A nuclear device in those days was . . . that he could do it within five years*: Broad, *Teller's War* (New York: Simon and Schuster, 1992), p. 45.

64 *In his classic 1974 book . . . two airliners loaded with jet fuel*: John McPhee, *The Curve of Binding Energy* (New York: Farrar, Straus and Giroux, 1974), p. 10.

4. Home Brew: Uncovering the Secrets of Uranium Production in Tennessee

68 *Oak Ridge dates back to the . . . original secret cities*: Richard Rhodes, *The Making of the Atomic Bomb*, p. 486.

68 *Since the end of the Cold War, the production complex . . . employ twenty-seven thousand people*: Congressional testimony of Clay Sell, Deputy Secretary of Energy, April 26, 2006.

69 *In the early 1990s, a* Wall Street Journal *reporter . . . how many people it employed"*: Bob Davis, "Into the Light: After Years of Secrecy, Nuclear-Arms Plants Show Off Technology," *Wall Street Journal*, December 4, 1990.

70 *"Three Mile Island, spiraling costs and . . . nuclear weapons plants has diminished"*: Lydia Chavez, "U.S. Nuclear Arms Makers Sour on Program," *New York Times*, June 9, 1982.

75 *Even after the war, problems continued . . . "vile cafeteria food"*: Russell B. Olwell, *At Work in the Atomic City* (Knoxville, Tenn.: University of Tennessee Press, 2004), p. 91.

76 *A 2004 report by the Department of Energy's inspector . . . a known*

carcinogen: Duncan Mansfield, "Beryllium Concerns Remain at Nuclear Weapons Plant," Associated Press State and Local Wire, April 21, 2003.

77 *Rocky Flats in Colorado, for example, seemed to be . . . the aforementioned FBI raid:* Tad Bartimus and Scott McCartney, *Trinity's Children* (New York: Harcourt Brace Jovanovich, 1991), p. 193.

77 *Although the legal wrangling continued . . . came to an ignominious end:* Wes McKinley and Caron Balkany, *The Ambushed Grand Jury* (New York: Apex Press, 2004), p. 79.

77 *One worker at K-25 nominated his demolition . . . bad boys of the chemical realm":* William Speed Weed, "Worst Science Jobs 2, Number 6: K-25 Demolition Worker," PopSci.com, accessed at www.popsci.com/popsci/science/5d7d0b4511b84010vgnvcm1000004eecbccdrcrd.html.

77 *In 2006, a worker was seriously injured . . . second story of the deteriorated structure:* Frank Munger, "K-25 Mishap Ruled Avoidable," *Knoxville News Sentinel*, March 7, 2006.

77 *According to the* Knoxville News Sentinel, *a 1999 explosion . . . the newspaper reported:* Munger, "Could Y-12 Accident Have Been Avoided?" *Knoxville News Sentinel*, February 2, 2000.

5. Where's the Big Board? Searching for Strategery in Nebraska

86 *During the Cold War, the logic of nuclear deterrence . . . that defied control or comprehension":* General George Lee Butler, speech to the National Press Club, Washington, D.C., February 2, 1998.

86 *Even the road we traveled from the Colorado border . . . in the event of a nuclear attack:* Address of Vice President Richard Nixon to the Governors Conference, Lake George, New York, July 12, 1954, accessed at www.fhwa.dot.gov/infrastructure/rw96m.htm.

87 *By the mid-1960s, for instance, Lincoln, Nebraska . . . prepare for nuclear Armageddon:* www.nebraskastudies.org/0900/frameset_reset.html?http://www.nebraskastudies.org/0900/stories/0901_0130.html.

89 *In its place was a strategy combining nuclear forces . . . and ballistic missile defense:* J. D. Crouch, special briefing on the Nuclear Posture Review, accessed at www.defenselink.mil/transcripts/transcript.aspx?transcriptid=1108.

89 *By fall 2006 . . . deployed warheads was estimated at around six thousand:* Amy F. Woolf, "U.S. Strategic Nuclear Forces: Background,

Developments and Issues," Congressional Research Service report, September 5, 2007.

91   *In the 1970s, when journalist Ron Rosenbaum explored . . . and whether we ought to obey":* Ron Rosenbaum, "The Subterranean World of the Bomb," *Harper's Magazine,* March 1978.

91   *That meeting reportedly would cover mini-nukes, . . . on the Nebraska plains:* Julian Borger, " 'Dr. Strangeloves' Meet to Plan New Nuclear Era," *Guardian,* August 7, 2003; "Secret Talks May Lead to Breaking Treaties," *Guardian,* February 19, 2003.

92   *"In the secret world of military planning . . . the defensive role of nuclear weapons":* William Arkin, "Not Just a Last Resort? A Global Strike Plan, with a Nuclear Option," *Washington Post,* May 15, 2005.

99   *According to the* Washington Post Magazine *. . . "the 'living SIOP' ":* R. Jeffrey Smith, "The General's Conscience: Why Nuclear Warrior George Lee Butler Changed His Mind," *Washington Post Magazine,* December 7, 1997.

6. A Cow Runs Through It: Visiting Missile Silos in the Great Plains

107   *"All wars end in tourism," observes Tom Vanderbilt . . . Cold War's architecture of survival:* Tom Vanderbilt, *Survival City* (New York: Princeton Architectural Press, 2002), p. 135.

112   *In 2006, the State Historical Society of North Dakota . . . to draw tourists to tiny Cooperstown (population: 1,100):* Judy Keen, "N.D. Nuke Site May Reopen as Museum," *USA Today,* December 27, 2006.

116   *Called the "steel balloon" . . . couldn't initially be launched from underground:* G. Harry Stine, *ICBM* (New York: Orion Books, 1991), p. 226.

125   *In 1988, they were allowed to serve with men . . . the vagaries of his own heart":* Daniel P. Moloney, *First Things: The Journal of Religion, Culture, and Public Life,* February 1, 2000, p. 45.

125   *The argument, according to Berry's defenders . . . that ran in the* Baltimore Sun: Robert L. Maginnis, "Saving Lieutenant Ryan Berry," *Baltimore Sun,* July 25, 1999.

125   *Bob Wyckoff . . . has adapted his verse to the post–Cold War era:* Association of Air Force Missileers, *AAFM Newsletter,* Vol. 14, No. 2, June 2006, pp. 7–8, accessed at www.afmissileers.org/newsletters/ NL2006/Jun06.pdf.

126   *Missileers maintain an active online forum . . . and morale appears to be*

at   an   all-time   low: www.missileforums.com/forums/viewtopic
.php?t=57, accessed on March 22, 2007.

126   *In one post, a missileer calling himself "Spank" celebrates . . . I get to
retire   a   MISSILEER!":* www.missileforums.com/forums/viewto
pic.php?t=36, accessed on March 22, 2007.

127   *Back in 2005, General Lance Lord . . . does winning the Cold War
change your mission?' It doesn't":* Speech in Washington, D.C.,
April 20, 2005, provided by the Air Force Space Command's public
affairs   office,   available   at   www.slate.com/id/2117172/sidebar/
2117203.

127   *As Fred Kaplan, author of* The Wizards *. . . desperately, looking for
something to do":* Fred Kaplan, "What's Next for Our Brave Missileers?" *Slate,* April 21, 2005, accessed at www.slate.msn.com/id/
2117172.

128   *According to at least one poll . . . the chances of an all-out nuclear war
are   remote:* 1998   CNN/USA   Today/Gallup   Poll,   accessed   at
www.cnn.com/ALLPOLITICS/1998/06/16/poll.

7. How We Learned to Stop Worrying About the Bomb in Pennsylvania: The Rebirth of Site R, the Government's Secret Nuclear Bunker

132   *As a 2000 profile of the facility in the* New York Times Magazine
reported . . . to ensure the continuity of government operations": Bill
Gifford, "Bunker? What Bunker?," *New York Times Magazine,* December 3, 2000.

133   *Asked about the site and its role in continuity-of-government . . . "And
I'll just leave it at that":* Department of Defense official news briefing,
March 27, 2002.

135   *"Reconstruction will begin . . . and most survivors will not envy the
dead":* Herman Kahn, *Thinking About the Unthinkable in the 1980s*
(New York: Simon and Schuster, 1984), p. 92.

135   In 1981, Deputy Under Secretary of Defense T. K. Jones . . . everybody's
going to make it": Joe Klein, "Unthinkable Chitchat," *New York Times,*
November 28, 1982.

135   *As* Time *noted in 1982, "Unlike the fallout-shelter mania . . . resuming
normal operations after a nuclear attack":* Time, "Dig a Hole," March
29, 1982, accessed at www.time.com/time/printout/0,8816,953410,00.
html.

135   *James Mann, author of the book* Rise of the Vulcans, *describes . . .*

U.S. nuclear strategists were planning to do to the Soviet Union": James Mann, "The Armageddon Plan," *Atlantic Monthly*, March 2004.

136   *As the GAO pointed out, one wayward agency's . . . articles for the Secretary and Deputy Secretary"*: GAO report, "Continuity of Operations: Improved Planning Needed to Ensure Delivery of Essential Government Services," February 2004.

136   *Fodor's even include the bunker at Raven Rock on its list . . . close to the actual facility:* www.fodors.com/wire/archives/002499.cfm.

138   *On September 11, 2001, as top defense officials . . . NORAD, was stuck in traffic:* Bruce Finley, "After 40 Years on Guard, Cheyenne Mountain to Stand Down," Denverpost.com, July 28, 2006; see also www.cooperativeresearch.org/entity.jsp?entity=ralph_eberhart.

140   *A heightened security regime—put in place before the Y2K . . . stopped conducting tours for the general public:* Alan Prendergast, "No Fighting in the War Room: After a Thirty-Year Open House, NORAD Declares Cheyenne Mountain Off-limits to Tourists," *Denver Westword*, March 25, 1999.

142   *Almost as soon as shelters were built . . . potentially vulnerable the day it was completed in 1965":* Tim Folger, "Shield of Dreams," *Discover*, November 1, 2001.

143   *During an exercise in 2005, Admiral Timothy Keating . . . "I can't be in two places at one time," the admiral complained:* Finley, "Military to Put Cheyenne Mountain on Standby," *Denver Post*, December 26, 2006.

143   Footnote: *As a GAO report noted, "The Air Force . . . about a 51 percent increase over initial estimates":* GAO report, "Defense Acquisitions: Further Management and Oversight Changes Needed for Efforts to Modernize Cheyenne Mountain Attack Warning Systems," July 2006.

150   *"Just how Congress was expected to reach the Greenbrier is unclear . . . the craziest thing I ever heard of":* Ted Gup, "Last Resort: The Ultimate Congressional Hideaway," *Washington Post Magazine*, May 31, 1992.

151   *According to military analyst William Arkin, . . . bunk beds will be assigned in 12-hour shifts":* William M. Arkin, "How to Pack for the Bunker; And Other Government Contingency Plans," *Los Angeles Times*, August 1, 2004.

152   *Other reporters, who have made it . . . could result in fines or jail time:* Steve Goldstein, " 'Undisclosed Location' disclosed: A Visit Offers Some Insight into Cheney Hide-out," Knight Ridder newspapers, July 20, 2004.

154   A Pittsburgh Post-Gazette *article describes "six-stories of . . . mysterious antennas, dishes and massive, steel doors":* Dennis Roddy, "Homefront: Site R Is Secure, But It's Not Undisclosed," *Pittsburgh Post-Gazette,* December 16, 2001.

154   *Author James Bamford writes of "a secret world of five buildings . . . and a subterranean water reservoir":* James Bamford, *A Pretext for War,* quoted in Michael Duffy, "One Expert's Verdict: The CIA Caved Under Pressure," *Time,* June 14, 2004.

154   *Underground worlds, once created, take on a life of their own . . . furtive conduits of power":* Tom Vanderbilt, *Survival City,* p. 148.

155   *Some cities took this as carte blanche . . . bring your own everything":* Jay Reeves, "Emergency Planners Renew Huntsville's Shelter Program," *Decatur Daily,* September 28, 2007.

8. Rocket City, USA: Huntsville's Space Odyssey

157   *The treaty was seen as a landmark of arms control . . . nuclear attack was massive retaliation:* "The Anti-Ballistic Missile (ABM) Treaty at a Glance," Arms Control Association fact sheet, January 2003, accessed at www.armscontrol.org/factsheets/abmtreaty.asp.

158   *Nike Zeus didn't work particularly well . . . armed with nuclear-tipped interceptors:* Ashton Carter and David N. Schwartz, editors, *Ballistic Missile Defense* (Washington, D.C.: Brookings Press, 1984), pp. 440–42; author interview with Philip Coyle, August 13, 2007.

159   *Six weeks later—as if on cue . . . alarming the U.S. intelligence community:* "National Missile Defense: An Overview (1993–2000)," Missile Defense Agency Historian's Office, accessed at www.mda.mil/mdalink/html/nmdhist.html.

163   *The center had embarked . . . bags of "Saturn V Coffee" as part of its fund-raising campaign:* U.S. Space and Rocket Center Foundation Web site, www.spacecamp.com/saturnv.

164   *The V-2 carried a one-ton (one-thousand-kilogram) high-explosive payload:* G. Harry Stine, *ICBM,* p. 46.

164   *the Redstone was designed to carry a thermonuclear warhead:* U.S. Army official online history of the Redstone program, accessed at www.redstone.army.mil/history/systems/redstone/welcome.html.

165   *While the Peenemünders later insisted the rocket . . . it would have had sufficient range to reach the United States:* Bob Ward, *Dr. Space* (Annapolis, Md.: U.S. Naval Institute Press, 2005), p. 52.

165 *"Stuhlinger spoke proudly . . . the garrulous old scientist suddenly clammed up"*: Ken Silverstein, "Huntsville's Missile Payload," *Mother Jones*, July/August 2001, accessed at www.motherjones.com/news/feature/2001/07/missile.html.

176 *After all, the "burn rate" at the time in Iraq . . . around eight billion dollars per month and climbing*: Bryan Bender, "Cost of Iraq War Nearly $2b a Week," *Boston Globe*, September 28, 2006.

9. Fantasy Island: Vacationing in the Marshall Islands

179 *The combined explosive power of the tests was over one hundred thousand kilotons . . . the total yield of all the nuclear tests in Nevada*: List of atomic tests in the Marshall Islands and their combined yield, fact sheet accessed at www.rmiembassyus.org/Nuclear%20Issues.htm.

184 *A reporter visiting the Marshall Islands for* Outside *. . . spend their days tracking death machines"*: Tad Friend, "Lost at Sea," *Outside*, March 1997.

184 *But perhaps most memorable for current residents . . . a less-than-flattering portrait of Kwajalein residents*: JoAnn Wypijewski, "Missile Defense Makes Its Mark in the Marshall Islands," *Harper's Magazine*, December 2001.

191 *The U.S. government invited twenty-two foreign observers . . . a boat-load of print and radio correspondents*: Jonathan M. Weisgall, *Operation Crossroads* (Annapolis, Md.: U.S. Naval Institute Press, 1994), pp. 142–144.

192 *They were banished to uninhabited Rongerik Atoll . . . restaged for the benefit of the newsreel cameras*: Ibid., p. 112–113.

196 *As a group of Harvard Law School student advocates noted . . . Marshallese residents who had suffered much higher levels of exposure*: Harvard Law Student Advocates for Human Rights, "Keeping the Promise: An Evaluation of Continuing U.S. Obligations Arising out of the U.S. Nuclear Testing Program in the Marshall Islands," April 2006.

196 *The United States and the Republic of the Marshall Islands had agreed . . . would provide a sustainable income for the country*: GAO Report, "Compacts of Free Association: Trust Funds for Micronesia and the Marshall Islands May Not Provide Sustainable Income," June 2007.

199 *Eugene Sims, a longtime civilian manager on Kwajalein . . . "all of those who have known the 'Kwaj condition'"*: Eugene Sims, *Kwajalein Remembered* (Eugene, Ore.: Eugene Print, 1993), p. 20.

10. Take Me to Your One-Eyed Baby: Promoting Nuclear Tourism in Kazakhstan

204 *After Borat warmed up a rodeo crowd in Salem . . . a tolerant, modernizing democracy:* Laurence Hammack, "Kazakhstan Official Hopes Roanoke Area Knows That 'Ali G' Has Nothing to Do with His Country," *Roanoke Times*, August 8, 2006.

207 *According to reported numbers, Kazakhstan in 1991 . . . an arsenal totaling 1,360 warheads:* Flight International, November 13, 1991.

207 *"Kazakhstan is a big country and it can't stand unarmed . . . Nazarbayev was quoted as saying":* Vincent J. Schodolski, "Republic Bolts Russian Nuclear Arms Deal," *Chicago Tribune*, April 10, 1992.

223 *"My name Borat Sagdiyev," he said . . . people with a bone in the middle of their brain":* "Borat Comes to Washington," video available at www.washingtonpost.com/wpdyn/content/video/2006/09/28/ VI2006092801279.html.

11. Barbarians at the Gate: In Search of Russia's Secret Nuclear Cities

227 *Russian facilities received over half a billion dollars . . . for facility security alone:* U.S. Department of Energy, Moscow Office, "Summary of DOE Programs in Russia: FY '04 Accomplishments and FY '05 Goals," February 2005; NNSA news release, April 11, 2001.

229 *Russia's nuclear arsenal, he had written, "is a guarantee . . . for all nations who cannot accept the American 'freedom and democracy'":* Viktor N. Mikhailov, "Russia Is a Nuclear Power," accessed at www.iss.niiit.ru/pub-eng/pub-05.htm.

229 *That spring, in fact, an article in* Foreign Affairs *. . . nuclear arsenals of Russia or China with a first strike":* Keir A. Lieber and Daryl G. Press, "The Rise of U.S. Nuclear Primacy," *Foreign Affairs*, March/April 2006.

231 *Russia still maintains a massive arsenal . . . according to a 2006 estimate prepared by the Natural Resources Defense Council):* Robert S. Norris and Hans M. Kristensen, "Nuclear Notebook: Russian Strategic Forces, 2006," *Bulletin of the Atomic Scientists*, March/April 2006.

231 *In October 1996, a despondent Vladimir Nechai . . . shot himself:* Michael R. Gordon, "A Top Russian Nuclear Scientist Kills Himself," *New York Times*, November 1, 1996.

232 *Many of the fears of nuclear watchers . . . in Novosibirsk, one of Russia's major scientific cities:* Margarita Antidze, "Georgia Says It Foiled Sale of Bomb-Grade Uranium," Reuters, January 25, 2007.

232 *But the most alarming—and most controversial—claim . . . had essentially gone missing:* Carey Sublette, "Alexander Lebed and Suitcase Nukes," discussion posted at www.nuclearweaponarchive.org/News/Lebedbomb.html.

241 *Those programs, under the broad mandate of "threat reduction," . . . selling their knowledge to rogue nations:* Amy Woolf, "Nonproliferation and Threat Reduction Assistance: U.S. Programs in the Former Soviet Union," Congressional Research Service report, February 23, 2007.

12. Got Nukes? Nuclear Junketeering in Iran

251 *"Upon permission granted by President Mahmoud Ahmadinejad . . . Iran's nuclear activities are peaceful":* Islamic Republic News Agency, October 4, 2006.

253 *A subsequent high-level overture from Tehran . . . was reportedly ignored by the White House:* "Washington 'Snubbed Iran Offer,'" BBC News, January 18, 2007.

257 *As part of the deal, the Europeans offered Iran . . . could be readily diverted to military use:* "Europe to Offer Iran Reactor if Tehran Shows Nuclear Program Is Peaceful," Agence France-Presse, October 20, 2004.

257 *In what foreshadowed an escalating battle of wills . . . resume their work at Esfahān:* Nuclear Threat Initiative, "Iran Profile," accessed at www.nti.org/e_research/profiles/Iran/3119_3150.html.

261 *Iran's history with nuclear energy was not always . . . read a 1970s advertising caption:* Accessed at www.iranian.com/Pictory/2006/May/guess.html.

261 *In the 1960s, the United States supplied a five-megawatt . . . went critical in 1967:* Nuclear Threat Initiative, "Iran Profile," accessed at www.nti.org/e_research/profiles/Iran/3119_3268.html.

262 *During the 1970s, as oil revenue flooded state coffers, . . . a European consortium's uranium enrichment facility in France:* Nuclear Threat Initiative, "Iran Profile", accessed at www.nti.org/e_research/profiles/Iran.

262 *In 1976, the* New York Times *reported . . . at a cost unofficially estimated at more than $20 billion":* Eric Pace, "Iran, with Oil Income Slipping, Shelves Some Ambitious Projects and Delays Others," *New York Times*, February 16, 1976.

262 *By the 1990s, Iran's younger generation . . . government of President Mohammad Khatami*: BBC News, "At-a-Glance: Iran's Vital Statistics," accessed at news.bbc.co.uk/2/shared/spl/hi/pop_ups/04/middle_east _iran0s_vital_statistics/htm 1/1.stm; James Whittington, "Youth Shapes Iran's Economy," BBC News, December 3, 2002.

263 Footnote: *The role of Jafarzadeh was one of the most curious . . . worked as a paid terrorism analyst for Fox News*: Elizabeth Rubin, "The Cult of Rajavi," *New York Times Magazine*, July 13, 2003.

263 *At the end of that year, Iranian officials signed . . . "snap inspections" of its nuclear facilities*: Nuclear Threat Initiative, "Iran Profile: Nuclear Overview," accessed at www.nti.org/e_research/profiles/Iran/1819 .html.

263 *In 2005, Secretary of State Condoleezza Rice put it succinctly: "Our view is that Iran needs no civil nuclear power"*: Remarks with Russian Foreign Minister Sergey Lavrov, Moscow, October 15, 2005, transcript accessed at usinfo.state.gov/xarchives/display.html?p=washfile-english& y=2005&m=October&x=20051015144505attocnich5.270022e-02.

264 *The following month, the government voted . . . relied on imported petroleum*: Gethin Chamberlain and Kay Biouki, "Iran Votes to Impose Petrol Rationing," *Sunday Telegraph*, March 11, 2007; "Petrol Ration- ing in Iran?," *Economist*, March 22, 2007.

266 *On August 8, 2005, two days after Ahmadinejad's inauguration . . . broke the IAEA seals at Natanz*: James Martin Center for Nonprolifera- tion Studies, "Chronology of Key Events Related to the Implementation of IAEA Safeguards in Iran," accessed at cns.miis.edu/pubs/week/ 060120.htm.

269 *Fereidoon Abbasi Davani . . . was on the top of that list*: UN Security Council Resolution 1747, adopted March 24, 2007, accessed at www .un.org/News/Press/docs/2007/sc8980.doc.htm.

Epilogue: Next Year in North Korea

278 *As nuclear weapons expert Joseph Cirincione noted . . . transfer of nuclear, biological, and chemical weapons"*: Joseph Cirincione, *Bomb Scare* (New York: Columbia University Press, 2007), p. 117.

279 *"There has been no presidential or cabinet–level statement . . . that argues the case for the RRW," the report states*: Bruce Tarter et al., "United States Nuclear Weapons Program: The Role of the Reliable Replacement Warhead," report of the Nuclear Weapons Complex

Assessment Committee, American Association for the Advancement of Science, 2007.

283 *The* Los Angeles Times . . . *a ten-million-dollar Nuclear City museum:* Don Lee, "Visiting China's Nuclear Past," *Los Angeles Times*, September 2, 2007.

284 *In January 2007, George Shultz, William Perry . . . consistent with America's moral heritage," they wrote:* George P. Shultz, William J. Perry, Henry A. Kissinger, and Sam Nunn, "A World Free of Nuclear Weapons," *Wall Street Journal*, January 4, 2007.

Select Bibliography

Allison, Graham. *Nuclear Terrorism: The Ultimate Preventable Catastrophe.* New York: Henry Holt and Company, 2004.

Alvarez, Luis. *Alvarez: Adventures of a Physicist.* New York: Basic Books, 1987.

Amundson, Michael A. *Yellowcake Towns: Uranium Mining Communities in the American West.* Boulder, Colo.: University Press of Colorado, 2002.

Anderton, Frances, and Chase, John. *Las Vegas: The Success of Excess.* Cologne, Germany: Könemann Verlagsgesellschaft, 1997.

Arkin, William M., and Fieldhouse, Richard W. *Nuclear Battlefields: Global Links in the Arms Race.* Cambridge, Mass.: Ballinger Publishing, 1985.

Bamford, James. *A Pretext for War: 9/11, Iraq, and the Abuse of America's Intelligence Agencies.* New York: Doubleday, 2004.

Barker, Holly M. *Bravo for the Marshallese: Regaining Control in a Post-Nuclear, Post-Colonial World.* Belmont, Calif.: Wadsworth/Thompson, 2004.

Bartimus, Tad, and McCartney, Scott. *Trinity's Children: Living Along America's Nuclear Highway.* New York: Harcourt Brace Jovanovich, 1991.

Bernstein, Jeremy. *Plutonium: A History of the World's Most Dangerous Element.* Washington, D.C.: Joseph Henry Press, 2007.

Bird, Kai, and Sherwin, Martin J. *American Prometheus: The Triumph and Tragedy of J. Robert Oppenheimer.* New York: Vintage Books, 2006.

Boyer, Paul. *By the Bomb's Early Light: American Thought and Culture at the Dawn of the Atomic Age.* New York: Pantheon, 1985.

Broad, William J. *Star Warriors: A Penetrating Look into the Lives of the Young Scientists Behind Our Space Age Weaponry.* New York: Simon and Schuster, 1985.

———. *Teller's War: The Top-Secret Story Behind the Star Wars Deception.* New York: Simon and Schuster, 1992.

Caldicott, Helen. *The New Nuclear Danger: George W. Bush's Military-Industrial Complex.* New York: New Press, 2002.

Carter, Ashton B., and Schwartz, David N., editors. *Ballistic Missile Defense.* Washington, D.C.: Brookings Press, 1984.

Cirincione, Joseph. *Bomb Scare: The History and Future of Nuclear Weapons.* New York: Columbia University Press, 2007.

Conant, Jennet. *109 East Palace: Robert Oppenheimer and the Secret City of Los Alamos.* New York: Simon and Schuster, 2005.

Conte, Robert S. *The History of the Greenbrier: America's Resort.* Charleston, W. Va.: Pictorial Histories Publishing, 1998.

Corera, Gordon. *Shopping for Bombs: Nuclear Proliferation, Global Insecurity, and the Rise and Fall of the A. Q. Khan Network.* New York: Oxford University Press, 2006.

Drell, Sidney D., and Goodby, James E. *The Gravest Danger: Nuclear Weapons.* Stanford, Calif.: Hoover Press, 2003.

Dyson, George. *Project Orion: The True Story of the Atomic Spaceship.* New York: Henry Holt and Company, 2002.

Finkbeiner, Ann. *The Jasons: The Secret History of Science's Postwar Elite.* New York: Viking, 2006.

FitzGerald, Frances. *Way Out There in the Blue: Reagan, Star Wars and the End of the Cold War.* New York: Touchstone, 2001.

Ghamari-Tabrizi, Sharon. *The Worlds of Herman Kahn: The Intuitive Science of Thermonuclear War.* Cambridge, Mass.: Harvard University Press, 2005.

Gusterson, Hugh. *Nuclear Rites: A Weapons Laboratory at the End of the Cold War.* Berkeley and Los Angeles: University of California Press, 1996.

————. *People of the Bomb: Portraits of America's Nuclear Complex.* Minneapolis and London: University of Minnesota Press, 2004.

Harris, Michael. *The Atomic Times: My H-Bomb Year at the Pacific Proving Ground.* New York: Ballantine Books, 2005.

Herken, Gregg. *Brotherhood of the Bomb: The Tangled Lives and Loyalties of Robert Oppenheimer, Ernest Lawrence, and Edward Teller.* New York: Henry Holt and Company, 2003.

Hersey, John. *Hiroshima.* New York: Alfred A. Knopf, 1985.

Hiro, Dilip. *The Iranian Labyrinth: Journeys Through Theocratic Iran and Its Furies.* New York: Nation Books, 2005.

Jafarzadeh, Alireza. *The Iran Threat: President Ahmadinejad and the Coming Nuclear Crisis.* New York: Palgrave Macmillan, 2007.

Johnson, Charles W., and Jackson, Charles O. *City Behind a Fence: Oak Ridge, Tennessee 1942–1946.* Knoxville, Tenn.: University of Tennessee Press, 1981.

Kahn, Herman. *Thinking About the Unthinkable in the 1980s*. New York: Simon and Schuster, 1984.

Kaplan, Fred. *The Wizards of Armageddon*. New York: Simon and Schuster, 1983.

Kuletz, Valerie L. *The Tainted Desert: Environmental Ruin in the American West*. New York: Routledge, 1998.

Langewiesche, William. *The Atomic Bazaar: The Rise of the Nuclear Poor*. New York: Farrar, Straus and Giroux, 2007.

Loeber, Charles R. *Building the Bombs: A History of the Nuclear Weapons Complex*. Albuquerque, N. Mex.: Sandia National Laboratories, 2002.

Mann, James. *Rise of the Vulcans: The History of Bush's War Cabinet*. New York: Viking, 2004.

McKinley, Wes, and Balkany, Caron. *The Ambushed Grand Jury: How the Justice Department Covered Up Government Nuclear Crimes and How We Caught Them Red Handed*. New York: Apex Press, 2004.

McMillan, Priscilla J. *The Ruin of J. Robert Oppenheimer and the Birth of the Modern Arms Race*. New York: Viking, 2005.

McPhee, John. *The Curve of Binding Energy*. New York: Farrar, Straus and Giroux, 1974.

Miller, Richard L. *Under the Cloud: The Decades of Nuclear Testing*. New York: Free Press, 1986.

Mycio, Mary. *Wormwood Forest: A Natural History of Chernobyl*. Washington, D.C.: Joseph Henry Press, 2005.

Nasr, Vali. *The Shia Revival: How Conflicts Within Islam Will Shape the Future*. New York: W. W. Norton and Company, 2006.

Nazarbayev, Nursultan. *Epicenter of Peace*. Hollis, N.H.: Puritan Press, 2001.

Olwell, Russell B. *At Work in the Atomic City: A Labor and Social History of Oak Ridge, Tennessee*. Knoxville, Tenn.: University of Tennessee Press, 2004.

Ordway III, Frederick I., and Sharpe, Mitchell R. *The Rocket Team*. Burlington, Ontario: Apogee Books, 2003.

Rhodes, Richard. *The Making of the Atomic Bomb*. New York: Touchstone, 1986.

—————. *Dark Sun: The Making of the Hydrogen Bomb*. New York: Touchstone, 1995.

Richelson, Jeffrey T. *Spying on the Bomb: American Nuclear Intelligence from Nazi Germany to Iran and North Korea*. New York: W. W. Norton and Company, 2006.

Ritter, Scott. *Target Iran: The Truth About the White House's Plans for Regime Change*. New York: Nation Books, 2006.

Rose, Kenneth D. *One Nation Underground: The Fallout Shelter in American Culture*. New York: New York University Press, 2001.

Rosenbaum, Ron. *The Secret Parts of Fortune: Three Decades of Intense Investigations and Edgy Enthusiasms*. New York: Random House, 2000.

Saudabayev, Kanat, et al. *Kazakhstan's Nuclear Disarmament: A Global Model for a Safer World*. Washington, D.C.: Nuclear Threat Initiative, 2006.

Serber, Robert. *The Los Alamos Primer: The First Lectures on How to Build an Atomic Bomb*. Berkeley and Los Angeles: University of California Press, 1992.

Shroyer, Jo Ann. *Secret Mesa: Inside Los Alamos National Laboratory*. New York: John Wiley and Sons, 1998.

Sims, Eugene C. *Kwajalein Remembered: Stories from the "Realm of the Killer Clam."* Eugene, Ore.: Eugene Print, 1993.

Smith, P. D. *Doomsday Men: The Real Dr Strangelove and the Dream of the Superweapon*. London: Allen Lane, 2007.

Stine, G. Harry. *ICBM: The Making of the Weapon That Changed the World*. New York: Orion Books, 1991.

Vanderbilt, Tom. *Survival City: Adventures Among the Ruins of Atomic America*. New York: Princeton Architectural Press, 2002.

Ward, Bob. *Dr. Space: The Life of Wernher von Braun*. Annapolis, Md.: U.S. Naval Institute Press, 2005.

Weisgall, Jonathan M. *Operation Crossroads: The Atomic Tests at Bikini Atoll*. Annapolis, Md.: U.S. Naval Institute Press, 1994.

APPENDIX

A Beginner's Guide to Nuclear Tourism

Most, though not all, of the places we visited for this book are accessible to tourists, and we provide details on our Web site (www.nuclearvacation.com). For those planning a nuclear itinerary, we also highly recommend the Bureau of Atomic Tourism Web site (www.atomictourist.com), which provides information on and links to many nuclear destinations. For the true nuclear junkie, there is the frighteningly comprehensive *Traveler's Guide to Nuclear Weapons*, by James M. Maroncelli and Timothy L. Karpin, available on CD for sale through the National Atomic Museum in Albuquerque. Basic tour information follows:

NEVADA: The National Nuclear Security Administration conducts bus tours of the Nevada Test Site on the last Thursday of every month; there is occasionally a waiting list, so be sure to contact the Nevada Site Office's Office of Public Affairs at (702) 295–0944 well in advance of a visit. The Atomic Testing Museum at 755 East Flamingo Road in Las Vegas is just minutes from the Strip.

NEW MEXICO: Trinity, where the world's first atomic device was detonated on July 16, 1945, is open to the public twice a year, on the first Saturdays of April and October. For more information, contact the Public Affairs Office at White Sands Missile Range at (505) 678–1134/1700.

Los Alamos National Bank sponsors a walking tour of downtown Los Alamos that includes key sites from the Manhattan Project. For more information, contact the Los Alamos Historical Society (www.losalamoshistory.org). Los Alamos National Laboratory runs the Bradbury Science Museum (www.lanl.gov/museum), a public facility that features exhibits on the history of the Manhattan Project, the first use of atomic weapons, and the era of nuclear testing.

Sandia National Laboratories is located on Kirtland Air Force Base. The base once housed the National Atomic Museum (soon to be renamed the

National Museum of Nuclear Science and History; www.atomicmuseum.com), now located in downtown Albuquerque.

CALIFORNIA: Lawrence Livermore National Laboratory conducts tours on Tuesdays and Thursdays. The tours last approximately two and a half hours (starting times vary), and tour participants must be at least eighteen years old. U.S. citizens need to register two weeks in advance. Non-U.S. citizens must register sixty days in advance. Tour request forms are available online through the Livermore Public Affairs Office (www.llnl.gov/pao).

TENNESSEE: Oak Ridge National Laboratory hosts regular public tours. Contact ORNL Visitor Services at x10visit@ornl.gov or (865) 574–7199. The city of Oak Ridge holds the Secret City Festival each June. The city is also home to the American Museum of Science and Energy (www.amse.org), dedicated to "peaceful uses of atomic energy."

NEBRASKA: The Strategic Air and Space Museum (www.strategicairandspace .com), which features a number of historic bombers, is located near Ashland, Nebraska, just off Interstate 80, and is open year-round.

MISSILE FIELDS: The Titan Missile Museum (www.titanmissilemuseum.org) in Sahuarita, Arizona, is the only publicly accessible Titan II missile site. To reserve a tour, contact the museum office at (520) 625–7736. In South Dakota, the National Park Service conducts tours of a decommissioned Minuteman II missile alert facility (www.nps.gov/mimi). Reservations can be made via the Minuteman Missile headquarters office at (605) 433–5552.

Private citizens can drive on public roads leading to current missile silos and missile alert facilities. While we don't encourage silo spotting (neither does the federal government), it also isn't illegal so long as you don't encroach on private property or restricted government land. Coordinates of the active silos are available at www.siloworld.com. The Web site also has information on decommissioned missile silos for sale (with asking prices in the two-hundred-thousand- to three-hundred-thousand-dollar range).

WEST VIRGINIA: Tours of the Greenbrier bunker are open to the general public as well as to registered hotel guests. For reservations, call the Bunker Office at (304) 536–7810 or visit www.greenbrier.com/bunker.

HUNTSVILLE, ALABAMA: The U.S. Space and Rocket Center (www.spacecamp .com) is located right off Interstate 65 and is open year-round.

MARSHALL ISLANDS: Continental Micronesia serves the Marshall Islands, with direct flights from Honolulu to Majuro. As of this writing, U.S. Army Kwajalein Atoll was off-limits to visitors without military orders. Bikini Atoll, however, is now open to tourists, allowing scuba divers to tour the atomic wrecks.

KAZAKHSTAN: Kazakhstan's National Nuclear Center (www.nnc.kz) organizes official excursions around the Semipalatinsk Test Site. Call 322 (51) 2–33–33. Tourists wishing to visit the test site can also simply hop a cab from the neighboring city of Semipalatinsk. For more information on Semipalatinsk, visit Aidar Samayev's Web site (semey2004.freenet.kz/welcome_to_the _centre_of_eurasia.htm).

RUSSIA: The Kurchatov Institute is located near the Oktyabrskoye Pole metro station in Moscow. For visitor information, contact museum director Sofia Yevgenievna Voinova at 7 (499) 196–99–02.

IRAN: Anyone interested in visiting Iran's nuclear facilities is advised to contact the nearest Iranian embassy or interests section and remind them of President Ahmadinejad's promise to open nuclear sites to tourism.

Acknowledgments

A Nuclear Family Vacation might have been nothing more than a whimsical idea had it not been for those who supported our writing and research.

We are forever grateful to Michelle Tessler of the Tessler Literary Agency, who helped shape the book concept, and Miles Doyle and Colin Dickerman at Bloomsbury, for their enthusiasm, suggestions, and careful editing. Thanks as well go to June Thomas, the foreign editor of *Slate*, who supported and nurtured the idea of nuclear vacationing through two series of articles published in 2005 and 2006. We are also grateful to the Nation Institute's Carl Bromley, who first suggested to us that our nuclear vacation would make for a good book, and Kim Nauer, who supported our travels in the former Soviet Union through the Nation Institute's Investigative Fund.

Robert Wall of *Aviation Week & Space Technology* and D. Brent Morris of the U.S. Air Force Academy both provided detailed comments and criticisms on the entire draft. Carl Akerlof, Ann Finkbeiner, John Robinson, Noah Shachtman, Mort Weiss, and Jane Phillips also gave us helpful comments and corrections, while Peter Zimmerman made a number of early suggestions that contributed to the development of questions posed in some of the chapters. Of course, any errors of fact or omission remain solely our responsibility.

These travels would not have been possible without the openness shown by both the Department of Energy and the Department of Defense. While we sometimes chafed at the limits of nuclear secrecy, it is to the United States' credit that our nuclear infrastructure is, in some respects, transparent and open. A particular thanks goes to Bryan Wilkes, director of public affairs for the National Nuclear Security

Administration, who expressed support early on for our travels and helped open doors at a number of sites. We're also indebted to Jim Danneskiold at Los Alamos National Laboratory; David Schwoegler at Lawrence Livermore National Laboratory; Michael Padilla and Neal Singer at Sandia National Laboratories; Bill Wilburn at Y-12; and Mike Bradley at Oak Ridge National Laboratory. Within the Department of Defense, we thank Lieutenant Denver Appelhans at U.S. Strategic Command; Staff Sergeant Kurt Arkenberg and Captain Nora Eyle at F. E. Warren Air Force Base; Major Thomas Veale at Cheyenne Mountain; Bill Congo and John Cummings of Space and Missile Defense Command in Huntsville; and Tamara Ward of U.S. Army Kwajalein Atoll. A special thanks goes to Anne Greene on Kwajalein, who opened a window for us into a closed community.

In Moscow, Valery Fadeyev and Pavel Bykov of *Expert* magazine and Lola Topchieva provided invaluable assistance in navigating a bureaucratic maze that we never quite comprehended. Roman Vassilenko of the embassy of Kazakhstan facilitated our trip to Semipalatinsk, while Aidar Samayev, with the very best of intentions, showed us his city. We also thank Leily and Rahman in Tehran.

The staff at the Greenbrier was enormously helpful, providing us with excellent background and history on the hotel's bunker.

A special acknowledgment goes to our family, both nuclear and extended, who were patient and supportive during our travels and throughout the process of writing this book.

Finally, though this book may offer a critique of nuclear policy, we have nothing but praise for those who work in the weapons complex. We met a large number of dedicated, patriotic, and intelligent people— both in the United States and abroad. A great many people spoke candidly to express their own professional doubts, frustrations, and hopes about working inside the nuclear infrastructure. If we came away with unique insights into the nuclear world, it is to the credit of those we interviewed. To them, we owe the greatest debt.

Index

A Note on the Authors

NATHAN HODGE is a Washington, D.C.–based staff writer for *Jane's Defence Weekly*. He has made frequent appearances on National Public Radio and the BBC. A regular contributor to *Slate*, he has reported extensively from Afghanistan, Iraq, and the former Soviet Union. His work has appeared in *Details*, the *Financial Times*, and *Foreign Policy*, among many other publications.

SHARON WEINBERGER is a writer for *Wired*'s national security blog, Danger Room. She is the author of *Imaginary Weapons: A Journey Through the Pentagon's Scientific Underworld*. Her writing on national security and science has appeared in the *Washington Post Magazine*, *Slate*, *Discover*, *Nature*, and *Aviation Week & Space Technology*.

A Note on the Type

The text of this book is set in Adobe Sabon, named after the type founder Jacques Sabon. The original version was designed by Jan Tschichold and jointly developed by Linotype, Monotype, and Stempel in response to a need for a typeface to be available in identical form for mechanical hot metal composition and hand composition using foundry type.

Tschichold based his design for Sabon roman on a font engraved by Garamond and Sabon italic on a font by Granjon. It was first used in 1966 and has proved an enduring modern classic.